A VIEW OF THE CONSTITUTION OF THE UNITED STATES OF AMERICA

By WILLIAM RAWLE LL.D.

2nd Edition

1829

◆ ◆ ◆ ◆ ◆

Secession as Taught at West Point Military Academy

◆ ◆ ◆ ◆ ◆ ◆ ◆ ◆ ◆ ◆ ◆ ◆

Edited and Annotated by James R. Kennedy and Walter D. Kennedy

A View of the Constitution of the United State of America
By William Rawle, LL.D.
Edited and Annotated by Walter D. Kennedy and James R. Kennedy

First Printing

The Scuppernong Press
PO Box 1724
Wake Forest, NC 27588
www.scuppernongpress.com

Cover and book design by Frank B. Powell, III

Printed in the United States of America

International Standard Book Number: ISBN 978-1-942806-28-8

Library of Congress Control Number: 2020908304

The foundation of a free government begins to be undermined when freedom of speech on political subjects is restrained; it is destroyed when freedom of speech is wholly denied.

William Rawle, LL.D.
Philadelphia, PA 1825

Editors' Introduction

The following book, *A View of the Constitution of the United State of America*, 1829 edition, by William Rawle, LL.D.,[1] was first published in 1825, and it has been more than 190 years since it was last published. In editing and annotating Mr. Rawle's book, we have endeavored to make his work understandable to those who are reading it in the early part of the 21st century. In doing so, we have corrected those parts of his text which he had noted were incorrect, and on rare occasions, we have substituted words more in keeping with modern usage. The changes have been made with an eye toward maintaining the meaning and spirit of his original work. It is our intention to protect the truth and integrity of his work. The following is an example of some of the words changed: tranquillity changed to tranquility, defence changed to defense, and colour changed to color.

To assist the reader in the study of Rawle's book, we have divided his text into eight sections, with each section containing brief prefatory remarks about Rawle's discussion. Also, we have added notes and references from the works of the authors debating the adoption of the Constitution as well as from works relating to the material being discussed. Our notes will be indicated by italicized text. On pages 1 through 292 editor's notes appear in italics, Rawle's in standard font. Editor's annotation notes appear, in italics, at the bottom of the page. Rawle's notes, in the text, appear at the end of each chapter.

SECTIONS

1 *Legum Doctor* ("teacher of the laws" in Latin or Doctor of Laws in English) is a doctorial-level academic degree, as opposed to a *Juris Doctor* or Doctor of Jurisprudence (J.D. or D.Jur), which is not a terminal degree.

Foreword
Secession As Taught At West Point

With the government of the United States becoming more aggressive in domestic and international affairs, with the tax-and-spend mentality of Washington demanding more tribute from its tax serfs, and with a supreme Federal government that knows no limitation on its lust for power, now is the time to look to the early political writers of America for a proper definition of the true role of government in the life of a supposedly "free people." William Rawle's book on the Constitution of the United States is important today because it examines how the people of early America viewed the role of the State government, the Federal government, and the individual American.

William Rawle was a highly respected legal authority in early America. He was a Northerner, a friend of both Washington and Franklin, and an abolitionist. Yet, his *A View of the Constitution of the United States of America* could have been written by John C. Calhoun, Jefferson Davis, or any leader of the Confederate States of America. Many of the Confederate Generals defended their role as Confederates by stating they had been taught at West Point that secession was a right of the States. It is true, Mr. Rawle's textbook was used at West Point Military Academy, and it teaches that one of the reserved rights of the States is the right of secession. Early in the history of the United States, States' Rights was viewed as an American, not just a Southern, idea. The fact that a Northern Abolitionist defended the right of a State to secede from the Union is a clear indication that, in 1861, the South was Right!

Mr. Rawle's view of the Constitution was that of a Jeffersonian States' Rights man. In his view, the States were the prime movers in the formation of the Federal government, and all power that the Federal government exercised was so exercised by the permission and at the behest of the Sovereign States. Mr. Rawle clearly believed that, in those areas in which the States had delegated a portion of their sovereign power, the Federal government would be supreme. In all other areas, those which had not been delegated by the State's own actions to the Federal government, the States would be supreme. According to Rawle, as long as the Federal government's action was in pursuant of the powers delegated to it, its actions were supreme. But Mr. Rawle also noted, as did Hamilton and Madison,[2] that, in those actions in which the Federal government acted beyond (not in pursuant of) its constitutionally mandated powers, the Federal government's acts were void. So strong is Rawle's view of States' Rights that he included as the last chapter of his book on the Constitution of the United States a discussion of the right of a State to secede from the Union.

Introducing Mr. William Rawle

William Rawle was born April 28, 1757, in Philadelphia, Pennsylvania. In his early years, he was educated at the Friends Academy in Philadelphia. Since his family was of Tory allegiance during the American War for Independence, he went to England during the War and continued his studies in law at Middle Temple. After America's defeat of the British, he decided to return to his home in Philadelphia on a passport granted by Franklin on May 8, 1782, an event which proved to be the beginning of a friendship between Mr. Rawle and Mr. Franklin. One year later, Rawle was admitted to the bar in Philadelphia, and in 1789, he was elected to the Pennsylvania State Legislature. When Benjamin Franklin organized the Society for Political Inquiries, Rawle was invited to become a member. George Washington was also a member of the Society at that time, the Federal government being located in Philadelphia, and a warm relationship formed between these three men.[3]

President Washington appointed Rawle as the United States attorney for Pennsylvania in 1791. Rawle held the position of United States attorney for Pennsylvania for eight years. During that time, it became his duty to prosecute the individuals responsible for the Whiskey Rebellion in Western Pennsylvania.

In 1792, Rawle became an honorary member of the Maryland Society for Promoting the Abolition of Slavery. He became so involved with the issue of abolition that he became the president of that organization in 1818 and remained its president until his death in 1836. Rawle's active civic and professional life was replete with successful

---

2 Alexander Hamilton, James Madison, The Federalist No. 33 and No. 45, in *The Federals, Student Edition*, Carey & McCellan eds. (Dubuque, IA: Kendall-Hunt Pub. Co. 1990).

3 Dumas Malone, ed., *Dictionary of American Biography* (New York: Charles Scribner's Sons, 1935), XV: 400-01.

achievements and honors. His interest in law and government would inspire him to write a textbook on the Constitution of the United States. The first edition was published in 1825 and a second in 1829. Such a book from one who had been a Loyalist during the War for Independence and who later became an associate of both Franklin and Washington was bound to attract extensive attention.

Rawle's View of the Constitution

Rawle's first edition book is a concise volume of 347 pages (original text), consisting of thirty-one chapters and four appendices. His second edition (349 pages), was 32 chapters long because he included a chapter on treason. In 1826, the year after Rawle's *A View of the Constitution of the United States*,1825 edition, was first published, it was reviewed by the eminently respected Boston journal, *The North American Review*.[4] If Rawle's book was laced with radical secessionist views or seditious ideas, they were completely overlooked by the reviewer.

The only criticism offered by the reviewer of Rawle's work was in the mode of presidential election. It was Rawle's view that, in respect to the election of the president, the original intent of the "framers of the constitution, or expectations of the people, [had] been so completely frustrated."[5] The reviewer responded, "Now this language is much too strong .... Whatever difficulties, therefore, may have been encountered in the election of a president, it can hardly be said with truth, that the views of the framers of the constitution have been completely frustrated."[6] Except for taking issue with Rawle's view on how the presidential election should be held, the reviewer offered much praise for Rawle's book in a cordial review. He recommended it to foreigners who had little or no appreciation for the intricacies of the republican form of government (a condition not uncommon to the masses of American voters today) and as an introduction to a more "extended course of reading." In his summation, the reviewer notes "To those, who are desirous of studying the noblest monument of human wisdom, the Constitution of the United States, we recommend the treatise of Mr. Rawle as A SAFE AND INTELLIGENT

4 *North American Review* (1826: New York: AMS Press, Inc., 1965), XXII: 446-51.
5 Review, 448.
6 Review, 448.

GUIDE" (emphasis added).[7] Not only was Rawle's book warmly reviewed when it first appeared in print, but also, twenty-eight years later, it was still being recommended. In his book, *On Civil Liberty and Self-Government*, Francis Lieber, LL.D., recommends Rawle's book, among others, to his students and former students as a guide in Constitutional issues.[8] Note that Lieber's suggestion was made in 1853, only seven years before South Carolina seceded from the Union.

Rawle's text, having been so blessed by a member of Boston's civic orthodoxy and by a noted legal educator some twenty-eight years later, has much to say about the nature of the union which the Constitution created. In the introduction of his text, Mr. Rawle outlines how and under what circumstances republican institutions were created in America.

As to who has the right to make and unmake a government, Rawle unequivocally states, "A moral power equal to and of the same nature with that which make, alone can destroy . … So the people may, on the same principle, at any time alter or abolish the constitution they have formed."[9] But how can the American people "alter or abolish" a government? Is this to be a great democratic experience of the American Nation? Hardly so! The act of altering or abolishing is, according to Rawle, to be done by the same power, "which made" the constitution, that is, by the State. "It [ratification of the constitution] was not the simple act of a homogeneous body of men, either large or small. It was to be the act of many independent states, though in a greater degree the act of the people set in motion by those states; it was to be the act of the people of each state, and not of the people at large."[10]

Here we see Rawle restating a fundamental American idea about the nature of government that is, the people have the right to consent to the form of government under which they live. Although very American, this principle of "government by the consent of the governed" has many noble antecedents.

In the Huguenot treatise against absolutism, *Vindiciae Contra Tyrannos*, circa 1579, the author clearly demonstrates that the people

---

7 *Review*, 450.

8 Francis Lieber, *On Civil Liberties and Self-Government* (Philadelphia: J. B. Lippincott and Co., 1859), 270.

9 William Rawle, *A View of the Constitution of the United States* (Philadelphia: H. C. Carey & Lea, 1825), 12.

10 Rawle, (Philadelphia: H. C. Carey & Lea, 1825), 13.

are above the king ("king" being used here as a metaphor for government) because they established the king and it is from them the right to govern is granted. "He who is established by another is accounted under him who has established him, and he who receives his authority from another, is less than he from whom he derives his power. … [T]hey [kings or government] should acknowledge that for them, they, as it were borrow their power and authority."[11] For the Protestant Huguenots, the will of the people, as long as it was in harmony with God's sovereign will, was supreme.

Writing in defense of the English people's right to recall a tyrannical king, in another antecedent for the American experience, John Milton states, "The power of kings and magistrates is nothing else but what is only derivated, transferred, and committed to them in trust but the right remaining in [the people] to resume it to themselves, if by kings or magistrates it be abused."[12]

In 1664, Samuel Rutherford wrote *Lex Rex* in which he demonstrates the power of the king comes from the estates which elect him, and therefore the people acting through the "free estates" retain the prerogative to recall their delegated rights. "Those who have power to make have power to unmake a king."[13] Rutherford goes on to state the power exercised by established governments is "a power borrowed from (or a fiduciary power which is his by trust) the estates, who made him king."[14]

Rawle follows the same line of reasoning in his interpretation of the nature of government under the constitution as did the republicans of Europe in their struggle against centralized government as epitomized by absolute monarchy. Note all four treatise agree that legitimate government proceeds from the will of the people, and this will is expressed, not by the people *en masse*, but by people within their sovereign communities, that is within the estates or states. It is the will of the people as expressed through their agents, the States, as Rawle shows, would establish the Federal government. "Those who

---

11 Junius Brutus, *Vindiciae Contra Tyrannas* (1689: Edmonton, AB, Canada: Still Waters Revival Books, 1989), 59-60.

12 John Milton, "The Tenure of Kings and Magistrates," qtd. in Kennedy & Kennedy, *The South Was Right!* (Baton Rouge: Land and Land Pub., 1991), 126; also, in second edition (Pelican Publishing Co., Gretna, LA: 1994), 190.

13 Samuel Rutherford, *Lex Rex* (1644; Harrisonburg, VA: Sprinkle Publications, 1982), 126.

14 Rutherford 126-27.

have the power to make, have the power to unmake . . . ."

Throughout his introduction, Rawle leaves little room to question the fact of who created the Federal government. He clearly states each State existed as a free and sovereign entity before and after the ratification of the Constitution.

> Each state was naturally tenacious of its own sovereignty and independence, which had been expressly reserved in their antecedent associations, and of which it was still meant to retain all that it did not become unavoidably necessary to surrender . . . . [T]he people, formed into one mass, as citizens of the union, yet still remaining distinct, as citizens of the different states, created a new government, without destroying those which existed before . . . . [15]

The act of forming the Federal government was as Rawle stated, "the act of many independent states . . . ."

In the preceding paragraphs, we have recounted Rawle's view on the nature of the American Union at its inception. But what about his views on the overt act of secession by a State from the Union?

Rawle On Secession Of A State From The American Union

After a careful and precise investigation of the Constitution of the United States, Rawle, in the final chapter, discussed the nature of the American Union. Chapter XXXI of the first edition is entitled "Of the Union." In the second edition, this chapter (XXXII) is entitled "Of the Permanence Of The Union."

Rawle opens the final chapter by stating, " . . . we shall conclude with adverting to the principles of its cohesion, and to the provisions it contains for its own duration and extension."[16] The maintenance of the Union, according to Rawle, is predicated upon the existence of the republican institutions within the United States. As Rawle explains the issue, these United States are a republic of republics. The first duty that each State has to the other members is to assure the maintenance of a republican form of government within the United States.

---

15 Rawle, (Philadelphia: H. C. Carey & Lea, 1825), 14.

16 Rawle, (Philadelphia: H. C. Carey & Lea, 1825), 288.

> The Union is an association of the people of republics; its preservation is calculated to depend on the preservation of those republics. The people of each pledge themselves to preserve that form of government in all. Thus each becomes responsible to the rest, that no other form of government shall prevail in it, and all are bound to preserve it in every one.[17]

The power of maintaining a republican form of government is lodged with the Federal government. As Rawle notes, by common consent each State delegated this authority to the Federal government. But under what circumstances could this power be used? The Federal government is not licensed to interfere at will in the political life of a State. Only upon application of the legislature or executive of a State could Federal force be applied within a State to protect it against "domestic violence." As long as a State remains within the Union, it is subject to its common compact (the Constitution) and must maintain its republican form of government.

> If a faction should attempt to subvert the government of a state for the purpose of destroying its republican form, the paternal power of the Union could thus be called forth to subdue it. Yet it is not to be understood that its [Federal government's] interposition would be justifiable, if the people of a state should determine to retire from the union, whether they adopted another or retained the same form of government, or if they should, with the express intention of seceding, expunge the representative system from their code, and thereby incapacitate themselves from concurring according to the mode now prescribed, in the choice of certain public officers of the United States.[18]

Rawle, in this section, explains that, if a State remains within the Federal Union, it is held accountable to all members of that Union to maintain a republican form of government. Representative governments are so commonplace today that it may be difficult to understand just why the Founding Fathers of the republic feared the loss of republican institutions. Today, in the Western World, republican

17 Rawle, (Philadelphia: H. C. Carey & Lea, 1825), 288.
18 Rawle, (Philadelphia: H. C. Carey & Lea, 1825), 289.

governments are the norm, whereas in the early history of the United States, monarchy was the accepted rule in Europe. Republics were considered weak, fragile, and of short duration in the nineteenth century. Americans in that age had a great fear of monarchy, much like Americans feared Communism during the Cold War; this fear of monarchism resulted in the insistence of maintaining republican institutions as outlined in the Constitution.

As Rawle notes, when a State withdraws from the Union, it is no longer constrained by the former association. When a State is no longer a part of the United States, it resumes all of its formally delegated rights and may perform any and all acts of sovereignty. Once out of the Union, its will is then unquestioned. But in all cases, the will of the people of the State is supreme, and Rawle explains why this is the case.

> To deny this right [secession from the Union] would be inconsistent with the principle on which all our political systems are founded, which is, that the people have in all cases, a right to determine how they will be governed.[19]

According to Rawle, if a majority of the people of a State peacefully and deliberately "resolve to relinquish the republican form of government, they ceased to be members of the Union." But if a faction or small group of people takes control of a State by violence and thereby destroys republican government, at that time "the Union is bound to employ its power to prevent it." The only pretext for the Federal intervention in the affairs of a State is when the will of the majority of established electors has been usurped.

Rawle understood the danger to the liberty of the people of the States if the Federal government were allowed to meddle in State affairs. Rawle made the following statement:

> . . . [I]n order that such interference may not wantonly or arbitrarily take place, that it shall only be on the request of the state authorities: otherwise the self-government of the state might be encroached upon at the pleasure of the Union, and a small state might fear or feel the effects of a combination of larger states against it under the color of constitutional authority.[20]

19 Rawle, (Philadelphia: H. C. Carey & Lea, 1825), 289.
20 Rawle, (Philadelphia: H. C. Carey & Lea, 1825), 292.

Here we see how the Constitution is designed to protect the "self-government of the state" from being "encroached upon at the pleasure of the Union."

We find in Rawle's examination of the Constitution his theory of how the people of a State would initiate its secession from the Union. Rawle always recurs to the idea that the people within the sovereign community, that is, the State, have the right to determine their own political destiny.

> The secession of a state from the Union depends on the will of the people of such state. The people alone as we have already seen, hold the power to alter their constitution . . .. Still, however, the secession must in such case be distinctly and peremptorily declared to take place on that event . . .. But in either case the people is the only moving power.[21]

In language which cannot be misunderstood, Rawle instructed his readers not only upon the right of a State to secede from the Union but also upon the formula for how a State should execute the project. True to his republican principles, Rawle demands the people, the electors of the State, should have the final voice in the act of withdrawing from the Union.

After explaining in what manner a State should discharge its responsibility in the act of seceding, Rawle then warns his readers of the dangers of such an act. It must be remembered Rawle was not advocating secession "for the fun of it" but only as an option available to the State in defense of the liberty of its people. A State must consider whether the wrongs inflicted are sufficient to warrant the loss of "the benefits (and they are known to be many), deprives herself of the advantages (and they are known to be great), severs all the ties of affection (and they are close and enduring), which have bound her to the Union . . .."[22]

---

21 Rawle, (Philadelphia: H. C. Carey & Lea, 1825), 296-96.

22 Jefferson Davis, "Farewell Address to U.S. Senate," qtd. in Kennedy & Kennedy *The South Was Right!* (Baton Rouge, LA: Land and Land, 1991), 149-50; also, second edition (Pelican Publishing Co., Gretna, LA: 1994), 315.

> Separation would produce jealousies and discord, which in time would ripen into mutual hostilities, and while our country would be weakened by internal war, foreign enemies would be encouraged to invade with the flattering prospect of subduing in detail, those whom, collectively, they would dread to encounter.[23]

Thus, Rawle invokes the plea of maintaining the common good as the premise for maintenance of the Union. It is clear from reading his book this common good is never sufficient enough to negate the will of the people of the State. The warning he gives is an appeal for sober reasoning when the question of secession arises. As Rawle and Rutherford have already stated, "Those who have the power to make have the power to unmake." The noble example of self-government given the world by America "ought never to be withdrawn while the means of preserving it remain."[24] This self-government could only be maintained by the good will and intent of the parties of the agreement. Thus, as Burke had taught the English, one cannot in the name of freedom destroy another man's freedom because "… you impair the object by your very endeavors to preserve it. The thing you fought for is not the thing which you recover, but depreciated, sunk, wasted, and consumed in the contest."[25] The Union as a free association of sovereign States cannot be enforced at the point of a bloody bayonet because force precludes volition.

Rawle at West Point

The idea that a "secessionist" textbook on the United States Constitution was used at West Point Military Academy has caused much discomfort and embarrassment to the victors of the War for Southern Independence. It has been asserted by some that no such book was ever used at West Point, while others have stated that most of the "Confederate" graduates were taught the right of secession at West Point from Rawle's textbook. As in most controversies, the truth

23 Rawle, (Philadelphia: H. C. Carey & Lea, 1825), 299.

24 Rawle, (Philadelphia: H. C. Carey & Lea, 1825), 300.

25 Edmund Burke, "Speech on Conciliation With the Colonies," qtd. in M. H. Adrams, ed., *The Norton Anthology of English Literature* (New York: W. W. Norton & Co., 1974), 2356.

in this matter is difficult to ascertain.

As to the question, "Was Rawle's textbook ever used in West Point?" a qualified "yes" can be given. In *The Centennial of the United States Military Academy at West Point*, we find the following note in reference to Rawle's *A View of the Constitution of the United States of America*:

> The text-book of the law department, from (?) to (?). A copy of this book owned by the Library U.S. Military Academy makes it very probable that it was used as a textbook.[26]

As can be seen from this statement, the records of the Academy are not absolute as to what textbook was in use early in the history of West Point. What appears to be the case is that Rawle's textbook was used no less than one year and no more than fifteen years, but this fact cannot be verified by records at West Point. The hard evidence of its use comes from a copy of a textbook containing marginal notations in the possession of the library at West Point and from notations in the journal of Cadet (later General) S. P. Heintzelman. In Heintzelman's journal, which he kept as a cadet at West Point, he refers to "recitation and examination in Rawle on the Constitution."[27] General (U.S.) Heintzelman was in the graduating class of 1825 and was a classmate of Confederate General Albert Sidney Johnston.

Charles Francis Adams, the grandson of President John Quincy Adams, in his booklet *The Ethics of Secession* states the "official" use of Rawle's textbook at West Point covered a time span from 1825 through 1840. In 1909, Charles F. Adams modified that statement as follows:

> Rawle's "View" never was an established and authorized textbook at the Academy for any course of instruction; but between 1825 and 1832, the question of Nullification and the right of secession were freely discussed among the students, and Rawle's view was certainly accepted by the Southern students, and in all probability, by the mass of both students and instructors. I have equally little question that frequent refer-

26 *The Centennial of the United States Military Academy at West Point, New York, 1802-1902* (Washington: Government Printing Office, 1904), I: 441.
27 S. P. Heintzelman, qtd. in Edgar S. Dudley, "Was 'Secession' Taught at West Point?" *The Century Magazine*, (New York: The Century Co., 1909), LXXVIII 633.

> ence was made to the book . . .[28]

Many Southerners confirm the story of Rawle's textbook being used at West Point. None other than President Jefferson Davis agrees that this text was in common use at West Point. President Davis states:

> Rawle on the Constitution was the textbook At West Point, but when the class of which I was a member entered the graduating year Kent's Commentaries were introduced . . .[29]

General Fitzhugh Lee made the following statement about the use of Rawle's textbook:

> My recollection is that Rawle's *View of the Constitution* was the legal text-book at West Point when Generals Lee, Joseph E. Johnston and Stonewall Jackson were cadets there and later on was a text-book when I was a cadet there.[30]

General Dabney H. Maury stated the following:

> Mr. Davis and Sidney Johnston and General Joe Johnston and General Lee and all the rest of us who retired with Virginia from the Federal Union, were not only obeying the plain instincts of our nature and dictates of duty, but we were obeying the very inculcations we had received in the National School. It is not probable that any of us ever read the Constitution or any exposition of it except this work of Rawle, which we studied in our graduating year at West Point. I know I did not . . .[31]

Colonel Edgar S. Dudley, Judge-Advocate, United States Army, reviewed the matter of Rawle's textbook being used at West Point

---

28 Charles Francis Adams, qtd. in Edgar S. Dudley, "Was 'Secession' Taught At West Point?" *The Century Magazine*, (New York: The Century Co., 1909), LXXVIII 631,
29 Jefferson Davis, qtd. in Edgar S. Dudley, "Was 'Secession' Taught At West Point?" *The Century Magazine* (New York: The Century Co. 1909), LXXVIII 633.
30 Fitzhugh Lee, qtd. In Edgar S. Dudley, "Was 'Secession' Taught At West Point?" *The Century Magazine* (New York: The Century Co. 1909), LXXVIII 634.
31 Dabney H. Maury, qtd. In Edgar S. Dudley, "Was 'Secession' Taught At West Point?" *The Century Magazine* (New York: The Century Co. 1909), LXXVIII 634.

Military Academy. Colonel Dudley made the following report in his findings published in 1909:

> It is undoubtedly true that the question of the right of a State to secede was under discussion by cadets and that Rawle's work was often referred to in these discussions and its views quoted in support of the right of secession . ... The results of this examination of the records of the United States Military Academy, and of their view of statements of both sides of the subject shows conclusively, to my mind, that Rawle's work "*A View of the Constitution of the United States*" was introduced as a text-book by the professor of geography, history, and ethics for one year only (1826) and was then discontinued . ...[32]

The fact that Rawle's book was in use as a textbook at West Point cannot be realistically denied. The evidence also supports the theory Rawle's textbook was used as a reference work years after it was discontinued as an official textbook. Rawle's textbook was superseded by *Kent's Commentaries on American Law*, which served as a text not only for constitutional law but also for international law.[33] It should be noted Kent's textbook does not contradict the teaching found in Rawle's textbook. Rather than contradict, Kent and Rawle are in agreement on three major areas of constitutional government:

(1) The people have the right to be judge of what type of government they are to live under, and the duration of that government. Kent states,

> When the government established over any people becomes incompetent to fulfill its purpose, or destructive to the essential ends for which it was instituted, it is the right of that people . . . to throw off such government, and provide new guards for their future security.[34]

---

32 Edgar S. Dudley, "Was 'Secession' Taught At West Point?" *The Century Magazine* (New York: The Century Co. 1909), LXXVIII 633-35.

33 *The Centennial of the United States Military Academy At West Point*, New York, 1802-1902 (Washington: Government Printing Office, 1904), I 195-96.

34 James Kent, *Commentaries on American Law* (1826; New York: Da Capo Press, 1971), I: 195-96.

Kent and Rawle see this principle of "government by the consent of the governed" as a basic principle and right of mankind.

(2) Both Kent and Rawle believe in the States' Rights theory of American government, that is, the States as sovereign entities acting in their sovereign capacities, were the prime movers in the establishment of the United States. In respect to the sovereign nature of the States, Kent leaves no doubt how he feels "... the state governments would clearly retain all those rights of sovereignty which they had before the adoption of the constitution . . . and which were not by that constitution EXCLUSIVELY DELEGATED TO THE UNION [emphasis added]."[35]

(3) The maintenance of the Union was to be predicated upon mutual respect among the States, and not by brute force. According to Mr. Kent, how the Union was to be maintained was "... for on the concurrence and good will of the parts, the stability of the whole depends."[36] The CONCURRENCE and GOODWILL, not bayonets, would hold the Union together.

Kent's *Commentaries on American Law* continued in use at West Point until 1880. In 1886, Cooley's *The General Principles of Constitutional Law in the United States*, was substituted as the textbook on constitutional law.[37] Cooley had already proven himself to be a loyal advocate of government by centralized power (see T. M. Cooley, *A Treatise on Constitutional Limitations*).[38] Cooley wrote in favor of the then ongoing socialist revolts in Europe (circa 1848). It is important to note the teachings of men such as Cooley could become the general rule in the United States only after the military defeat of the South and the resultant extermination of the South's pre-war conservative political influence in Congress.

The Meaning of Rawle's Textbook Today

What is the significance of Mr. Rawle's 1829 textbook to those of us living in the first part of the 21st century? First, his book offers an insight into the mindset of early Americans *vis-à-vis* the act

35 Kent, 363.

36 Kent 369.

37 *The Centennial of the United States Military Academy at West Point, New York, 1802-1902* (Washington: Government Printing Office, 1904), I: 441.

38 Thomas M. Cooley, *A Treatise On The Constitutional Limitations* (1866; New York: Da Capo Press, 1972), 5-6.

of secession. We have here a book written by a close associate of two of America's greatest political leaders, George Washington and Benjamin Franklin, a leader in the abolition movement, one who was alive during the great constitutional debate which formed the Union, and a member of a well-established Northern family.

The uniqueness of his work is not in the fact a textbook was used at West Point that advocated the right of secession as a reserved right of the States, but the fact a Northerner is advocating the right of a State to secede is of great significance. Well before Rawle, many Southerners had written very similar statements about secession. In the preface to his edition of *Blackstones Commentaries*, St. George Tucker (1803) states,

> … the union is in fact, as well as in theory, an association of states, or, a confederacy. … [Each State] is still a perfect state, still sovereign, still independent, and still capable, should the occasion require, to resume the exercise of its functions as such, in the most unlimited extent.[39]

In 1957, the renowned Southern writer, Richard M. Weaver, noted that "… the prime purposes of the idealistic founders of the nation was to check the growth of a centralized, autonomous power."[40] For well more than two hundred years, Southerners have known these facts. Regrettably, the South cannot offer one of its own as a means of defending its cause, regardless of qualifications, because a Southerner's opinion will be suspected as not being impartial. Mr. Rawle, being from the North and an abolitionist, cannot be accused of such bias. He is indeed a Good Yankee!

Beyond the use of Rawle's work as a means of correctly interpreting Southern (Confederate) history, Rawle's book is an excellent course of study for modern Americans. When a government has so much power that its will becomes law, the spirit of constitutions and the limits imposed on governments by those documents are dead. The United States today is more than twenty-one trillion dollars in debt, and no one seems capable of reining in this Leviathan. Levia-

---

39 St. George Tucker, qtd. in Jesse T. Carpenter, *The South as a Conscious Minority* (New York: The New York University Press, 1930), 202.

40 Richard M. Weaver, "The South and the American Union," G. M. Curtis, III and J. J. Thompson, Jr., eds., *The Southern Essays of Richard M. Weaver* (Indianapolis, IN: Liberty Press, 1987), 246.

than's will has become absolute law. Now is the time, as never before in the history of this nation, to study the intent of the founders of the Constitutional Republic of 1787. By revisiting our constitutional roots, we may yet come to a place where once again the people will not live in fear of their government.

Deo Vindice

Walter D. Kennedy and James R. Kennedy, March 2020

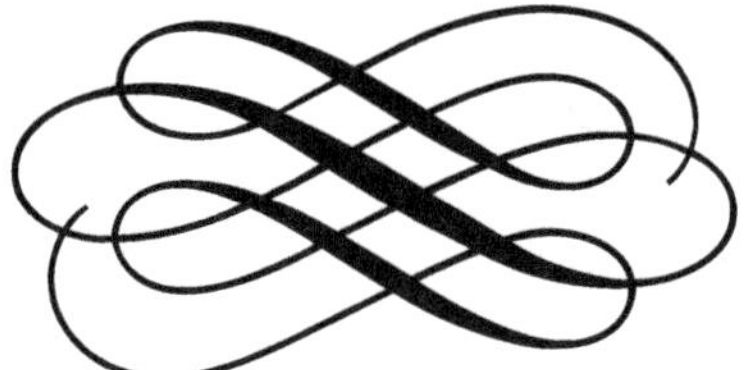

The following text is from Rawle's 1829, (first edition published in 1825). The second edition (1829) of his book was published with the following notation by Mr. Rawle:

> In this edition, the principles laid down in the first, remain unaltered. The author has seen no reason for any change of them. A small variation in the arrangement, and the correction of some typographical errors, will principally distinguish it from the first.

Thus we have the testimony of William Rawle, LL.D., four years after the first edition was published. In his own words, " … the principles laid down in the first [edition], remain unaltered." The principles laid down in his day were those which Americans fought for in 1776 and Confederates fought to defend in 1861. Let us hope the day will never dawn when Americans will be so ideologically depraved and self-centered as not to feel a patriotic flush at the thought of those principles.

Preface

IF the following work shall prove useful, as an elementary treatise to the American student, the author will be gratified.

IF foreigners are enabled, by the perusal of it, to obtain a general idea of the merits of the constitution, his satisfaction will be increased.

To the American public in general, its value may chiefly consist in the exhibition of those judicial decisions, which have settled the construction of some points that have been the subjects of controversy.

In this edition, the principles laid down in the first, remain unaltered. The author has seen no reason for any change of them A small variation in the arrangement, and the correction of some typographical errors, will principally distinguish it from the first.

Table of Contents

Section I
Introduction

Rawle begins his study of the United States Constitution with a discussion of the nature of government. He investigates under what condition and for what reasons people come together to form governments, and he reviews the early political history of the colonies. The central theme of Rawle's introduction is a reaffirmation of the principle of "government by the consent of the governed."

INTRODUCTION.

OF POLITICAL CONSTITUTIONS IN GENERAL OF THE NATURE OF COLONIAL GOVERNMENTS, AND OF THE BRITISH COLONIES IN NORTH AMERICA.

By a constitution we mean the principles on which a government is formed and conducted.

On the voluntary association of men in sufficient numbers to form a political community, the first step to be taken for their own security and happiness, is to agree on the terms on which they are to be united and to act. They form a constitution, or plan of government suited to their character, their exigencies, and their future prospects. They agree that it shall be the supreme rule of obligation among them.[41]

This is the pure and genuine source of a constitution in the republican form. In other governments the origin of constitutions is not

41 *The Constitution is therefore said to be the supreme law of the land. Only that law which is in keeping with (pursuant to) the agreed-upon constitution is lawful. In The Federalist No. 33, Hamilton noted any act which was not in keeping with the constitution would be a usurpation of American rights. Hamilton states, " ... it will not follow ... that acts of the larger society which are not pursuant to its constitutional powers, but which are invasions of the residuary authorities of the smaller societies [States], will become the supreme law of land. These will be merely acts of usurpation, and will deserve to be treated as such." Therefore, any act that is not made according to the regulation and or stipulation agreed upon in the Constitution cannot be said to be valid.*

always the same.

A successful conqueror establishes such a form of government as he thinks proper.[42] If he deigns to give it the name of a constitution, the people are instructed to consider it as a donation from him; but the danger to his power, generally induces him to withhold an appellation, of which, in his own apprehension, an improper use might be made.

In governments purely despotic, we never hear of a constitution. The people are sometimes, however, roused to vindicate their rights, and when their discontents and their power become so great as to prove the necessity of relaxation on the part of the government, or when a favorable juncture happens, of which they prudently avail themselves, a constitution may be exacted, and the government compelled to recognize principles and concede rights in favor of the people.

The duration of this relief is wholly dependent upon political events. In some countries the people are able to retain what is thus conceded; in others, the concession is swept away by some abrupt revolution in favor of absolute power, and the country relapses into its former condition. To rectify abuses, without altering the general frame of government, is a task, which though found more difficult, yet is of less dignity and utility, than the formation of a complete constitution.

To alter and amend, to introduce new parts into the ancient texture, and particularly new principles of a different and contrary nature, often produces an irregular and discordant composition, which its own confusion renders difficult of execution. The formation of a constitution founded on a single principle, is the more practicable from its greater simplicity.

Whether this principle is pure monarchy, aristocracy, or democracy, if it be steadily kept in view, the parts may be all conformable and homogeneous.

In a pure monarchy all the power is vested in a single head. He may be authorized to make and expound, and execute the laws. If this be the result of general consent, such countries possess a constitution. The same may be said of an aristocracy if the people agree to deposit all power in the hands of a select number; and of a democracy, in

42 *The people of the conquered South were forced, post-war, to accept new state and federal constitutions. The state governments thus created were in fact illegitimate, puppet governments doing the bidding of their Republican masters in Washington, DC.*

which they retain, in such manner as they hold most conducive to their own safety, all sovereignty within their own control. The difficulty in either case is to regulate the divisions of the authority granted, so that no portion of it, vested in one branch or one body of men, shall bear an undue relation to the others. Each must be sufficient to support itself, yet all must be made to harmonize and co-operate.

A constitution may combine two of the foregoing principles, like those of ancient Rome, some of the Grecian Republics, and in modem times, Geneva and some of the small communities of Italy: or, like the present government of England, it may combine the three principles.

The high authority which has been often quoted[1] in favor of the last mentioned form, may be allowed its full weight, without impugning the obvious position, that the whole power which is conceded to an hereditary monarch, may be vested by a democratic republic in an elective magistrate, and all the benefits derived from it, enjoyed without the dangers attending hereditary succession.

If an hereditary monarch abuses his power, the people seldom obtain relief without insurrection; and thus, between the ambition of princes on the one side, and the sense of injury on the other, the peace of the country is constantly endangered. If the monarch be elected for life, a young aspiring prince may continue the grievances of the state for a long time, and unless there be an express provision for deposing him, the choice of another in his place, would involve the whole body in tumult and disorder.

The power of choosing another supreme magistrate at the end of a reasonable time, obviates these objections. The substantial difference between a mixed monarchy and a republic formed on a proper distribution of powers, is therefore confined to the term of service of the supreme magistrate.

The powers of every government are only of three kinds; the legislative, executive, and judicial. This natural division, founded upon moral order, must be preserved by a careful separation or distinction of the powers vested in different branches. If the three powers are injudiciously blended; if for instance, the legislative and executive, or the executive and judicial powers are united in the same body, great dangers may ensue, and the effect would be the same, whether such powers are devolved on a single magistrate or on several. In the wise distribution of these powers, in the application of suitable aids and checks to each, we may attain the *optime constituta respublica*, [the best constitution for a republic] which is the object of general desire and admiration.

It has been reserved for modern times and for this side of the Atlantic, fully to appreciate and soundly to apply the principle of representation in government. The advantages, which occasionally arise to an individual, of being able to commit his cares and concerns to another, who in the exercise of such authority is considered as the principal himself, are elevated and ennobled by being transferred to the concerns of an entire community. Without the representative principle, one of two consequences must follow; either the whole body must be assembled and act together, or a few, who may have possessed themselves of sufficient force, will undertake to dictate and give laws to the whole. But a wise people sees and dreads its own danger in large assemblies. Experience tells them that they cannot trust themselves when thus collected together; that sudden bursts of feeling are likely to predominate over their own judgment; that facts and causes are often misrepresented or misunderstood, and the deliberate judgment, which alone ought to be solely exercised, is overpowered by unaccountable excitement and precipitate impulse. It was forcibly said in reference to the popular assemblies of Athens, that if every Athenian were a Socrates, still every Athenian assembly would be a mob.

A people sagacious enough to discover this imperfection in itself, avoids the danger by selecting a suitable number to act for it, upon full consideration and with due caution; and while it authorizes them to express what are to be considered its own sentiments, it gives to that expression the same effect as if it proceeded immediately from itself The virtue of this salutary principle is impaired if it be divided. If it extend only to a part of the government; if there are other component parts which have an equal or superior power, independent of the representative principle, the benefit is partial.

In England, of three co-ordinate parts, one only is supposed by the constitution to represent the authority of the people, and at what time this representation was introduced among them, is not clearly settled by their own jurists and antiquarians. That it existed before the Norman Conquest in some form, now not exactly ascertained, is indeed agreed; but on the subversion of the Saxon institutions, effected by William, the practice was, at least, suspended until the reign of Henry III. The provincial constitutions of America were, with two exceptions, modelled with some conformity to the English theory; but the colonists of Rhode Island and Providence Plantations were empowered to choose all their officers, legislative, executive, and judicial; and about the same time a similar charter was granted to Connecticut. "And thus," complains Chalmers, a writer devoted to regal principles, a mere democracy or rule of the people was established. Every power deliberative and active was invested in the freemen or their delegates, and the supreme executive magistrate of the empire, by an inattention which does little honor to the statesmen of those days, was wholly excluded." He expresses his own doubts whether the king had a right to grant such charters.[2]

But, although in all the other provinces, the charters were originally granted or subsequently modified so as to exclude the principle of representation from the executive department, these two provinces, at the time, of our revolution, retained it undiminished. The suggestion of the full unqualified extension of the principle of representation may therefore be justly attributed to the example of Rhode Island and Connecticut, which, when converted into States, found it unnecessary to alter the nature of their governments, and continued the same forms, in all respects, except the nominal recognition of the king's authority, until 1818, when Connecticut made some minor changes and adopted a formal Constitution. Rhode Island, however, is still satisfied with the charter of Charles II from which it has been found sufficient to expunge the reservation of allegiance, the required conformity of its legislative acts to those of Great Britain, and the royal right to a certain portion of gold and silver ores, which happily for that state, have never been found within it.

As representation is sometimes partial in respect to the proportion of the powers of government to be exercised, so it is sometimes confined to a portion only of those governed. In this respect it is perhaps still more objectionable. The power of electing the great officers of the state belonged in Venice to a few families; the people at large had no voice, and it was therefore indifferent to the Venetians, whether they became the subjects of France, or were ceded by her to Austria, or whether they continued to be governed by those in whose appointments they had not the least share. With us, representation is in its nature universal, but in practice there are some exceptions which will be noticed in a subsequent place. They are few, and do not impair the principle.

It is not necessary that a constitution should be in writing; but the superior advantages of one reduced to writing over those which rest on traditionary information, or which are to be collected from the acts and proceedings of the government itself are great and manifest. A dependence on the latter is indeed destructive of one main object of a constitution, which is to check and restrain governors. If the people can only refer to the acts and proceedings of the government to ascertain their own rights, it is obvious, that as every such act may introduce a new principle, there can be no stability in the government. The order of things is inverted; what ought to be the inferior, is placed above that which should be the superior, and the legislature is enabled to alter the constitution at its pleasure.

This is admitted by English jurists to be the case in respect to their own constitution, which in all its vital parts may be changed by an act of parliament; that is, the king, lords, and commons may, if they think proper, abrogate and repeal any existing laws, and pass any new laws in direct opposition to that which the people contemplate and revere as their ancient constitution. No such laws can be resisted or disobeyed by the subject, nor declared void by their courts of justice as unconstitutional. A written constitution which may be enforced by the judges and appealed to by the people, is therefore most conducive to their happiness and safety.

Vattel [3] justly observes, that the perfection of a state, and its aptitude to fulfil the ends proposed by society, depend on its constitution — the first duty to itself is, to form the best constitution possible, and one most suited to its circumstances; and thus it lays the foundation of its safety, permanence and happiness.[43] But the best constitution which can be framed with the most anxious deliberation that can be bestowed upon it, may, in practice, be found imperfect and inadequate to the true interests of society. Alterations and amendments then become desirable — the people retains — the people cannot perhaps divest itself, of the power to make such alterations.

A moral power equal to and of the same nature with that which made, alone can destroy.[44] The laws of one legislature may be repealed by another legislature, and the power to repeal them cannot be withheld by the power that enacted them. So the people may, on

---

43 *Madison in The Federalist No. 43 states, "... the safety and happiness of society are the objects at which all political institutions must be sacrificed." Madison makes it clear that the safety and happiness of society are to take precedence over any institution of government or even government itself.*

44 *Samuel Rutherford in* Lex Rex *states, "Those who have power to make have the power to unmake a King." In* Lex Rex, *"King" is a metaphor for government. This idea was restated for Americans by Jefferson in the Declaration of Independence.*

the same principle, at any time alter or abolish the constitution they have formed. This has been frequently and peaceably done by several of these states since 1776.[4] If a particular mode of effecting such alterations has been agreed on, it is most convenient to adhere to it, but it is not exclusively binding. We shall hereafter see the careful provision in this respect, contained in the Constitution of the United States, and the cautious and useful manner in which it has hitherto been exercised. Indeed it is a power which, although it cannot be denied, ought never to be used without an urgent necessity. A good constitution is better understood and more highly valued, the longer it continues. Frequent changes tend to unsettle public opinion, and in proportion to the facility with which they are made, is the temptation to make them. The transactions in France since the year 1791 support these remarks.

The history of man does not present a more illustrious monument of human invention, sound political principles, and judicious combinations, than the Constitution of the United States. In many other countries, the origin of government has been vaguely attributed to force, or artifice or accident, and the obscurities of history have been laboriously developed to trace the result of these supposed causes. But America has distinctly presented to view the deliberate formation of an independent government, not under compulsion, or by artifice, or chance, but as a mean of resisting external force, and with a full and accurate knowledge of her own rights, providing for, and securing her own safety. It is not, however, intended to assert that this instrument is perfect, although it is deemed to approach as near to perfection as any that has ever been formed. If defects are perceived they may readily be accounted for.

Great and peculiar difficulties attended its formation. It was not the simple act of a homogeneous body of men, either large or small. It was to be the act of many independent states, though in a greater degree the act of the people set in motion by those states; it was to be the act of the people of each state, and not of the people at large. The interests, the habits, and the prejudices of the people of the different states were in many instances variant and dissimilar. Some of them were accustomed chiefly to agriculture, others to commerce; domestic slavery was reprobated by some, by others it was held lawful in itself, and almost necessary to their existence. Each state was naturally tenacious of its own sovereignty and independence, which had been expressly reserved in their antecedent association, and of which it was still meant to retain all that it did not become unavoidably necessary to surrender. Different local positions and different interests were therefore the sources of many impediments to the completion of this great work, which at last resulted in the combination of mutual and manly concessions: the representatives of each state, deeply impressed with the necessity of giving strength and efficiency to their union, yielded those points which by them were deemed of inferior magnitude. That every state should be fully satisfied was scarcely to be expected; but every state was bound to consider, that not its own peculiar interests only, but those of the whole were to be regarded, and that what might be supposed to be particular sacrifices, were compensated by the general advantage, in which they were to participate.

The constitution thus became the result of a liberal and noble sacrifice of partial and inferior interests, to the general good; and the people, formed into one mass, as citizens of the Union, yet still remaining distinct, as citizens of the different states, created a new government, without destroying those which existed before, reserving in the latter, what they did not surrender to the former, and in the very act of retaining part, conferring power and dignity on the whole.

It will contribute to a proper understanding of the nature of this government, to consider the political situation of the country and its colonial dependence on Great Britain, before the great event of its final separation.

An explanation of the legal nature of colonies in general, will not only serve as an introduction in this view, but will be useful to the student, as the United States, possessing vast tracts of uncultivated land, are in the constant habit of forming colonies therein, under the appellation of territorial governments.

A colony is a portion of the population of a country, either expressly sent or permitted to go to a distant place for the purpose of forming a dependent, political body. Dependence necessarily enters into the description of a colony, for a body of men may emigrate, either with the view of uniting themselves to a foreign community, or of setting up a government of their own, in neither of which cases would the parent country be bound to protect them, or be entitled to interfere with their internal government or control their trade.

The Greeks, the Carthaginians, and the Romans, established numerous colonies, sometimes of a military nature, to secure distant conquests, but more generally of a civil kind and for commercial purposes, or to furnish an outlet for a superabundant population.

In the former instance, the removal was compelled, in the two latter voluntary, but in all, the parent country retained and exercised certain rights over her colonists, founded on the express or implied engagement to protect them. The colony always continued so much a part of the parent country that, if she entered into war, the colony was rendered a party to it, and an attack upon the latter, without any hostile declaration against the parent, was held to be an attack upon the parent.

This relation produced certain consequences which were considered beneficial to both. The internal administration of the colony was either immediately directed by the parent state or subjected to her revision, and its trade was either confined to their mutual intercourse, or sparingly allowed to be shared with other countries.

We are not clearly informed, in what manner a revenue for the benefit of the parent state was extracted from them. In some mode it was probably attained, since it is reasonable that those who receive protection out of the public purse, should proportionally contribute to the public expense. One important political feature in these institutions is, that the members of the parent state are entitled to participate in the civil rights of the colony. An Athenian was received as a citizen at Crotona, and a Corinthian at Corcyra; and vice versa, the colonist continues a subject or a citizen of the parent state. A Frenchman or an Englishman, born in either of their colonies, is a natural born subject of the country from which his ancestors migrated.[5]

The Romans alone made some distinctions on this subject, which did not long continue, and are now merely interesting as a matter of history.

But a stranger who joined a colony, gained only those rights which would have appertained to him in the parent country, and hence if an alien cannot hold lands in the United States, he cannot, without an express legislative dispensation, hold land in any of our territories where the feudal tenures prevail.

There are instances in ancient history of colonies increasing in population and strength so as to send out new colonies to adjacent territories, who still however, partook of the original relation to the parent country, and there also are examples of Greek colonies, when they had become populous and strong, throwing off their subjugation to the states from which they sprung.

With us it is a standing and a sound rule, to erect our colonies into states, and receive them into the Union as soon as they acquire a sufficient population; a subject to which we shall again have occasion to advert.

The discoveries made in America by Europeans, being considered as conferring an exclusive right of occupancy on the sovereign under whose authority they had sailed, various parts of this continent were appropriated by the British crown to the establishment of colonies; sometimes by extensive grants to favored individuals, sometimes by encouraging settlers at large, reserving the general domain to the crown.

Hence two sorts of provincial governments ensued. 1. Those denominated Royal Governments, in which the executive officers were appointed by the crown, but the legislative power was vested in the people, subject however to the control of the king in council. This form prevailed in those provinces where the general domain continued in the crown until it was, from time to time, granted to the settlers. 2. Proprietary Governments, where a large territory was at once granted by the crown to one or more individuals.

Of the latter, Maryland granted to Lord Baltimore, and Pennsylvania to William Penn, are instances; it likewise embraces the provinces of New England, as the territory was collectively termed, which was afterwards subdivided into New Hampshire, Massachusetts, Rhode Island and Providence Plantations, and Connecticut. New Jersey, North and South Carolina were also granted to private companies. Charters were granted by the different monarchs, more or less liberal in their terms, but all founded on the general relation of subjection to the crown, sometimes expressly declared, but omitted in others from a conviction that it was unnecessary.

In some of them the power of legislation was uncontrolled by the parent state. In others, the laws that were passed were to be transmitted to England, and if disallowed by the king in council, they lost their force; but until his disapprobation was announced, they were binding on the colony, if enacted according to their respective charters. In most of the colonies, appeals were allowed to the same authority, from the decisions of the highest provincial tribunals. There is no reason to believe that these appeals were in general otherwise decided than the justice of the case required; but the power of rejecting the acts of the legislature, was sometimes capriciously exercised. It may perhaps have been deemed expedient by the English ministry, to keep alive the sense of colonial dependence whenever the charter afforded the opportunity.

In general the courts of Vice Admiralty were retained under the direction of the crown, who appointed the judges of them and exercised exclusive jurisdiction as well in relation to the proper subjects of maritime jurisdiction, as the collection of so much of the revenue as arose from trade, the exclusive power of regulating which was uniformly understood to be reserved. Little direct commercial intercourse was allowed between the colonies and any other than the British dominions: their mutual or internal commerce and their manufactures, were seldom interfered with, yet one or two regulations calculated to promote the interests of English manufactures, were justly complained of, although they were peaceably submitted to.

But, for a long time, Great Britain abstained from imposing internal taxation. On some great public exigencies, when their own safety was endangered, the colonists spontaneously rendered assistance to the extent of their ability, and with these filial efforts, and with the revenue derived from imposts on trade, the parent country appeared to be satisfied. But at length the increase and prosperity of the colonies suggested to the ministry, the idea of a new contributory fund, to be subject to their own power and not to be dependent on voluntary grants. The principle that the right of taxation depends on representation, one of the greatest beauties in the ancient constitution of England, though now reduced almost to a shadow, was disregarded, or the British subject was supposed to have suspended his claim for it, by residence in a distant colony. The chartered rights, which in the reign of the Stuarts had been frequently trampled on, were again set at naught, and a scheme of internal taxation was adopted, which it was supposed might be easily enforced, and would gradually introduce a systematic extraction of internal revenue. Stamp duties were imposed on most of the instruments in common use, and were to be paid to officers appointed by the crown. But the people of America were too sagacious not to perceive the danger of submitting to the first inroads upon their rights, and too firm not to resist them. By a simultaneous impulse, from one end of our continent to the other, a concerted abstinence from the use of stamps and the resignation of many of the officers employed, the measure was rendered impracticable.

The common danger suggested the idea of an union for common defense. A precedent for a congress of the provinces was not wanting. In the year 1753, deputies from several of them had assembled at Albany for a different purpose. The apprehensions of a war between

France and Great Britain, in which, as we have already observed, the colonies of each would be necessarily involved, led to this assembly, the object of which was to increase the means of defense by forming an union of the provinces. The plan was disapproved by the British ministry, because it was apprehended that it might produce a concert of measures opposing the supremacy of the mother country.[6] In 1765, the object of a congress was still defense, but against an enemy of a different description; against the invasion of a ministry supported by acts of parliament which they could procure at pleasure. Remonstrance and entreaty were, however, the only weapons wielded, and these, combined with the practical opposition everywhere experienced, produced a change in the ministry and an abandonment of the measure. But although the law was repealed, the ministry thought it expedient to assert by a declaratory act, the right to bind their colonies, by acts of parliament, in all cases whatever; a declaration disregarded by the colonists who now began to feel their own power, till it was endeavored to be enforced by the imposition of a duty on tea, glass, and a few other articles, expressly for the purpose of raising a revenue to defray part of the colonial expenses. The spirit which had been raised was not however easily allayed. The same indications of resistance were now renewed, but the military force in this country was increased by detachments from the regular army in Great Britain — and the ministry avowed a determination to persevere. Another congress was convened, and a second course of complaint and supplication, unavailingly pursued. The language was still that of faithful, though injured subjects: their grievances were imputed not to the monarch, but to his ministers — and in the ardent expressions of hope that they should not be deprived of the rights enjoyed by their fellow subjects, they admitted their own subjection. Even after the fatal blow was struck at Lexington in 1775, and the whole country was in arms, the most dutiful language of subjects towards a sovereign was retained. But this incongruity ceased, when the people, perceiving no relaxation of the efforts to subdue them, boldly resolved to throw off a yoke too heavy to be borne, and no longer contenting themselves with claiming the rights of British subjects, asserted those of independent man.

By this great measure the congress of provinces became at once the congress of so many sovereign states — entitled to places in the catalogue of nations; and a meeting of humble, complaining colonists terminated in the formation of an empire.

It soon was found expedient to devise some explicit form of association, by which the powers granted to the congress or retained by the new states, should be distinctly ascertained. Articles of confederation were therefore prepared, (and with the exception of one state, which, however, afterwards came into them,) speedily adopted, by which the United States were formed into a federal body, with an express reservation to each state, of its freedom, sovereignty and independence, and of every power, right, and jurisdiction, not expressly delegated to the United States, in Congress assembled. The federal powers were declared to be those of making war and peace, coining money and issuing bills of credit, establishing courts of admiralty, building and equipping a navy, ascertaining the number of men to be raised for the army, making requisitions on each state for its quota, regulating the trade and managing all affairs with the Indians, establishing post-offices, and some other matters of less importance but for many of these, even for agreeing on the number of ships to be built, and the appointment of a commander in chief of the army or navy, the consent of at least nine states, in congress assembled, was requisite. From this outline it is obvious that the congress still continued in a great degree dependent on the individual states, which alone possessed the means of raising supplies. The power to coin money, when it did not possess the bullion, to emit bills of credit when it had no funds to redeem them, was purely nominal. Even the expenses of its own members, were to be defrayed by the respective states which sent them, and which retained the dangerous power to recall them at pleasure. Yet such was the fervor of freemen engaged in a common cause, that, while the war continued, the mere recommendations of congress carried with them the force of mandates, and it was not until after the peace of 1783, that the necessity of giving to the head of the union the means of supporting its own government was universally felt and acknowledged. After some ineffectual substitutes had been proposed, a convention of delegates from the different states was assembled at Philadelphia in 1787. The members were appointed by the legislatures of the respective states. The result of their deliberations was again to become a matter of recommendation which required the assent of the people to give it effect. It was communicated by the convention to congress, and by congress to the several legislatures, in order to be submitted to a convention of delegates chosen in each state by the people. This course, which had been recommended by the general convention itself, eventuated in its final adoption by all the states.

But the assent of nine was sufficient for its But the assent of nine was sufficient for its commencement, and on the 2d of July, 1788, congress was informed, that nine states had adopted it. On the 13th of September, they fixed the time for the appointment and meeting of electors, and "commencing proceedings under the new constitution."

CHAPTER NOTES
INTRODUCTION

1. Cicero de Republica

2. Political Annals of the British Colonies

3. Book 1 ch. 3

4. New Hampshire, New York, Pennsylvania, Delaware, South Carolina, Georgia, Connecticut, have altered their constitutions since that period.

5. The only exception that occurs with us is, as to the right of the inhabitant of a territory to maintain an action against a citizen of one of the states in the United States' court, but this is owing to the particular structure of the Judiciary system of the United States.

6. Marshall's *Life of Washington*, Vol. I, p. 300, Vol. II, p. 90

SECTION II
Chapters I-VI

In the following chapters, Rawle investigates the nature of the government the Constitution established, he discusses how the States relate to each other, and how they relate to the new Federal government.

According to Rawle, the imperfections of the Articles of Confederation required a change in the type of government of the United States. The change was made in order to form a more perfect union in which the blessings of liberty would belong to Americans and be passed on to their posterity. As he notes, a new system was formed without destroying the previous organization of the States. It was indeed an act of the States which was to form the new government. The people of the States acting through their agents, the States, delegated a portion of their rights to form a "more perfect union." But note, Rawle clearly states that "... the sovereignty of the states is not altered."

The unique nature of the Constitutional Republic is that, in America, citizens owe their allegiance to the Federal government only in those areas in which the States have freely empowered the Federal government. In all areas not delegated to the Federal government, the States are supreme. As Rawle states, "The supremacy of the union in all those points that are thus transferred, must therefore be considered as two coordinate qualities, enabling us to decide on the true mode of giving a construction to the Constitution."

CHAPTER I.

THE CONSTITUTION OF THE UNITED STATES.

THE government, formed under the appellation of the United States of America, is declared in the solemn instrument which is denominated the Constitution, to be "ordained and established by the people of the United States, in order to form a more perfect union, establish justice, insure domestic tranquility, provide for the common defense, promote the general welfare, and secure the blessings of liberty to themselves and their posterity."

In this distinct exposition of principles, most of which are common to all freemen, and some peculiar to the situation of our country, we perceive the motives, and are guided in the construction of the instrument. We find the intention to create a new political society, to form a new government which the necessities and dangers of our country loudly required. The imperfect and inefficient confederation of 1779, is intended to be abandoned. The states are no longer to be known to each other merely as states. The people of the states unite with each other, without destroying their previous organization. They vest, in a new government, all the powers necessary for the attainment of the great objects to which the states separately or confederated, had been found incompetent. They reserve to the state governments, or to themselves, only what is not necessary for the attainment of those objects. In all other respects the sovereignty of the states is unaltered. The obligations of duty and allegiance to them are not impaired; but in all those instances which are within the sphere of the general government, the higher obligations of allegiance and duty to it, supersede what was due to the state governments, because from the nature of the case they cannot be co-equal. Two governments of concurrent right and power cannot exist in one society. Superiority must, therefore, be conferred on the general government, or its formation, instead of promoting domestic tranquility, would produce perpetual discord and disorder.[45]

The principles of this constitution to be thoroughly understood should be frequently contemplated. The composition of such a government presents a novel and sublime spectacle in political history. It is a society formed not only out of the people of other societies, but in certain parts, formed by those societies themselves. The state is as much a member of the Union, and forms as much a part of the greater society as the people themselves, yet the state does not enter into the Union upon federate principles; it does not send represen-

45 *A common question asked about a citizen's allegiance in Rawle's time was to which does a citizen owe allegiance, the State or Federal government? In 1776 Americans turned away from a strong, centralized government and formed a Republic of Sovereign States. As Rawle demonstrates (in the second edition, Chapter XXXII), as long as the Federal government acts within the limits of its delegated powers, AND as long as a State remains in the Union, citizens owe their allegiance to the Federal government in those areas which the States have agreed the Federal government would be supreme; but, in all other areas, their allegiance belongs to the State. In The Federals No. 51, Madison called this arrangement the "compound republic of America."*

tatives in the nature of federal delegates, or ambassadors; it cannot, at its own pleasure, increase or diminish their number. When the appointment is made, the person appointed becomes an officer of the United States, not of the state which sends him, and he is not politically responsible to his immediate constituent. In one case only is a vote taken by states, and the immediate representatives of the people, in that case represent the state.[46]

It will be seen that in some cases a state has the right to claim the aid of the judicial power of the Union, and in all, it is bound to support the legislative and executive acts of the general government when consistent with the constitution. As therefore it is neither a stranger, nor properly speaking a confederate, it seems to follow that it must be considered as part of the greater nation, a term, which in the course of this work we shall chiefly use in reference to the United States, because although every political body, governed only by its own laws or internal regulations, may denominate a nation, yet the states, not possessing that absolute independence, cannot with full propriety be so designated. But a name is of little importance if the substance be retained; and if Virginia or Pennsylvania are not known abroad as nations, it does not affect their power at home as states. In this relation every state must be viewed as entirely sovereign in all points not transferred by the people who compose it, to the government of the Union: and every exposition that may be given to the constitution, inconsistent with this principle, must be unsound. The supremacy of the Union in all those points that are thus transferred, and the sovereignty of the state in all those which are not transferred, must therefore be considered as two co-ordinate qualities, enabling us to decide on the true mode of giving a construction to the constitution.[47] As different views have prevailed, different theories of

---

46 *See Madison, The Federalist No. 39, where he explains how the new government would be a mixture of a Federal, National, and Confederation. Madison clearly states that "Each State ... is considered as a sovereign body, independent of all others ... bound by its own voluntary act." The recognition of States' Rights was an integral part of the formation of the new "more perfect union."*

47 *In The Federalist No. 32, Hamilton declares "An entire consolidation of the States into one national sovereignty would imply an entire subordination of the parts; and whatever power might remain in them, would be altogether dependent on the general will. But as the plan of the convention aims only at a partial union or consolidation, the State governments would clearly retain all rights of sovereignty which they before had and which were not, by that act exclusively delegated to the United States." Both Rawle and Hamilton view the States as independent actors in the formation of the*

construction have been formed. Some have contended that it should be construed strictly; others have asserted, that the most liberal construction should be allowed. By construction we can only mean the ascertaining the true meaning of an instrument, or other form of words, and by this rule alone ought we to be governed in respect to this constitution. A strict construction, adhering to the letter, without pursuing the sense of the composition, could only proceed from a needless jealousy, or rancorous enmity. On the other hand, a liberal construction may be carried to an injurious extreme; concessions of power may be conceived, or assumed, which never were intended, and which therefore, are not necessary for its legitimate effect. The true rule therefore seems to be no other than that which is applied in all cases of impartial and correct exposition; which is to deduce the meaning from its known intention and its entire text, and to give effect, if possible, to every part of it, consistently with the unity, and the harmony of the whole.

In many respects we have the benefit of the learned elucidations of judicial tribunals, and wherever the supreme court of the United States has pronounced its solemn decision upon constitutional points, the author has gladly availed himself of this irrefragable authority; but where a guide so certain, cannot be found, recourse can only be had, to an anxious and serious endeavour to display and expound, with truth and justice, the main features of a constitution, which must always be more admired, as it is more considered, and better understood. If these examinations produce the same effect upon the reader, that they have upon the author, the attachment to it, of our native citizens, and its attractions to foreigners will be increased; and those who are now here, and those who may hereafter be here, will concur to venerate and support a government, eminent above all others in promoting the freedom and the happiness of man.

---

new Union. This independence is never lost, nor can we find in the writings of the Founding Fathers such an assertion. Hamilton, in The Federalist No. 31, hoped that the American people would "... preserve the constitutional equilibrium between the general and State governments."

CHAPTER II.

OF THE LEGISLATIVE POWER.

THE course proposed to be pursued, is first, to consider the legislative power as it resides in the senate and house of representatives; to what extent the president participates in general legislation, and his power in conjunction with the senate relative to making treaties, with the operation and effect of treaties; we shall then proceed to those powers of general legislation which are implied by the Constitution, or expressly enumerated, and conclude this head with a view of the restraints under which both the United States and the states severally, are constitutionally placed.

The legislative power is vested in the congress of the United States, consisting of the senate and house of representatives. The first paragraph evinces that it is a limited government. The term "all legislative powers herein granted," remind both the congress and the people, of the existence of some limitation. The introduction displays the general objects. The Constitution itself enumerates some of the powers of congress, and excludes others which might perhaps fall within the general expressions of the introductory part. These prohibitions are in some degree auxiliary to a due construction of the Constitution. When a general power over certain objects is granted, accompanied with certain exceptions, it may be considered as leaving that general power undiminished in all those respects which are not thus excepted.

The value and effect of this proposition may be adverted to hereafter.

The legislative body possesses with us a great advantage over that of those countries where it may be adjourned or dissolved at the pleasure of the executive authority. It is self-moving and self-dependent. Although it may be convened by the executive, it cannot be adjourned or dissolved by it. The time of its assembling is fixed by the Constitution, until which, unless a law has been passed appointing an earlier day, or the president on extraordinary occasions has thought proper to convene it, the action of the legislature cannot commence; but if in their opinion the public good shall require it, they may continue uninterruptedly in session, until the termination of the period for which the members of the house of representatives are elected, and they may fix as early a time for the meeting of the next congress as they think proper. A similar principle prevails in all the state constitutions, and it is only where it exists, that a legislature is truly independent. It is as inconsistent with sound principles for the executive to suspend, at its pleasure, the action of the legislature, as for the latter to undertake to deprive the executive of its constitutional functions.

But without a constitutional limit on its duration, it must be conceded, that a power in the legislature to protract its own continuance, would be dangerous. Blackstone attributes the misfortunes of Charles I. to his having unadvisedly passed an act to continue the parliament, then in being, till such time as it should please to dissolve itself, and this is one of the many proofs that the much praised constitution of that country wants the character of certainty. No act of congress could prolong the continuance of the legislature beyond the term fixed by the Constitution.

CHAPTER III.

OF THE SENATE.

THE senate, on account of its more permanent duration and various functions, will receive our first attention. If the infusion of any aristocratic quality can be found in our Constitution, it must be in the senate; but it is so justly tempered and regulated by other divisions of power, that it excites no uneasiness. The mounds and safeguards with which it is surrounded must be violently broken down, before any political injury can arise from the senate.

The senators are appointed from time to time, by the legislatures of the different states;[48] but if a vacancy happens during the recess of the state legislature, the executive thereof may make temporary appointments until the next meeting of the legislature, which shall then fill such vacancies.

The vesting this power in the state legislatures is the only material remnant of the federative character of the late congress; but the delegates then appointed possessed the whole power; those now appointed, hold but a part of the powers of the general government. It is recommended by the double advantage of favoring a select appointment, and of giving to the state governments, such an agency in the formation of the general government as preserves the authority of the former, and contributes to render them living members of the great body [1]. Whether the appointment shall be made by a joint or a concurrent vote of the two branches, when the legislature of a state consists of two branches, as it now universally does, the Constitution does not direct. The difference is, that in a joint vote, the members of both houses assemble together and vote numerically. A concurrent vote is taken by each house voting separately, and the vote of one receiving the assent of the other branch.

The person appointed must be at least thirty years of age, have

---

48 *With the adoption of the Seventeenth Amendment on April 8, 1913, the election of United States Senators was changed from being elected by the State legislatures to election by statewide vote. In either case, the election of senators by the States is a tacit recognition by the Federal government of the independent and sovereign nature of each State. According to international law, every Sovereign State has the right and must be accorded the right of an equal, regardless of size or population, in council with other Sovereign States.*

been a citizen of the United States nine years, and at the time of his election, he must be an inhabitant of the state by which he shall be chosen. The senatorial trust requiring great extent of information and stability of character, a mature age is requisite. Participating immediately in some of the transactions with foreign nations, it ought to be exercised by those who are thoroughly weaned from the prepossessions and habits incident to foreign birth and education. The term of nine years is a reasonable medium between a total exclusion of naturalized citizens, whose merits and talents may claim a share of public confidence, and an indiscriminate and hasty admission of them, which might possibly create a channel for foreign influence in the national council [2].

Each state, whether more or less populous, appoints two senators — a number which would have been inconvenient, if the votes in the senate were taken, as in the former congress, by states, when, if the delegates from a state were equally divided, the vote of the state was lost; and which of course rendered an uneven number preferable: but in the senate, a numerical vote is taken in all cases, and the division of opinion among those who represent particular states, has no influence in the general result. If the senate should be equally divided, the casting vote is given by the Vice President, whose office it is to preside in the senate. The equality of states in this respect, is not perhaps defensible on the principle of representing the people, which ought always to be according to numbers; but it was the result of mutual concession and compromise, in which the populous states, enjoying the advantages of proportional numbers in the house of representatives, by which they are enabled to control the interests of the smaller states, yielded as a compensation, the principle of equality in this branch of the legislature, which enjoys in most respects equal, in some respects greater powers.

No other political league or community is known to have possessed as wise adjustment of its capacities and qualities. In Europe, different states or cities have always stood as individual members of the league, and the majority which decided, was the majority of the league, not of the representatives who attended. This composition of both is peculiar to our country, and has been found in practice, neither productive of schism nor deficient in energy. A perfect independence of sentiment has been uniformly manifested by the members, and great superiority to local interests and impressions, particularly sought for in the senate, has always been found there.

It may not be improper to observe in this place, that some of the state legislatures appear to have viewed the relative duties of the senators whom they have appointed, in a more restricted light than it is apprehended the Constitution implies. It seems to have been supposed that the senators were bound to obey the directions of the state legislatures, and the language of some resolutions has been, that the senators be "instructed," and the members of the house of representatives from the particular states "requested," to make or support certain propositions. But surely the opinion is erroneous. A senator is no more bound to obey the instructions of the state legislature, in opposition to his own judgment, than a representative of the people in the other house, is bound by the occasional instructions of his constituents. They are both elected for the purpose of freely and honestly exercising their own judgments according to the best of their capacities.

The moment they take their seats, they commence the task of legislating for the Union, including the state from which they are delegated, whose peculiar interests and desires, it may often be necessary to postpone to the general benefit. On the contrary, the state contemplates and urges its own interests; its inhabitants or the electoral sections of its inhabitants, in like manner, consider and pursue theirs, and it is perfectly proper that they should be represented to and directly pressed upon, the persons so delegated. But, the powers and the duties of those delegates are essentially altered if such requests are converted into binding instructions. In respect to senators, the impropriety of the measure seems peculiarly striking. If one state possesses a right to direct the votes of its senators, every other state must have the same right, and if every state were to exercise such right, no portion of the legislative power would really reside in the senate, but would be held by the states; thus relapsing into the principles of the old confederation, or falling into something worse.

The appointment of a senator is for six consecutive years, but if a vacancy happens, an appointment is made by the executive of the state, for the proportion of the term of service which remains. Under the direction of the Constitution, the senators were at their first meeting divided into three classes: the seats of those of the first class to be vacated at the end of two years, of the second class at the end of four, and of the third at the end of six years; the reason of which was, that the senate should always continue a permanent body. The house of representatives, at the expiration of two years is at an end: a new house, though it may consist of the same members, then succeeds; but the public service requires, for many purposes, that there should always be a senate. In executing the directions of the Constitution, it was so arranged, that two senators from the same state, should not go out at the same time.

The senate at first sat with closed doors, but it was afterwards conceived to be more conformable to the genius of a free country, that the deliberations of both the legislative bodies should be openly conducted, with the exception, however, of its consideration of treaties and appointments to offices on the President's nomination.

On these points, their deliberations would be very improperly exposed to public notice; the national interest is better promoted by waiting for the result.

A majority of the senate constitutes a quorum; that is, a majority of the members of the senate, not a majority of the states. The power of legislation might therefore be suspended by the willful absence of a majority; but what effect this would have on the government, in other respects, will hereafter be considered.

In respect to the single function of legislation, a deep and serious discussion might be had on a point which has not yet occurred, and it is fervently hoped may {never arise in this country. If the legislatures of a} majority of the states were to omit or refuse to appoint senators, the question would be, whether the majority of those who were actually in office, excluding from the computation the number to which the non-appointing states were entitled, would be sufficient, within the spirit of the constitution, to uphold the legislative power. It is sufficient to state, without presuming to decide the question.

CHAPTER NOTES
III

1. Federalist, No. 62. The author avails himself of the first occasion to quote this excellent work, to unite in the general homage that has been paid to it. The letters signed Publius were the production of three enlightened statesmen, Jay, Madison, and Hamilton. They were collected and published under the title of the Federalist, and contain the soundest principles of government, expressed in the most eloquent language.

2. Federalist, No. 62.

CHAPTER IV.

OF THE HOUSE OF REPRESENTATIVES.

THE house of representatives was founded on the principle of the representation of the people; yet not purely and abstractedly, but with as much conformity to it as was practicable.

It is composed of representatives of the people of the several states, not of the people at large; and in this respect there is still something of a federative quality. If the whole had been thrown into one mass, it would certainly have been more consistent with a full representation of the entire people, but many would have been the objections to it. It would have been desirable that the qualifications of the electors should be uniform, but considerable variety of opinion and practice in this respect exists. In some states, the system of universal suffrage prevails; in others a freehold or other estate is required of more or less value. Residence for a longer or shorter time is requisite in different states, and when the constitution was framed, different qualifications were required in two of the states for electors of the different branches of the legislative body. The people of each state were naturally attached to their own institutions, and would unwillingly have surrendered them in favor of others. Indeed, if the qualification of property had been required, the people of those states wherein universal suffrage was established, would probably have refused altogether to accede to the Union.

Again. If the representatives were to be all chosen by a general ticket, the consequences would be that thousands of voters must give their suffrages in favor of persons of whom they had no knowledge. If it was required that the candidate should reside in a particular district, the inhabitants of Georgia would either have to select a resident of Massachusetts on their own judgment, or implicitly follow the suggestions of the voters in Massachusetts.

Under these difficulties the principle of exact representation was necessarily abandoned, and in lieu of it, representation was apportioned among the several states. The medium of not more than one representative for 30,000 inhabitants, was first agreed on, and is a fundamental part of the system by which the inhabitants of every state, although it might possess a fractional part however large of

30,000, consented to relinquish the benefit of the ultra number.[49] But every state is to be represented; and if any one should by casualties be reduced below that number, she is still to have one representative, as she will still retain two members of the senate. [1].

At one time it was conceived by congress, that without invading the constitution, the principle of apportionment might be reformed to advantage. The object was to prevent the loss in the number of representatives arising from the fractional parts.

With a sound political view to retain the just relation of representation to numbers, it is provided in the Constitution, that within three years an actual enumeration should be made of the inhabitants of the United States, which should be repeated every ten years. In fixing the number of the first house of representatives, the population was estimated, not ascertained. When the census, (as it is now commonly termed,) was taken in 1790, it appeared that, in many states, there would be considerable fractional parts, which, whether the quotient was fixed at 30,000, or a greater number, would be unrepresented. To increase the number of the house of representatives as far as the constitution would permit, was deemed most conducive to the public security, against the preponderancy of executive influence, which however was denied and resisted by a considerable minority. A bill, after great struggles, passed both houses, which it seems difficult to reconcile to the Constitution.

The whole number of inhabitants according to the recent census being ascertained, it was divided by 30,000, and produced the number of one hundred and twenty representatives, which were, in the first place, apportioned among the several states, until as many representatives as it would give were allotted to each. The residuary numbers were distributed among the states having the highest fractions. But the correct and independent mind of the illustrious man who then held the office of president, rejected the bill. It was returned to the house of representatives, with the observation, that the Constitution had provided that the number of representatives should not exceed one for 30,000, which is to be applied to the respective numbers of the states, and the bill allotted to eight of the states more than one for 30,000.

---

49 *Originally, the Constitution provided for sixty-five Representatives, each representing approximately 30,000 citizens. That number was set at 435 by the "Reapportionment Act of 1929." Today each Federal Representative represents between 500,000 to a maximum of 900,000 citizens in the state of Montana as of 2020. Lobbyists have more influence/control in Congress today than the average citizen.*

As there was not a constitutional majority to pass it again, the effort failed, and probably will never be renewed. Another law was immediately passed, allotting one member to 33,000 inhabitants, which still left some fractional parts unrepresented.

The same objection also exists in the representative bodies of states, where the apportionment is made among counties — but a state legislature possesses the power of enlarging or reducing counties, and of adding two or more together, whereas the United States have no power to alter the boundaries of a state, although they may give their assent to an alteration by the state itself the enumeration, at stated intervals, as required by the Constitution is, like many other parts of it, deserving of praise both for its wisdom and its novelty. It is not to be found in the Constitution of any of the European governments, and if occasionally practiced, it is not obligatory on them to continue it.

The census of Rome was directed by a law passed three hundred years after the commencement of the state was occasionally intermitted, and finally abolished; but the institution itself was rather of a military than a representative character.

By conforming the representation to the actual number of citizens, as it is ascertained from time to time, the evils experienced in the country, to which, on account of its bearing the greatest resemblance to our civil polity, we so frequently allude, are avoided. The decline of population in some parts of England, and its increase in others, have produced the utmost inequality in the formation of their house of commons. London, which contains about one-seventh of the inhabitants of England, is entitled to send four members to parliament. The inconsiderable united borough of Weymouth and Melcombe Regis, containing seventeen hundred inhabitants, sends the same number. Manchester and Birmingham, two very populous towns, have no representatives, while the small deserted borough of Old Sarum, without a house or an inhabitant, is the vehicle through which two members obtain their seats; the largest county in the kingdom sends only two.

Thus a rigid adherence to an ancient system of representation, which may perhaps have been not unsound at the time it was formed, is now productive of the grossest abuses. The name, the tegument are preserved, when the substance that ought to be enclosed, is almost entirely gone.

The beneficial effects of our system will appear by referring to the following tabular view, in, which the increase of general population may be deduced from the increased number of representatives from most of the states.

TABLE.

STATES	Number of Representatives. 1789.	1791.	1803.	1813.	1823.
New Hampshire	3	4	5	6	6
Massachusetts	8	14	17	20	13
Rhode Island	1	2	2	2	2
Connecticut	5	7	7	7	6
New York	6	10	17	27	34
New Jersey	4	5	6	6	6
Pennsylvania	8	13	18	23	26
Delaware	1	1	1	2	1
Maryland	6	8	9	9	9
Virginia	10	19	22	23	22
North Carolina	5	10	12	13	13
South Carolina	5	6	8	9	9
Georgia	3	2	4	6	7
Kentucky, (separated from Virginia, 1791)		2	6	10	12
Vermont, from (New Hampshire and New York, 1791)		2	4	6	5
Tennessee, (from North Carolina, 1796)		2	3	6	9
Ohio, (from a territory, 1802)			1	6	14
Louisiana, (from a territory, 1812)				1	3
Indiana, (from a territory, 1816)					3
Mississippi, (from a territory, 1817)					1

STATES	Number of Representatives. 1789.	1791.	1803.	1813.	1823.
Illinois, (from a territory, 1818					1
Alabama, (from a territory, 1821)					3
Missouri, (from a territory, 1822)					1
Maine, (from MA, 1822)					7
Territories sending Delegates.					
Michigan					1
Arkansas					1
Florida					1

There is, however, one anomaly in our system with which we are sometimes reproached. The representative proportions are made to depend on adding to the whole number of free persons in each state, including those bound to service for a term of years, and excluding Indians not taxed, three-fifths of all other persons, that is, that fifteen slaves shall be considered as equal in the ratio of representation to nine freemen.

It would now be unseasonable and useless to consider or to answer the arguments on either side. It has been agreed to, and the question is for ever at rest.

It only remains to observe, that to guard against a refractory disposition, should it ever arise in the legislatures of the states, in respect to the times, places, and manner of holding elections for senators and representatives, congress is empowered at any time, to make or alter by law such regulations, except as to the place of choosing senators. This exception was proper, as congress ought not to have the power of convening the state legislature at any other than its usual place of meeting. We have already observed, that when the Constitution was adopted, different qualifications were prescribed in some of the states for electors to their different legislative branches. As the house of representatives is the most numerous branch of the general legislature, it was judiciously provided that the electors of it should have the qualifications requisite for the electors of the most numerous branch of the state legislature.

When vacancies happen, the executive authority of the state, issues writs for elections to be holden to fill them.

Both the senate and house of representatives possess the usual powers to judge of the elections, returns and qualifications of their own members, and to punish them for disorderly behavior, which may be carried to the extent of expulsion, provided two-thirds concur.

It has not yet been precisely settled what must be the disorderly behavior to incur punishment, nor what kind of punishment is to be inflicted; but it cannot be doubted that misbehavior out of the walls of the house or within them, when it is not in session, would not fall within the meaning of the Constitution.

Expulsion may, however, be founded on criminal conduct committed in any place, and either before or after conviction in a court of law.

But a power extending beyond their own precincts, and affecting others than their own members, has been exercised by both houses, and has been decided in the supreme court to be constitutional.

It is a maxim in the practical application of government, that the public functionaries should be supported in the full exercise of the powers entrusted to them. Attempts to bribe or to intimidate them constitute offences against the public. They amount to more than contempts or breaches of privilege against. the legislative bodies, and they undoubtedly subject the offenders to the usual course of prosecution and punishment in the courts of law. But this liability does not exclude the immediate jurisdiction of the legislative body, which is supported by strong considerations of public policy. The people are entitled to the utmost purity and integrity in the conduct of their representatives. The house is a guardian of the public interests in this respect. It is its duty to make immediate inquiry as to any attempt to assail the freedom or corrupt the integrity of any of its members. From the duty to inquire arises the right to punish; it needs not to be devolved on the ordinary tribunals. It is true that no power to this effect is expressly given by the Constitution, nor does the judicial or criminal power given to the courts of the United States in any part, expressly extend to the infliction of punishment for such offences. But it is not therefore to be inferred that no such power exists any where. If the courts of the United States would possess it by implication, there is no reason for refusing it to the legislative body itself, unless it should be discovered to be wholly inconsistent with the construction or nature of that body, or with some clause in the Constitution. But the reverse of the first position is the truth. It would be inconsistent with the nature of such a body to deny it the power of protecting itself from injury or insult. If its deliberations are not perfectly free, its constituents are eventually injured. This power has never been denied in any country, and is incidental to the nature of all legislative bodies. If it possesses such a power in the case of an immediate insult, or disturbance preventing the exercise of its ordinary functions, it is impossible to deny it in other cases, which although less immediate or less violent, partake of the same character, by having a tendency to impair the firm and honest discharge of public duties.

Those clauses in the Constitution which provide that the trial of all crimes shall be by jury, in the state and district where the offence has been committed, are ever to be held sacred — but it would be doing violence to them to carry them further than the plain meaning, that trial by jury shall be preserved in criminal prosecutions in the ordinary courts; otherwise it would be impossible to support the jurisdiction given to the senate in cases of impeachment, wherein no trial by jury takes place. It appears then that this implied power of punishing what are termed contempts and infringements of the privileges of the houses, is in reality the useful institution of a summary jurisdiction for the punishment of offences substantially committed against the people, and that it is correctly deduced from the Constitution.

The following express provisions, which require no elucidation, are inserted to close this part of the subject —

A majority of each house shall constitute a quorum to do business, but a smaller number may adjourn from day to day and may be authorized to compel the attendance of absent members in such manner and under such penalties as each house may provide.

Neither house without the consent of the other shall adjourn for more than three days, nor to any other place than that in which the two houses shall be sitting.

Each house shall keep a journal of its proceedings, and from time to time publish the same, excepting such parts as may in their judgments require secrecy, and the yeas and nays of the members of either house shall, at the desire of one-fifth of those present, be entered on the journal.

CHAPTER NOTES
IV

1. In the articles of confederation it was also a fundamental provision that each state should have one vote, (art. iv,) and this was made an express condition in the instructions given by the state of Delaware to its delegates in the convention of 1787.

CHAPTER V.

OF THE PRESIDENT'S PARTICIPATION IN THE LEGISLATIVE POWER.

THE president partakes of the legislative power under wise and cautious qualifications, founded, as the whole frame of our government is founded, on their tendency to promote the interests of the people. He does not originate laws or resolutions; he takes no part in the deliberations on them during their progress; he does not act in relation to them indirectly by advice or interference of any sort, until they have passed both houses: it is only when their operations are concluded that his power begins.

A view of his other functions will belong to other parts of this work, but as preparatory to the whole, it is necessary to set forth the manner of his being elected.

To call an individual from private life in order that he may preside over the interests of millions; to invest him with the various dignified functions, and the extensive patronage which appertain to a station so exalted; to secure as completely as possible, the free exercise of the people's rights; to discourage and prevent the artifices of party, and of individual ambition; and to accomplish all this by means of a fixed and practicable system which should neither be misunderstood, perverted nor resisted, was a task of no small difficulty.

Hereditary succession has its advocates among the lovers of peace and regularity; and the turbulent elections of Poland have often been quoted by those who did not distinguish between a military aristocracy and a well ordered republic. But we had among ourselves more appropriate examples in the elections of the governors of states, which an experience, short but satisfactory, pointed out as models that might be carefully consulted.

The immense territory over which this officer was to preside, the population already great, and annually increasing beyond the relative growth of most other countries, the divisions of states, each separate and independent, and the necessity of admitting to some extent the sensations of local identity even in the act of general and consentaneous suffrages, suggested certain combinations of the elective faculty which in a single state would be useless and unwieldy.

To effect these purposes, an excellent theory was adopted. Each state is to appoint in such manner as the legislature may direct, a number of electors equal to the whole number of senators and representatives to which the state may be entitled in congress, and these electors are to choose the President, and Vice President by ballot only.

In thus fixing the proportional number of electors, we perceive a due attention to the preservation of the state character, without impairing the universality of action incident to the election itself.

The people of each state had created their respective legislatures according to the forms of their own constitutions. Those legislatures are to direct in what manner the electors shall be appointed, and there is no restriction upon them in this respect, because it is one of those instances in which it was right to leave a certain free agency to the state.

We have seen that in the appointment of senators, the state acts by the legislature alone. The legislature cannot divest itself of the duty of choosing senators when the occasion requires it. It cannot devolve the choice upon electors or on the people.

But the duties of the senate though dignified and exalted, are not so various as those of the president. Their participation in the executive business is small and at uncertain intervals. The president comes into daily contact with the people, by his daily executive functions, yet it was conceived that he might feel a greater dependence on the people than the public interests would warrant, if his election sprung immediately from them. On the other hand, if his election depended entirely on the legislatures, it would carry the state character beyond its reasonable bearings, and create a sense of dependency on them alone, instead of a relation to the people at large. Under the old confederation, the president was chosen by the members of the congress, and not by the state legislatures who appointed those members.

From these coincidences it was found expedient that he should owe his election, neither directly to the people, nor to the legislatures of states, yet that these legislatures should create a select body, to be drawn from the people, who in the most independent and unbiassed manner, should elect the president. As the election would thus in effect become in a certain sense, the combined act of the legislatures and of the people, it was further considered that while the latter were thus brought into action, the state character was further to be maintained, and hence two electors were, at all events, to be secured to each state. Thus as an equal representation in the senate was already secured to each state, however small the state might be, a certain degree of respectability and effect was also secured to the smallest state, in the number of electors. This concession to the small states could not, however, be allowed, without allowing it also to the largest, since all are constitutionally equal.

The manner in which these great objects were to be effected is now to be exhibited.

It is directed that the electors shall meet in their respective states. The particular place of meeting is properly to be fixed by the legislature, but it cannot be out of the state; if the legislature should inadvertently or designedly omit to designate the place of meeting, or if any moral or physical cause should render it impossible for the electors to assemble there, nothing appears in the Constitution to prevent them from meeting at a place of their own choice.

The election is to be by ballot, the mode of proceeding best calculated to secure a freedom of choice.

Of the two persons voted for, one at least shall not be an inhabitant of the same state with the electors. The votes being transmitted to the senate were to be opened by its president in the presence of the senate and house of representatives. The person having the greatest number of votes was to be president if such number was a majority of the whole number of electors appointed, and if there was more than one who, had such majority and had an equal number of votes, the house of representatives were immediately to choose by ballot one of them for president. If no person had a majority, the house should in like manner choose the president out of the five highest on the list. The votes of the house were to be taken not individually, but by states, the representatives from each state having one vote. A quorum to consist of a member or members from two-thirds of the states, and a majority of all the states was necessary for a choice.

The mode of proceeding was somewhat different as to the vice president. After the choice of the president, the person having the greatest number of votes was to be vice president. If there remained two or more who had an equal number of votes, the senate and not the house, were to choose from them by ballot the vice president, and as it is not directed that in this respect they shall vote by states, it follows that they vote individually as in ordinary cases.

Such was the original plan of the constitution, but it has been usefully altered by providing that the ballots of the electors shall be separately given for president and vice president, and that the vice president shall be elected, as in the case of the president, by a majority of the whole number of electors appointed.

The number of candidates out of whom the selection is to be made by the house of representatives, is reduced from five to three. The senate in respect to vice president is confined to the two highest in votes.

In regard to the final choice of the president, it was deemed expedient that the house of representatives should vote by states, because there would always be reason to suppose that if the people at large were much divided in opinion, their immediate representatives would be incapable of coming to a decision, and no other mode of removing the difficulty occurred than in this manner to refer it to the states. In the senate, where the representation is equal, the same inconvenience was not to be apprehended, and by reducing the ultimate candidates to a smaller number, those who represented states in which the votes had been lost, would be much less influenced, even if such influence existed at all.

Another benefit also resulted from it. By the first mode of proceeding the senate was restrained from acting until the house of rep resentatives had made their selection, which if parties ran high, might be considerably delayed by the amendment, the senate may proceed to choose a vice president immediately on receiving the returns of the votes. If under the old mode, the house of representatives did not choose a president before the fourth day of March next ensuing, the vice president then in office was to act as president. So that although the public confidence might have been wholly withdrawn from him, he would become president in effect whereas on the present plan, if no president is elected by the house of representatives, the vice president who will fill the office, will have the fresh suffrages of the people.

So far therefore as relates to this part of the plan for choosing the president and vice president, the arrangement seems now settled as judiciously as the nature of our Constitution will admit, although one difficulty not provided for, may possibly some day occur. If more than three of those highest in votes for president, or than two of those voted for as vice president should be equal in number of votes, it is not directed how the selection shall be made. In the original text it is declared, that the votes of the house of representatives and the senate shall be by ballot, and. so it still continues as to the house of representatives, but it is not directed in the amendment, how the votes of the senate shall be given. It is probable, however, that a vote by ballot, would be adopted.

At present, (1824,) the electors are chosen by the people in seventeen out of the twenty-four states, either by a general ticket, or in districts fixed by the legislature. In the remaining seven, the legislature has reserved to itself the power of appointing them. The former mode seems most congenial with the nature of our government, and the popular current now sets so strongly in favor of it, that the practice will probably become general. [1]

Vacancies in the office of president are provided for. "In case of the removal of the president from office, or of his death, resignation or inability to discharge the powers and duties of the office, it shall devolve on the vice president," and congress shall have power to provide for the concurrent vacancies of both.

This power has been executed by authorizing the president *pro tempore* of the senate to perform those functions. The president *pro tempore* of the senate is chosen by the senate during the absence of the vice president, or when he executes the office of president, and it has become usual for the vice president to retire from the senate a few days before the close of the session, in order that a president *pro tempore* may be chosen, to be ready to act on emergencies. If however there should happen to be vacancies in all these three respects, the speaker of the house of representatives is next empowered to assume the office of president, and beyond this no provision has been made.

If the vice president succeeds to the office of president, he continues in it till the expiration of the time for which the president was elected; but if both those offices are vacant, it becomes the duty of the secretary of state to take measures for the election of a president.

The effect of the last amendment has not been adverted to by congress. As the Constitution now stands a vice president cannot be elected till the regular period.

Notification is to be given, as well to the executive of each state as in one at least of the public newspapers printed in each state, that electors of a president shall be appointed or chosen within thirty-four days next preceding the first Wednesday in the ensuing December, unless there shall not be two months between the date of the notification and the first Wednesday in the ensuing December, in which case the election shall be postponed till the ensuing year. But if the term of the office of the president and vice president would have expired on the third of March next following such vacancies, no extra election is necessary, as the regular election will then take place on the same day which the secretary of state is otherwise directed to notify.

For the office of both president and vice president is fixed to commence on the fourth of March in each year, and the regular election takes place on the first Wednesday of the preceding December.[50]

Under these multiplied provisions, no inconvenience can be apprehended. It can scarcely ever happen that there shall be at one and the same time no president, vice president, *pro tempore* president of the senate, and speaker of the house of representatives.

It must however be acknowledged that in no respect have the enlarged and profound views of those who framed the constitution, nor the expectations of the public when they adopted it, been so completely frustrated as in the practical operation of the system so far as relates to the independence of the electors.

It was supposed that the election of these two high officers would be committed to men not likely to be swayed by party or personal bias, who would act under no combination with others, and be subject neither to intimidation or corruption. It was asserted that the choice of several persons to form an intermediate body of electors, would be much less apt to convulse the community with extraordinary movements, than the choice of one who was himself to be the final object of their wishes. [2]

Whether ferments and commotions would accompany a general election by the whole body of the people, and whether such a mode of election could be conveniently practiced in reference to the ratio of representatives prescribed in the constitution, is yet to be ascertained; but experience has fully convinced us, that the electors do not assemble in their several states for a free exercise of their own judgments, but for the purpose of electing the particular candidate who happens to be preferred by the predominant political party which has chosen those electors. In some instances the principles on which they are chosen are so far forgotten, that electors publicly pledge themselves to vote for a particular individual, and thus the whole foundation of this elaborate system is destroyed.

Another innovation has also been introduced. Members of congress, entrusted only with the power of ordinary legislation, have frequently formed themselves into a regular body at the seat of gov-

50 *Amendment 20 of the Constitution, which was adopted on January 23, 1933, sets the beginning of the President's term of office at noon on January 20.*

ernment, and undertaken to point out to the people certain persons as proper objects of their choice. Although the mild and plausible garb of recommendation is alone assumed, yet its effect is known and felt to have been often great and sometimes irresistible.

If the Constitution, as originally proposed, had contained a direct provision that the president and vice president should be chosen by a majority of the two houses of congress, it is not probable that this part of it would have been adopted.

That the chief executive magistrate should be the creature of the legislature; that he should view in them the source from which he sprung, and by which he was to be continued, would at once destroy the dignity and independence of his station, and render him no longer what the Constitution intended, an impartial and inflexible administrator of the public interests. To the people alone he would no longer consider himself responsible, but he would be led to respect, and would be fearful to offend, a power higher than the people.

Such principles cannot be found in the Constitution; and it is wholly inconsistent with its spirit and its essence, to effectuate indirectly, that which directly is not avowed or intended. These instances fully prove that the safety of the people greatly depends on a close adherence to the letter and spirit of their excellent Constitution; but it is probable that a late failure will prevent a renewal of the last-mentioned attempt. And in reference to the election of 1828, it has not been renewed, but, with a strict adherence to the forms prescribed, the voice of a great majority of the people has decided the choice.

Before we close the subject, it is proper to add that, in one respect, the caution of the Constitution cannot be violated — no senator or representative or person holding an office of trust or profit under the United States can be an elector, and therefore the vote of every such person would be void.

CHAPTER NOTES
V

1. There are now (1829) but two states, *viz.* Delaware and South Carolina in which the electors are appointed by the legislature.

2. Fed. No. 8.

CHAPTER VI.

OF THE MANNER OF EXERCISING THE LEGISLATIVE POWER.

THE two houses possess co-equal powers in regard to originating laws, except those for raising revenue, which originate only in the house of representatives, but the senate may propose or concur with amendments as in other bills. Some doubts have existed as to the policy, or at least the necessity of this exception. It is introduced, however, into most of the state constitutions, and may be founded on the utility of keeping this frequent subject of legislation in a regular system, in order that public credit may not be impaired by the suggestion of discordant plans, or needless innovations. In addition to which, it was probably supposed that the members of the house of representatives, coming more frequently from the body of the people, and from their numbers combining a greater variety of character and employment, would be better qualified to judge not only of the necessity, but also of the methods of raising revenue.

On all other subjects, a bill may originate in either house, and after having been fully considered, it is sent to the other. If amendments are proposed, the bill is sent back for concurrence. If the two houses disagree, either to the bill, as originally trained, or as amended, a conference usually takes place, and if neither house will recede, the bill is lost. It is not usual to bring forward another bill on the same subject during the same session, but it may be done, as it is a mere matter of parliamentary regulation, and not prohibited by the Constitution.

When a bill has passed both houses, it is presented to the president, and his share of the legislative duty commences, but it is wisely and prudently guarded. If he possessed the right of imposing an absolute negative, it would vest in him too great a power. If he sent back the bill, with or without its reasons for refusing his assent, and the same numbers that originally passed it, were still sufficient to give it the effect of a law, the reference to him would be an empty form. It is therefore most judiciously provided, that not only every bill which has passed both houses, but every order, resolution, or vote, on which the concurrence of both is necessary, except on questions of adjournment, may, if not approved by him, be returned with his objections to the house in which it originated. These objections are to be entered at large on their journal, and the house is then to proceed to reconsider the bill or resolution; if after such reconsideration, two-thirds of that house shall agree to pass the bill or resolution, it shall be sent, together with the objections, to the other house, by which it shall likewise be reconsidered, and if approved by two-thirds of that house also, the bill becomes a law, and the resolution becomes absolute. But in all such cases, the votes of both houses shall be determined by yeas and nays, and entered on the journals. While this great share of the legislative power is given to the president, it would be improper to leave it to him indefinitely to exercise it, without some control in point of time, and therefore it is provided that if such bill or resolution, are not returned by him within ten days, (Sundays excepted,) the resolution shall take effect, or the bill shall become a law, unless congress by their adjournment prevent it; a consideration which ought to induce the two houses, whenever it if possible, to prepare matters of importance in either shape, for the consideration of the president, at least ten days before the time of their adjournment, otherwise, and particularly when the duration of the session is limited, measures of high interest may be frustrated for a season.

We might here draw a comparison much to our advantage between our system and those of the European monarchies, where the absolute negative of the king depends solely on his own will and pleasure, or on the other hand, with those ancient republics in which the chief executive magistrates did not in the smallest degree participate in the legislative power. Our scheme judiciously steers a middle course. Laws do not originate with the president, although it is his duty to recommend subjects for consideration when the public good requires it; but as laws may be unadvisedly and too precipitately passed even by a double legislature, it may be often salutary to call them to a reconsideration of their measures, and by requiring the objections to be entered on the journal, and the yeas and nays to be recorded, the people, who are the ultimate judges, are enabled to decide on the soundness of conduct on the part of all. The remedy takes place at the next election.[51]

---

51 *The people of a state may be burdened with a Senator who does not represent the people of their state but, in a federal system with real states' rights, this could be resolved by state legislation allowing for the recalling via a state ballot initiative.*

SECTION III
Chapters VII-X

In these four chapters, Rawle describes the powers which were delegated by the States to the United States Congress. As Rawle explains, the most supreme act of a Sovereign State is the act of delegating to another entity a portion of its sovereign power. Rawle reminds us this act of delegating powers to the Federal government was carried out by the free and voluntary actions of independent States. By their own will, the States limited their power in certain areas and provided the means for a Federal government to achieve those goals the States desired of it. This act of delegating a portion of their power by the States to the Federal government resulted in the formation of what the author of The Federalist No. 51, refers to as the "compound republic of America."

This compound republic of America results in greater protection of American liberty because the power delegated by the people is first divided between "two distinct governments," State and Federal. The portion allotted to each government is further divided among different departments, i.e., the Legislative, Executive, and Judicial.

In Chapter VII, Rawle examines the treaty-making power of Congress, who can make a treaty, and the mechanics of enacting a treaty. In Chapter VIII, Rawle reviews how and under what conditions laws are enacted by Congress. In Chapter IX, Rawle reviews the enumerated powers of Congress chief among which are:

1. *Lay ad collect taxes, duties, impost, and excises;*
2. *Borrowing money on the credit of the United States;*
3. *Regulate commerce with foreign nations and among the several States.*

In Chapter X, Rawle reviews the restrictions the States placed on the Federal government and the restrictions to which they mutually agreed to place upon each State.

CHAPTER VII.

OF THE TREATY MAKING POWER.

WE will now proceed to consider the legislative powers vested in these bodies.

Treaties being, next to the Constitution, the supreme law of the land, properly fall into this class. They are laws, in making which the house of representatives has no original share; whether their subsequent concurrence in any shape is necessary will hereafter be examined.

The language of the Constitution is, that "he [the president,] shall have power by and with the advice and consent of the senate to make treaties, provided two-thirds of the senators present concur."

This, at first view, would imply that a treaty, like an act of congress, should in its progress be the subject of joint deliberation, but the practice has necessarily been otherwise.

Treaties, if made abroad, are effected through the medium of our ministers to foreign courts under instructions from the president. If made here, the business is transacted by the secretary of state, under like instructions, with the ministers from foreign courts. The senate is not consulted in the first process: when the treaty is agreed on, the president submits it to the senate, in whose deliberations he takes no part, but he renders to them, from time to time, such information relative to it as they may require. The senate may wholly reject it, or they may ratify it in part, or recommend additional or explanatory articles, which, if the president approves of them, again become the subject of negotiation between him and the foreign power; and finally, when the whole receives the consent of the senate, and the ratifications are exchanged between the respective governments, the treaty becomes obligatory on both nations.

The proceedings of the senate during this process are with closed doors, and the contents of the treaty and the information connected with it ought in good policy to be kept secret. But the Constitution does not in express terms require it, and, in one particular instance, when the public mind was greatly agitated, disclosures, not only of the contents of the treaty itself, but of some of the proceedings of the senate in regard to it took place, the propriety of doing which was admitted or denied according to the opposing opinions of the day. [1]

The nature and extent of this constitutional power underwent full examinations [2] in the state conventions. The most general terms are used in the Constitution. The powers of congress in respect to making laws we shall find are laid under several restrictions. There are none in respect to treaties. Although the acts of public ministers, less immediately delegated by the people than the house of representatives; the president constitutionally and the senate both constitutionally and practically, two removes from the people, are by the treaty making power, invested with the high and sole control over all those subjects which properly arise from intercourse with foreign nations, and may eventually affect important interests at home. To define them in the Constitution would have been impossible, and therefore a general term could alone be made use of, which is, however, to be scrupulously confined to its legitimate interpretation. Whatever is wanting in an authority expressed, must be sought for in principle, and to ascertain whether the execution of the treaty making power can be supported, we must carefully apply to it the principles of the Constitution from which alone the power proceeds.

In its general sense, we can be at no loss to understand the meaning of the word treaty. It is a compact entered into with a foreign power, and it extends to all those matters which are generally the subjects of compact between independent nations. Such subjects are peace, alliance, commerce, neutrality, and others of a similar nature. To make treaties is an essential attribute of a nation.[52] One which disabled itself from the power of making, and the capacity of observing and enforcing them when made, would exclude itself from the international equality which its own interests require it to preserve, and thus in many respects commit an injury on itself. In modern times and among civilized nations, we have no instances of such absurdity. The power must then reside somewhere. Under the articles of confederation it was given with some restrictions, proceeding from the nature of that imperfect compact, to congress, which then nominally

---

52 *Sovereign American States delegated to the Federal government, via Article I, Section 10, of the Constitution, their treaty making authority. One cannot delegate something one does not legally possess. Free, independent, and sovereign states delegated certain and specific portions of their authority and, in so doing, created their agent — the Federal government. Sovereign States created a government "between the States" not over the states, see Article VII paragraph one U.S. Constitution.*

exercised both the legislative and executive powers of general government. In our present Constitution no limitations were held necessary. The only question was where to deposit it. Now this must be either in congress generally, in the two houses exclusive of the president, in the president conjunctly with them or one of them, or in the president alone.

The formation of a treaty often requires secrecy and dispatch, neither of which could be found in the first or second mode, and a contrary plan would be inconsistent with the usages of most nations. It remained then either to vest it in the president singly, or to unite one of the other bodies with him. The latter was obviously preferable, and all that remained was to select that one whose conformation appeared most congenial to the task. The senate is a smaller body, and therefore whenever celerity was necessary, the most likely to, promote it — it was a permanent body; its members, elected for a longer time, were most likely to be conversant in the great political interests which would be agitated, and perhaps it was supposed, that as representatives in one point of view, rather of the states than of the people, a federative quality appertained to them not wholly unconnected with the nature of a foreign compact.

From these and other considerations, the power was vested where we find it; and whenever objections are raised against the extensive operations of a treaty, on account of the source from which it springs, we must remember that it was the will of the whole body of the people to place it there.

The legal effect of a treaty constitutionally made is, that next to the Constitution itself, it prevails over all state laws, state constitutions, and acts of congress.

This is expressed in the following words —

"This Constitution and the laws of the United States which shall be made in pursuance thereof, and all treaties made or which shall be made under the authority of the United States, shall be the supreme law of the land, and the judges in every state shall be bound thereby, any thing in the Constitution or laws of any state to the contrary notwithstanding."[53]

---

53 *Article VI, Section 2 is the so-called "supremacy clause" which consolidationists use to claim that Federal laws are supreme to state laws. Actually, the clause does the exact opposite. The operative words are "laws...made in pursuance" to the Constitution. As High Federalists, Alexander Hamilton, noted in Federalist No.33, if a law is made that is not in "pursuance" to the Constitution, then that law is null and void. The words*

There is a variance in the words descriptive of laws and those of treaties — in the former it is said those which shall be made "in pursuance of the Constitution," but treaties are described as having been made, or which shall be made "under the authority of the United States."

The explanation is, that at the time of adopting the Constitution, certain treaties existed, which had been made by congress under the confederation, [3] the continuing obligations of which it was proper to declare. The words "under the authority of the United States," were considered as extending equally to those previously made, and to those which should subsequently be effected. But although the former could not be considered as made pursuant to a Constitution which was not then in existence, the latter would not be "under the authority of the United States," unless they are conformable to its Constitution.

It has been observed, that it is not distinctly declared whether treaties are to be held superior to acts of congress, or whether the latter are to be co-equal with or superior to the former. The mere collocation of the words would tend to give the superiority to the laws, but higher ground must be taken for the decision of the question.

Having felt the necessity of the treaty making power, and having fixed on the department in which it shall be vested, the people of course excluded from all interference with it, those parts of the government which are not described as partaking of it. The representation held out by our Constitution to foreign powers, was, that the president with the advice and consent of the senate, could bind the nation in all legitimate compacts: but if pre-existent acts, contrary to the treaty, could only be removed by Congress, this representation would be fallacious; it would be a just subject of reproach, and would destroy all future confidence in our public stipulations. The immediate operation of the treaty must therefore be to overrule all existing legislative acts inconsistent with its provisions.

But this is not inconsistent with a power to pass subsequent laws, qualifying, altering, or even wholly annulling a treaty. Such a power may be supported on another ground. Congress alone possesses the right to declare war; and the right to qualify, alter, or annul a treaty being of a tendency to produce war is an incident to the right of declaring war. Such measures may be essential to the interests of the

---

"supreme law of the land" are the result of the former — they are explanatory not mandatory. "In pursuance" are the operative words.

nation, and it is impossible to find them in any other part of the Constitution than in the general powers held by Congress. But in these procedures, the senate must necessarily, and the president may eventually be parties, and they are essentially different from laws to carry a treaty into effect, which suppose the treaty imperfect, till they are passed. The former laws on the contrary, consider the treaty as complete and effective, and are passed as the only means of counteracting it under a change of circumstances, at the hazard indeed of exciting the complaints, resentment, or hostilities of the foreign power.

In the years 1795 and 1796, the house of representatives was much agitated on account of the treaty of November 19th, 1794, between the United States and Great Britain. A resolution was passed requesting the president to lay before them a copy of his instructions to the minister who negotiated the treaty, with the correspondence and other documents relative to that treaty, excepting such papers as any existing negotiations may render it improper to disclose.

The illustrious individual who then held the office, answered, that he had never had but one opinion on the subject, and that his conduct had always conformed to it. His opinion was, that the power of making treaties is exclusively vested in the president, by and with the advice and consent of the senate, provided two-thirds of the senators present concur, and that any treaty so made and promulgated. thenceforward becomes the law of the land.

It is thus, he added, that the treaty making power has been understood by foreign nations; and in all the treaties made with them, we have declared, and they have believed, that, when ratified by the president, with the advice and consent of the senate, they become obligatory. In this construction of the Constitution every house of representatives had acquiesced, and until the present time, not a doubt or suspicion had appeared, to his knowledge, that this construction was not the true one.

With some further remarks, be concluded by observing, that as it was perfectly clear to his understanding that the consent of the house of representatives is not necessary to the validity of a treaty, as the treaty with Great Britain exhibited in itself all the objects requiring legislative provision, and on these the papers called for could throw no light; and as it is essential to the due administration of a government, that the boundaries fixed by the Constitution between the different departments should be preserved, a just regard to the Constitution and to the duties of his office forbade a compliance with their request. [4]

The principles thus laid down were so far acquiesced in by the house, that they passed a resolution disclaiming a power to interfere in making treaties, but asserting the right of the house of representatives, whenever stipulations are made on subjects committed by the Constitution to congress, to deliberate on the expediency of carrying them into effect. And subsequently, though not without much acrimonious debate, and by a small majority, it was declared to be expedient to pass the laws necessary to carry the treaty into effect.

From that time, the question remained undisturbed, until the session of 1815-16, when in relation to another treaty with Great Britain, the house of representatives, after much debate, passed a bill particularly enacting the same stipulations on one subject as those which were contained in the treaty. This, as a dangerous innovation on the treaty making power, was warmly opposed by the minority, and disagreed to by the senate. But after conferences between the two houses, it terminated in a sort of compromise, which it is difficult to reconcile with a sound construction of the Constitution. The act, (which was passed on the 1st of March, 1816,) shortly declares, that so much of any act as imposes a duty on tonnage, contrary to the provisions of a convention between the United States and his Britannic Majesty, shall from and after the date of that instrument, and during its continuance, be of no force or effect.

Thus a precedent was set, which a dissatisfied house of representatives may hereafter resort to; and although the judicial tribunals would probably consider the law as being wholly unnecessary, and a nullity in itself, it may be the cause of future legislative attempts producing more difficulty.

Yet however manifest these principles may appear, it must be confessed that another part of the Constitution presents an apparent difficulty which requires examination.

By the 9th sect. of the 1st article, it is expressly declared, that "no money shall be drawn from the treasury but in consequence of appropriations made by law."

A treaty may be made, by which a sum of money is engaged to be paid to a foreign power, on considerations beneficial to the Union; can such a contract be fulfilled without an act of congress? Three eventual cases may be stated:

Where there is a sufficient sum of money in the treasury, not under any specific appropriation.

Where there is a sufficient sum, but actually appropriated to different objects.

Where there is no money in the treasury, but a sufficient sum must be raised in some manner to fulfil the contract.

In the second and third of these supposed cases, it would seem that the treaty could not be carried into effect by its own power. Taxation, direct or indirect, can only be the work of congress.

By Art. 1. § viii. the congress shall have "power to lay and collect taxes, duties, imposts, and excises."

No such power is given to the president and senate in direct terms.

By another section, (the 7th,) of the same article, "All bills for raising revenue shall originate in the house of representatives." A nice disquisition might here be introduced, whether the fulfillment of a contract with a foreign power, was to be considered as raising revenue. The term ought to be interpreted in its broad and general sense, and in reference to the spirit and meaning of the whole Constitution. By revenue we must understand whatever is produced by taxes, duties, imposts, and excises, for public use. The moneys so raised may be applied to defray the expenses of government, to pay the principal or interest of the public debt, to maintain an army and navy, to pay for acquisitions of territory, (as in the recent instance of the purchase of Florida from Spain, when by treaty we assumed the payment of the money to which our own citizens were justly entitled, by reason of the injuries inflicted on them by that country,) to preserve peace and harmony with foreign powers, as the barbarous states of Africa, and a variety of other cases. It is still revenue, and congress alone can raise it. and the bill can only originate in the house of representatives. If, therefore, a new tax must be laid, or a specific appropriation already made by congress superseded, it seems obvious that it cannot be done by the president and senate.

The first of the three cases supposed will seldom happen, but should it ever take place, and a sum, which by treaty the United States were bound to pay to a foreign power, could be discharged out of moneys lying in the treasury, unfettered by appropriation, the difficulty would not yet be subdued. If the surplus in the treasury arose from a tax, laid with a view to the fulfillment of treaties which were thereafter to be concluded, great doubts might be entertained whether such a law would be constitutional. To extract money from the people for a purpose so indefinite, and to place those moneys at the disposal of the treaty making power, might possibly be supported by the authority given to congress to provide for the common defense and general welfare. But even this, as it would amount to a concurrence of congress in effectuating the treaty, would leave the question unresolved. The original difficulty remains, if the moneys thus found in the treasury, consisted of a surplus unappropriated by congress in any manner, or to any object whatever. Now we must keep in view, that a treaty with a foreign power, is not of itself an appropriation of moneys in the treasury of the United States, any more than it would be an appropriation of moneys in the treasury of the foreign power. It is evidently not an appropriation in a constitutional sense, for it can only be made (so far as relates to other subjects) as the act of both houses, and in the solemn form of a law. However strong, therefore, the obligation of good faith may be on the nation to fulfill the treaty, it does not seem that it has invested in the president and senate a full effectuating power. And if the president alone, or conjunctly with the senate, were to draw on the treasury for the sum necessary to fulfill it, such draught would not appear to be within the direction of the Constitution. [5]

On the whole, the conclusion seems to be, that in this single instance, the payment of money, the concurrence of the house of representatives is necessary to give effect to the treaty. But an engagement to pay a sum of money would not be, like the engagement to cede a part of the territory of the United States, unconstitutional and void. When it should receive the sanction of congress, and the means are provided, the treaty may be effected. It is reserved for congress alone "to dispose of the territory of the United States," if by this general expression we are to understand the alienation of any part of the territory, which we shall hereafter consider.

In another shape the same question was agitated in the year 1798. Parties at that time ran high; the house of representatives was much divided. It was conceived or alleged, that the expenses incurred by the multitude of our foreign ministers, were greater than necessary. The practice always had been, and still continues, to make an annual appropriation of a gross sum for the expenses of foreign intercourse, without further interference than to limit the compensation to ministers of different grades, but leaving it implicitly to the president, with the concurrence of the senate, to send ministers to such courts as they, who were best acquainted with the subject, should deem expedient. An effort was made to confine the higher rate of compensation to the ministers of three specified courts, and to allow all the others only half the same amount. It was warmly contended that congress, by having the exclusive power to raise and appropriate, was authorized to grant only so much money as they should think necessary. Happily for the interests and character of our country, the effort failed, and it is hoped will never be renewed.

There can be no doubt of the spirit and true intent of the Constitution, in respect to all pecuniary supplies required to support the exercise of the treaty making power. It is incumbent on congress to furnish those supplies. The Constitution has vested exclusively in the president and senate the duty of foreign intercourse. The interference of congress in any shape is not warranted further than to afford the means of carrying on that intercourse to the extent which the president and senate hold to be requisite for the national interest, and of furnishing the means of effectuating treaties constitutionally made, when, as has been seen, their intervention is absolutely necessary. It is true that there is no express direction to this effect, neither is there as to many other applications of the public revenue. But wherever there is a duty pointed out in general terms, and adequate powers given to any department of government for performing it, common sense indicates the course to be pursued, and those who are thus authorized, must be considered as bound to perform the duty. If it be refused, the general operations of government will be affected with greater or less injury according to circumstances; and the remedies can only be subsequently and perhaps tardily applied. These remedies must be a constitutional change of the public agents. But this is not peculiar to the American Constitution. Short of actual violence, it never is effected but by the mild, yet firm, exhibition of the sovereign power, if, as with us, it still remains in the people, by the substitution of others for those whose conduct has occasioned a diminution of public confidence.

The effect of a treaty on state constitutions and state laws cannot be questioned. Without considering whether it operates directly as a repeal of them, we are warranted in saying that an act done under a state law, in opposition to a treaty, cannot be set up as a legal bar to a proceeding founded on a treaty.

The inability of the Confederation to enforce the treaties made by them was severely felt. Many state laws which had been passed, during, or shortly after the war of the revolution, were inconsistent with some of the articles of the treaty of peace with Great Britain, and that power, complaining of injuries sustained in consequence thereof, postponed the fulfilment of the treaty in some points on their part. The inadequacy of the powers of congress to enforce it were then sensibly felt, and a serious declaration that a treaty, in virtue of the confederation, was part of the law of the land and obligatory on the several legislatures, was transmitted to all the states, with an urgent recommendation that the states themselves would repeal all those acts and parts of acts that were repugnant to the treaty. [6] In this respect the want of a judicial power was strongly perceived.

After the adoption of the Constitution, its retrospective effect upon the opposing laws of a state, passed even before the treaty, was speedily and fully established by the Supreme Court of the United States. [7]

As a law, the president enforces a treaty by his executive power when necessary. This took place in several instances during the war between France and Great Britain, after the president, in a legitimate execution of the duties of his high office, had issued a proclamation of neutrality. Some of the belligerent captures and other acts, so far as they occasionally interfered with the obligations of our treaties with either nation, were ratified by his interventions. [8]

The wisdom, impartiality, and firmness manifested on the part of our government, during the whole of that difficult period, entitled it to the highest applause, and there could be no better proof of its merits, than the dissatisfaction alternately expressed by each of the great contending powers. It is also due to the executives of the several states to declare that although there were at the time strong popular impressions in favor of one, and to the prejudice of the other nation, all considerations of that kind were suppressed in a prompt and efficient compliance with the directions emanating from the president. An accurate and comprehensive collection of the acts of our government during the whole of that war would be an useful addition to the stock of public information, and would afford precedents which no foreign cabinet could justly disdain to follow.

CHAPTER NOTES
VII

1. Relative to the British treaty of 1794.
2. See particularly the debates of the Virginia convention.
3. With France, the United Netherlands, and particularly the treaty of peace with Great Britain.
4. Message, Match 30, 1796, and see Marshall's *Life of Washington*, vol 5.
5. When lands are purchased of the Indian tribes through treaties made with them, the money is always paid under appropriations by acts of congress.
6. See the journal of congress, March 21, and April 13, 1787. The letter from congress prepared by Mr. Jay, then secretary for foreign affairs, is admirable in style and reasoning. See the Appendix.
7. Calder v. Bull, 3d Dallas, 386, and Brailsford v. Meade, ib. 1. The Supreme Court of Pennsylvania, in the case of Gordon, affirmed the same principle, 1 Dall. 233.
8. See Sergeant on Constitutional Law, p. 216. 397.

CHAPTER VIII.

OF LAWS ENACTED BY CONGRESS.

LAWS enacted by congress form the third rule of obligation. The power of legislation vested in congress, is conformable to the high objects of its formation, some of which are expressly enumerated, and some included in the extensive authority to provide for the common defense and general welfare; but this broad declaration has been considered by some as restrained by an amendment which has since become part of the constitution to the following effect: "The powers not delegated to the United States by the constitution, nor prohibited by it to the states, are reserved to the states respectively or to the people."

The question is not completely settled by this article. "The nature of a constitution requires "that only its great outlines should be marked, its important objects designated, and the minor "ingredients, which compose those objects, be deduced from the nature of the objects themselves. "If it contained an accurate detail of all the subdivisions of which its great powers will admit, and "of all the means by which they may be carried into execution, it would partake of the prolixity of "a legal code, and rather than to embarrass than to elucidate. Whether any particular power is "delegated to the general government or prohibited to the states, must depend on a fair construction "of the whole instrument." [1] The amendment does not speak of powers expressly delegated, and is in fact to be considered rather in the light of a cautious and special reservation of what is not granted, conceived in terms as general as the grant itself. But whatever is already granted, either generally or by express words, is not intended to be abridged, and therefore, in effect, this clause has no operation on the grant itself.[54]

54 *Because the Articles of Confederation state that "all powers not expressly [emphasis added] delegated to the Federal government" were to remain with the States, and whereas the Constitution in the tenth amendment states "The powers not delegated to the United States ... " are to remain with the States, some people maintain that the deletion of the word "expressly" from the Constitution means that the States can have only those rights which are allowed by a "fair" interpretation of the Constitution. Of course, by "fair" the advocates of centralized power mean a liberal or loose construction by which all power is given to the Federal government and the States are stripped*

In a variety of instances, the legislative power is not left to depend on general inferences. Express enumeration removes the difficulty as to the subject, and it is only in respect to what may be termed the excess of practical legislation, beyond the subject expressed, that any doubt can arise.

The style and composition of statues in modern times, have frequently been complained of; it has been observed that they sometimes obscure the sense by a multiplicity of words intended to produce the opposite effect, and the brevity and simplicity of ancient times have been held up as examples to be followed. But perhaps the peculiar character of our government may justify more minuteness in the legislative acts, than in those of a government not under similar limitations. Although verboseness, productive of perplexity, should be scrupulously avoided, yet the enactments of a law frames under limited authority, should clearly appear to be confined to that authority, and as little as possible be left for general construction. The acts hitherto passed by congress have not often created doubts as to their true meaning.

CHAPTER NOTES
VIII

1. See M'Culloch v. Maryland, 4 Wh. 316. Anderson v. Dunn, 6 Wh. 225.

---

of all reserved power. In The Federal Government: Its True Nature and Character, *Able Upsher addresses the assertion of the advocates of centralized power; he states that "The Constitution provides that congress shall have power to pass all laws which shall be necessary and proper for carrying into effect the various powers which it grants. The power to provide a navy is not, in itself, the power to build a dry dock; but, as dry docks are necessary and proper means for providing a navy, Congress shall have power to authorize the construction of them. But if the word 'expressly' had been used in the tenth amendment, it would have created a very rational and strong doubt of this. ... Hence the necessity of omitting the word 'expressly' in the tenth amendment. It left free from doubt and unaffected the power of congress to provide the necessary and proper means of executing the granted powers,* ***while it denied to the Federal Government every power which was not granted****"* [emphasis added].

CHAPTER IX.

OF THE ENUMERATED POWERS OF CONGRESS.

THE enumerated powers, which we now proceed to consider, will be all found to relate to, and be consistent with, the main principle; the common defense and general welfare.

The first is to lay and collect taxes, duties, imposts, and excises.[55] The three latter must be uniform throughout the United States; but there is no description of the subjects to be taxed nor any limitation of the amount to be raised.

The necessity of vesting this power in the union, seems to be too obvious to require much argument. No government can be supported without the means of raising an adequate revenue. It must possess this power in itself, and must not be dependent on others for their concurrence. We have seen in our own history the inefficient condition to which we were reduced, when the necessary income for the most important national objects, could only be obtained by requisitions of the several states.

Of the amount necessary to be raised, the government itself can be the only judge. In governments under a single head, when a separate purse may be kept, in which the people have no share, restrictions, if practicable, may be useful. Here, where the only treasury is that of the people, where compensations to public officers are scrupulously fixed, and a severe accountability is a permanent principle, no such limitations are necessary. And if the money should be faithlessly intercepted in its way to the treasury, or fraudulently withdrawn from it afterwards, the defaulter is always liable to legal coercion.

It was not thought necessary to define what shall be the exclusive subjects of taxation, although in some instances a part of the revenue of a state may be interfered with, by the exercise of the power; for it is better that a particular state should sustain an inconvenience

---

55 *Hamilton, in Federalist No. 30 through 36, explains the proper mode of taxation by Congress and how this process relates to the States. It is noteworthy that, although Hamilton was the foremost advocate of political centralism in America, in the above-mentioned papers, he unequivocally recognizes the "complete sovereignty" of the States (Federalist No. 31). In Federalist No. 32, he states " ... the State governments ... clearly retain all rights of sovereignty which they before had, and which were not, by that act exclusively delegated to the United States.*

than that the general wants should fail of supply. It was manifestly intended that congress should possess full power over every species of taxable property, except exports. The term taxes is genetical, and was made use of to confer a plenary authority in all cases of taxation. The general division of taxes is into direct and indirect; the latter term is not to be found in the Constitution, but the former necessarily implies it. Indirect is opposed to direct. There may possibly be an indirect tax on a particular article that cannot be comprehended within the description of duties, imposts, or excises, but if such case can arise, it will be comprehended within the general denomination of taxes. The term tax includes, 1st. direct taxes, which are properly capitation taxes and taxes on land, although direct taxes may perhaps be laid on other things that generally pervade all the states in the union. 2dly. duties, imposts, and excises. And 3dly. all other classes of an indirect kind. Indirect taxes affect expense or consumption, those who reduce their consumption of an article so taxed, reduce the amount of their tax. [1] A direct tax is independent of consumption or expense, and is to be apportioned among the several states, according to their respective numbers, which is to be determined by the same rule that, as already observed, is applied to representation. Indirect taxes do not admit of this apportionment, but they are to be uniform throughout the United States on the subject taxed. Thus, if Congress think proper to raise a sum of money by direct taxation, the quota of each state is to be fixed according to its census. If indirect taxation is preferred, the same duty must be imposed on the article whether its quantity or consumption is greater or less in the respective states. Whether direct or indirect taxation is most consistent with the genius and interests of our republic, has been much discussed, but it is a question now of little moment to us, since a Constitution authorizing both has been formed.

The next enumerated power is that of borrowing money on the credit of the United States.

When this Constitution was formed, the United States were considerably indebted to foreign nations, for the expenses of the war, and its own citizens had heavy claims, as well on the Union as on individual states, for services and supplies during the same eventful period. To combine and consolidate these debts, to discharge some and secure the rest, was necessary for the public faith and interest both abroad and at home. But to avail itself of the power of taxation, in order to accomplish such extensive objects at once, would have been injurious to the community. It was foreseen that many public creditors, whether distant or domestic, would be satisfied with the assumption or recognition of the principal and the payment of the interest. By the terms thus introduced, congress received power to make the necessary provisions for such objects. In case of future exigencies, the expenses of war or the failure of part of the usual revenue; a similar mean of continuing the operations and the character of government is also thus provided.

To regulate commerce with foreign nations, among the several states, and with the Indian tribes, is the third power. This, from its nature, must be considered as exclusive. If each state retained a power to regulate its own commerce with foreign countries, each would probably pursue a different system. Heavy duties or total prohibitions in respect to some articles, irregular and changeable codes of commerce, mutual rivalries, and other obvious inconveniences would naturally ensue. A common head can alone cure these evils. A common head can alone form commercial treaties with foreign powers, for to no other would a foreign power give sufficient credence.

In like manner the commerce between the different states is the proper subject of a general regulation.

In the term commerce are included not merely the act of buying and selling or exchanging merchandise, but also the navigation of vessels, and commercial intercourse in all its branches: it extends to vessels, by whatever force they are propelled or governed, whether wind, or steam, or oars; to whatever purposes they are applied, whether the carrying of goods or of passengers, or proceeding in ballast only. A general, unconfined power to regulate a subject, is in its nature exclusive of the action of others on the same subject.

These principles are so fully and clearly explained by Chief Justice Marshall in a recent case, [2] that we shall make no apology for inserting a large extract from his opinion.

"Commerce, as the word is used in the Constitution, is a unit, every part of which is indicated by the term.

"If this be the admitted meaning of the word, in its application to foreign nations, it must carry the same meaning throughout the sentence, and remain a unit, unless there be some plain, intelligible cause which alters it.

"The subject to which the power is next applied is to commerce 'among the several states.' Commerce among the states cannot stop at the external boundary line of each state, but may be introduced into the interior.

"These words do not, however, comprehend that commerce which is completely internal, which is carried on between man and man in a state, or between different parts of the same state, and which does not extend to, or affect other states.

"Comprehensive as the word 'among' is, it may very properly be restricted to that commerce which concerns more states than one. The phrase would probably not have been selected to indicate the completely interior traffic of a state, because it is not an apt phrase for that purpose; and the enumeration of the particular classes of commerce to which the power was to be extended, would not have been made had the intention been to extend the power to every description. The enumeration presupposes something not enumerated; and that something, if we regard the language or the subject of the sentence, must be the exclusively internal commerce of a state. The genius and character of the whole government seem to be, that its action is to be applied to all the external commercial concerns of the nation, and to those internal concerns which affect the states generally; but not to those which are completely within a particular state, which do not affect other states, and with which it is not necessary to interfere for the purpose of executing some of the general powers of the government. The completely internal commerce of a state may be considered as reserved for the state itself.

"But in regulating commerce with foreign nations the power of congress does not stop at the jurisdictional lines of the several states. It would be a very useless power if it did. The commerce of the United States with foreign nations is that of the whole United States. Every district has a right to participate in it. If congress has the power to regulate it, that power must be exercised wherever the subject exists. If it exists within the states, if a foreign voyage may commence or terminate at a port within a state, then the power of congress may be exercised within a state.

"This principle is, if possible, still more clear when applied to commerce 'among the several states.' They either join each other, in which case they are separated by a mathematical line; or they are remote from each other, in which case other states lie between them. What is commerce 'among' them, and how is it to be conducted? Can a trading expedition between two adjoining states commence and terminate outside of each? And if the trading intercourse be between two states remote from each other, must it not commence in one, terminate in the other, and probably pass through a third? Commerce among the states must, of necessity, be commerce within the states. In the regulation of trade with the Indian tribes, the action of the law, especially when the Constitution was made, was chiefly within a state. The power of congress, then, may be exercised within the territorial jurisdiction of the several states."

In respect to commerce with the Indian tribes, we are to adopt the same broad interpretation; but it is applicable only to independent tribes. It is immaterial whether such tribes continue seated within the boundaries of a state, inhabit part of a territory, or roam at large over lands to which the United States have no claim; the trade with them is in all its forms, subject exclusively to the regulation of congress, and in this particular also we trace the wisdom of the Constitution. The Indians, not distracted by the discordant regulations of different states, are taught to trust one great body, whose justice they respect, and whose power they fear.

The power to establish an uniform system of naturalization is also an exclusive one.

In the second section of the fourth article it is provided that the citizens of each state, shall be entitled to all privileges and immunities of citizens in the several states, and the same rule had been ambiguously laid down in the articles of confederation. If this clause is retained, and its utility and propriety cannot be questioned, the consequence would be, that if each state retained the power of naturalization, it might impose on all the other states, such citizens as it might think proper. In one state, residence for a short time, with a slight declaration of allegiance, as was the case under the former constitution of Pennsylvania, might confer the rights of citizenship: in another, qualifications of greater importance night be required: an alien, desirous of eluding the latter, might by complying with the requisites of the former, become a citizen of a state in opposition to its own regulations, and thus in fact, the laws of one state become paramount to that of another. The evil could not be better remedied than by vesting the exclusive power in congress.

It cannot escape notice, that no definition of the nature and rights of citizens appears in the Constitution. The descriptive term is used, with a plain indication that its meaning is understood by all, and this indeed is the general character of the whole instrument. Except in one instance, it gives no definitions, but it acts in all its parts, on qualifies and relations supposed to be already known. Thus it declares, that no person, except a natural born citizen, or a citizen of the United States at the time of the adoption of this Constitution, shall be eligible to the office of president — that no person shall be a senator who shall not have been nine years a citizen of the United States, nor a representative who has not been such a citizen seven years, and it will therefore be not inconsistent with the scope and tendency of the present essay, to enter shortly into the nature of citizenship.

In a republic the sovereignty resides essentially, and entirely in the people. Those only who compose the people, and partake of this sovereignty are citizens, they alone can elect, and are capable of being elected to public offices, and of course they alone can exercise authority within the community: they possess an unqualified right to the enjoyment of property and personal immunity, they are bound to adhere to it in peace, to defend it in war, and to postpone the interests of all other countries to the affection which they ought to bear for their own.

The citizens of each state constituted the citizens of the United States when the Constitution was adopted. The rights which appertained to them as citizens of those respective commonwealths, accompanied them in the formation of the great, compound commonwealth [56] which ensued. They became citizens of the latter, without ceasing to be citizens of the former, and he who was subsequently born a citizen of a state, became at the moment of his birth a citizen of the United States. Therefore every person born within the United States, its territories or districts, whether the parents are citizens or aliens, is a natural born citizen in the sense of the Constitution, and entitled to all the rights and privileges appertaining to that capacity. It is an error to suppose, as some (and even so great a mind as Locke) have done, that a child is born a citizen of no country and subject of no government, and that be so continues till the age of discretion, when he is at liberty to put himself under what government he pleases. How far the adult possesses this power will hereafter be considered, but surely it would be unjust both to the state and to the infant, to withhold the quality of the citizen until those years of discretion were attained. Under our Constitution the question is settled by its express language, and when we are informed that, excepting those

56 *The Federal government is here described by Rawle as a "compound commonwealth." In Federalist No. 51, it is referred to as a "compound Republic," and in Federalist No. 69 "Confederated America." In other places it has been referred to as a "Republic of Republics" and a "Republic of Sovereign States."*

who were citizens, (however the capacity was acquired,) at the time the Constitution was adopted, no person is eligible to the office of president unless he is a natural born citizen, the principle that the place of birth creates the relative quality is established as to us.

The mode by which an alien may become a citizen, has a specific appellation which refers to the same principle. It is descriptive of the operation of law as analogous to birth, and the alien, received into the community by naturalization, enjoys all the benefits which birth has conferred on the other class.

Until these rights are attained, the alien resident is under some disadvantages which are not exactly the same throughout the Union. The United States do not intermeddle with the local regulations of the states in those respects. Thus an alien may be admitted to hold lands in some states, and be incapable of doing so in others. On the other hand, there are certain incidents to the character of a citizen of the United States, with which the separate states cannot interfere. The nature, extent, and duration of the allegiance due to the United States, the right to the general protection and to commercial benefits at home and abroad, derived either from treaties or from the acts of congress, are beyond the control of the states, nor can they increase or diminish the disadvantages to which aliens may, by such measures on the part of the general government, be subjected.

Thus if war should break out between the United States and the country of which the alien resident among us is a citizen or subject, he becomes on general principles an alien enemy, and is liable to be sent out of the country at the pleasure of the general government, or laid under reasonable restraints within it, and in. these respects no state can interfere to protect him.

The duration of the quality of citizen, both in the native and in him who is naturalized, is a subject of considerable interest.

The doctrine of indefeasible allegiance has a deeper root in England than in any other country in Europe: the term is indeed almost peculiar to the English law, and in discussing the extent to which they carry it, we shall find it useful to ascend to the source of their government, and the foundation on which this doctrine is placed.

Whatever repugnance may occasionally be felt at the avowal, the present government of England must be considered as founded on conquest, and perhaps it is justly observed by some of their historians, that in scarcely any instance has conquest by foreign arms been pushed to a greater extent than with them.

The reluctance with which a brave and generous nation submitted to the yoke, increased the exasperation, and the tyranny of their conqueror. Their property was almost completely transferred to his military followers, their ancient laws were soon disregarded, although sometimes promised to be restored, and the pure feudal system of tenure was substituted to the ancient allodial estates, or perhaps the imperfect feuds of the Saxons.

With this system the Norman doctrine of allegiance is considered by some to have been introduced, although others trace it up to antecedent periods, [3] but whether the solemn declaration of allegiance was practiced in the time of Arthur or of Alfred, whether it were the custom of the Britons or the Angles, the Saxons or the Danes, we have sufficient ground for believing that after the conquest, it was understood to be due only to the king or the ruling chieftain, and not to the nation.

In the conflicts by which the country was distracted after the departure of the Romans, each successful competitor exacted from those he had subdued, an oath of fidelity and submission.

From this practice the usage arose of requiring a similar engagement from their own followers, as they subsequently dispersed themselves through the country and when Harold was overthrown by the Bastard of Normandy, the necessity of exacting it became more obvious, not only from the discontent which his severities excited, but from the impression which the illegitimacy of his birth might make on his subjects.

The oath of fealty and homage necessarily accompanied the numerous grants of land, wrested from its original owners, and bestowed upon his adherents; the oath of allegiance was incorporated with the oath of fealty, and whoever will reflect on the condition of the times will be satisfied that allegiance was not sworn to the nation, but to the individual whose victorious arms had rendered him the ruler of the nation.

Hence certain consequences were understood to flow; the allegiance thus solemnly pledged could not be withdrawn, unless the protection which was implied in return, should be withheld or become impracticable.

If the monarch was driven out by a successful competitor, who took possession of the throne, the allegiance was considered as transferred to him, and the subject who disobeyed the reigning sovereign, was held to violate his oath.

But from this allegiance, either original or transferred, he could not withdraw himself; he was supposed never to cease being the subject of the reigning sovereign. Allegiance equally permanent was held to result from birth. The king could see none but his own subjects within his own domain. Bound as he alleged to protect all, all were bound to be faithful to him. But allegiance sprung from the birth of those only who were born under his dominion. It is observed by Coke, that if enemies were to obtain possession of a town or fort, and have issue there, that issue would not be subjects of the king of England, for they would have no claim to his protection. [4]

If this view of the subject be correct; if allegiance, at least since the Norman Conquest, is to be considered as proceeding from force and not from contract; if it is legally due to the king and not to the society which he governs, we can remain under no difficulty in respect to its inalienable quality according to their laws.

The rights or expectations of the people were seldom taken into account; the king might, by treaty with a foreign power, alienate an entire territory; and its inhabitants, without their previous knowledge or consent, be compelled to serve another sovereign. [5] Thus allegiance was rendered perpetual at the pleasure of the sovereign, not of the people; and the former, not the latter, possessed a sort of property in it; but with us its indefeasible nature rests on better grounds.

The instantaneous result on our political character, from the declaration of independence, was to convert allegiance from compulsion into compact, and while it still remained due to the sovereign, to see that sovereign only in the whole community.

In the native we have observed that it is coeval with life; in him who migrates from another country, it commences as a permanent duty with naturalization; in both it lasts till death, unless it is released by some procedure, mutual on the part of both the state and the individual.

Whether the individual alone may relinquish it, is a question which in this as well as other countries has been often discussed, and on which an opinion cannot be given without diffidence, since it has not yet received a decision in the highest tribunal of our country.

In the first place, we may dispose with little comparative difficulty of the case of the naturalized citizen. His accession is voluntary, and his engagement is neither in its terms nor in its nature limited to any time. He therefore binds himself by contract for his life, and the state, which differently from the doctrine of the English and other monarchies, cannot afterwards deprive him of the quality thus acquired, which cannot again by its own act, convert him into an alien is equally bound for the same term.

This is well expressed by Locke in his treatise on civil government. "He that has once by actual agreement and express declaration given his consent to be of any commonweal, is perpetually and indispensably obliged to be and remain unalterably a subject of it, and can never be again in the liberty of a state of nature, unless by any calamity, the government he was under shall be dissolved, or by some public act it cuts him off from being a member of it."

Under our Constitution the last would be impossible without his own consent, and the citizen can no more dissolve this contract than he can any other of less moment without the consent of the opposite party.

But there are two other classes of citizens, and we must examine whether the same principle can be applied to them. It would, perhaps, be sufficient to say, that if the obligation, to which the naturalized citizen subjects himself, is clearly an obligation for life; that of the native cannot be for a shorter term. Naturalization is but a mode of acquiring the right, subject to the duties of a citizen; it is the factitious substitution of legal form for actual birth, and it can neither exceed nor fall short of the capacities and obligations which birth creates. It would be absurd indeed, if the foreigner was given to understand, that by naturalization he had become bound for life, in the midst of native citizens, none of whom were under the same obligation.

But we need not rest on this postulate. The compact created among the citizens, by the declaration of independence, was well understood by themselves at the moment, not to be of a temporary nature, and in the power of the individual at pleasure to dissolve. It was essential not only to the permanence, but to the formation of the new government, that every one either taking an active part in its establishment, or giving evidence of his consent by remaining within it, should be considered as bound to it, so long as it continued. Their situation at the moment was not that of aliens, who were held by a prior allegiance, while they undertook another. He who thus united himself with the newly formed state, instantly ceased, in contemplation of our law, to be a subject of Great Britain. He could thereafter, justify no hostile measure against us by alleging his ancient allegiance. What he once owed to that power was now wholly transferred to the new state, with all its qualities and accompaniments, except one. The correlative of protection, could not, as before, be destroyed at pleasure by the receiver of the allegiance. The obligation was mutual and perpetual. If any qualification of it was intended, it would have been expressed, but we do not find in any of the state constitutions, or in that of the United States, the slightest suggestion that the allegiance to be paid to them, was less solemn, less entire, less permanent than that which was previously due to the monarch of Great Britain. Thus the question stands in respect to this class of citizens.

The next inquiry is, whether this contract was confided to the individual or extended also to his issue. So far as relates to the parent, an answer to this question may be found in the mere statement of it. No one can suppose that the parent intended, that while he was a permanent citizen of the state, his children should not partake of the same rights, enjoy the same liberty, and be protected be, the same government. Nature itself impresses on the parental mind, a desire to promote the interests of children, and causes it to revolt at the idea of withholding from them what may not only be shared with them, but what also becomes more valuable by being so shared. The pleasing sensation in the parent, of passing from the condition of an oppressed subject, to that of a citizen of a free republic, would surely be impaired by a consideration that his offspring would acquire no birthright in the community of his choice. In respect to him, therefore, we cannot doubt the desire, and have only to examine the power, of fixing the political relations of his descendants. The principle which next presents itself is, that what all the members of the state must have thus understood, must also have been so understood by the state, which is only the collection of those members. The compact so far as relates to the state, of course extends to the individual and to all his descendants, and therefore, as the child is entitled to the benefit of being recognized as a citizen, the state is entitled in its turn, to view the child as under its allegiance. It may however be urged, that an infant cannot bind itself by contract, but if it is necessary to answer the objection, it is sufficient to say that an infant may expressly bind itself for necessaries, as food and raiment, that a contract is always implied where such articles are furnished, and that the reciprocal compact of protection and allegiance, must be ranked among considerations of the highest order and first necessity. The dignity of the subject is however somewhat affected by resting it on a ground so narrow; and when we consider all the obligations cast on a political society by the voluntary formation of it, we may discard the smaller rules of private contract, and more safely rely on the broad basis of the general good, inherent in its nature, and necessary to its self-preservation.

When the child has attained an age sufficiently mature, according to civil institutions, to enable it to determine the choice, it would seem, in consistency with the principles already laid down, that the individual must be allowed a reasonable time to enable him to select the country in which he will reside, and the society to which he will adhere. Of his willingness to continue, no public declaration seems to be requisite. His acts demonstrate his choice; but there would be a great difficulty in fixing the time in which a contrary determination ought to be formed and declared. The law has assigned twenty-one years as the age of discretion; but in whom is the judgment sufficiently ripened at so early a period, to enable him to determine on a subject so momentous, and how long after that period has been reached, shall be allowed for deliberation? These difficulties appear to be almost insuperable, and seem to render the principle itself inadmissible, unless it should be specially provided for by the legislature. But where the adult has for a sufficient length of time, by every external act, manifested his adhesion to the political society in which he was born, there can exist no right in him to shake off his allegiance without the consent of the state, and become a stranger, or in the course of events, an enemy to his country. By his acts he has bound himself as closely as the alien who, seeking to be naturalized, has taken an express oath. The obligations resulting from his birth are rivetted by his voluntary conduct afterwards, and he cannot dispute the indissoluble tie, of which he has thus doubled the effect.

To these positions some objections may be made, which it will be endeavored to answer.

The leading one is the great act of July 4, 1776, by which two and a half millions of subjects threw off their allegiance to Great Britain, and it is argued that what might be done by them collectively, could be done by them individually; but an obvious fallacy appears in the very statement of this proposition.

When the protection of the crown was withdrawn; when the aspect and the arm of paternal power were converted into virtual exclusion from the pale of the British family; a right of collective resistance was created which, unless similar measures could be exerted against an individual, can never exist in an individual. Our case differed in form only from the cession of territories and their inhabitants already noticed. If either by cession to another or by unmerited severity to those who are normally retained as subjects, the legitimate protection is thus wholly withdrawn; the dissolution of allegiance is the act of the sovereign, and if assented to by its subjects, is binding on both. It depends therefore upon facts to determine whether the cause of our separation was sufficient, and on these facts no American mind can hesitate.

The treaty of 1783 may be safely referred to in confirmation of this opinion. In recognizing the independence of the United States, the right to declare it on the principles we asserted, may justly be considered as also recognized. Great Britain did not by professing to grant us independence, (a grant which would not have been accepted,) affect to release us from present allegiance; but on the contrary must be considered as retrospectively acknowledging that by her own act she had entitled us to discontinue it.[57]

Another objection arises from the acknowledged right of emigration, of which, with us, no inhabitant is deprived, while, in many other governments, express permission is necessary; but the error of this consists in supposing that emigration implies the dissolution of allegiance.

Emigration in its general sense, merely signifies removal from one place to another; its strict and more appropriate meaning is the removal of a person, his effects and residence: but in no sense does it imply or require that it should take place. with a view to become a subject or citizen of another country.

Motives of health or trade, convenience or pleasure, may lead to emigration; but if a deprivation of citizenship were the necessary and immediate consequence, (and unless it is, the argument is without weight,) emigration would often be a cause of terror and sometimes a punishment, instead of a benefit, in which sense the right is considered.

Those who contend for the affirmative of the proposition, must be able to prove that the quality of citizenship ceases at the moment of departure; that if the emigrant returns he cannot be restored to his former rank, without passing through the regular forms of naturaliza-

---

57 *The Thirteen American Colonies did not need Great Britain's permission to withdraw from its union with Great Britain. The right of secession, as explained and declared in the Declaration of Independence, exists and is legitimate when the current government, "...becomes destructive of these ends, it is the Right of the people to alter or to abolish it, and to institute new Government..."as per the Joint Declaration of Independence, 1776.*

tion; that if real estate had descended upon him during his absence, he could not inherit it without the aid of a law in favor of aliens, and that if the country to which he has removed, becomes engaged in war with us, and he did not choose to remain there, he would be liable on his return, to be treated as an alien enemy. In Virginia, what is termed expatriation is authorized by an act of assembly passed in 1792. [6] This is a fair compact which an independent state has a right to make with its citizens, and amounts to a full release of all future claims against the emigrant who, if taken in war against the state, would not be liable to the charge of treason. But the release is effective only so far as relates to the state which grants it. It does not alter his relation to the United States, and it was questioned in the case of Talbot v. Janson [7] how far such a law would be compatible with the Constitution of the United States.

The Virginia act makes no distinction between the time of peace and of war.

Whether the citizen, having formed the unnatural design of aiding the actual enemies of his country, could make use of its legal forms to enable him to commit such a crime with impunity, remains to be decided by the tribunals of that state.

A distinction certainly not unreasonable has been taken between citizenship and allegiance. Perpetual allegiance is a doctrine of less force and efficacy in some countries than in others. It depends on their respective systems of law.

The origin of allegiance in England has been already described. Its former extension through almost every part of this country is unquestionable, and in many states it continues unimpaired in its qualities and nature.

It is indirectly recognized in the Constitution of the United States, and by the acts of congress, which have been since passed. The indefeasible quality conceived to be incident to it has not yet been decided on by the Supreme Court of the United States; but in the Circuit Courts, Ellsworth, chief justice, declared, that a member of the community [8] cannot dissolve the social compact so as to free himself from our laws, without the consent or the default of the community. And in another case, Washington, J. declared that no citizen can throw off his allegiance to his country without some law authorizing him to do so. [9] But in those countries where the doctrine of allegiance, in the sense we affix to it, does not exist at all, or where it is a part of their law that it may be thrown off in certain cases, our positions do not apply.

It may still further be urged, that the renunciation of all foreign allegiance inserted in the oath of naturalization implies a power to renounce what is due to us as well as what is due to a foreign state.

If this were found in the Constitution, it might occasion some difficulty; but it is the language of congress, on whom it does not rest to give a binding exposition of the Constitution. It was not required in the first act prescribing the mode of obtaining naturalization, and it was probably introduced from political jealousy, and by way of caution to the new citizen. The necessity of retaining it is not very perceptible. If a naturalized citizen should commit treason against us, by uniting with a hostile country from which he had emigrated, he would not be more amenable to the law, because of his renunciation, nor less so, if it had never taken place; and it would have no effect in the country which he had left, either by way of aggravation or extenuation of any offence for which he might be responsible to them. [10]

The temporary allegiance, which began with his residence among us, is rendered perpetual by his naturalization, and the renunciation is an useless adjunct. [11]

The last objection which occurs to the author is, that independent of the oath of abjuration, the admission of a foreigner to naturalization among us implies that he may withdraw his allegiance from his native country, and that otherwise in case of war, he would be involved in the hardship of being obliged to commit treason against one or the other: but the satisfactory answer always given to this proposition is, that if the individual chooses to entangle himself in a double allegiance, it is his own voluntary act. He may reside among us without being naturalized, he may enjoy much of the protection, and some of the advantages of a citizen, yet retain, unimpaired even in sensation, his allegiance to his native country till the moment he chooses to leave us. If he determines completely to unite his character and his fortunes with ours, we receive him under the compact already explained, and his temporary allegiance becomes permanently binding.

Another point of considerable moment remains to be noticed. Having shown what a citizen, native or naturalized, may not do by way of withdrawing his allegiance. we will now proceed to show in what cases the state may not withdraw its protection.

Every person has a right to remain within a state as long as he pleases, except the alien enemy, the person charged with crimes in any of the other states, or in a foreign state with whom a treaty to that effect exists, and fugitives from service or labor in any of the states. To the two latter descriptions, no asylum can by the Constitution of the United States, be afforded.

The states are considered as a common family, whose harmony would be endangered, if they were to protect and detain such fugitives, when demanded in one case, by the executive authority of the state, or pursued in the other by the persons claiming an interest in their service.

In the case of alien enemies, the public good is consulted. The right of sending them away, is an incident to the right of carrying on public war. It is not mentioned in the Constitution, but it properly appertains to those who are to conduct the war.

Whoever visits or resides among us, comes under the knowledge that he is liable, by the law of nations, to be sent off, if war breaks out between his country and ours, before he is naturalized. So if there is any treaty in force, by which we are bound to deliver up a fugitive, charged by another nation with the commission of crimes within its territory, every one arriving among us is considered as having knowledge of such compact.

But whatever may be held by certain theoretical writers, there is no foundation for the opinion, that we are bound by the general law of nations, without such compact, to surrender a person charged with a crime in another nation.

The principles by which this conclusion is attained, are as follow. A criminal act, committed within the limits of a nation, is an offence against that nation, and not against any other. It is the duty of a nation to punish offences against itself, but not against others. If the offender escapes, it has no power to pursue him into the territories of another, nor any right, by the general rules of law, to require the other to deliver him up. The nation in which he seeks an asylum, may conscientiously retain and protect him. In legal acceptation, he has been received as an innocent man; he holds this character among us, till he forfeits it by the commission of a crime against us; he is then, on conviction, liable to punishment for such crime, but we cannot punish him for a crime committed in another country.

Nature gives to mankind the right of punishing only for their own defense and safety. Hence it follows, that he can only be punished by those he has offended.

To deliver the fugitive to the nation which claims, in order to punish him, is to assist the punishment, and therefore directly at variance with these principles. [12]

Yet it is not to be inferred, that one state has a right to transfer its criminals to another, and that the latter is bound to receive them. It rests with every independent state to open its doors to the admission of foreigners on such terms only, as it may think proper.

During our colonial dependency, the mother country assumed a privilege of transporting certain classes of her convicted offenders to the provinces, and the want of laborers at first induced us to receive them without complaint.

But it was soon discovered to be an alarming evil, and many of the provinces took measures to oppose it. One of the last acts of the congress under the confederation, was to recommend to the several states to pass proper laws for preventing the transportation of convicted malefactors from foreign countries into the United States. Perhaps the power implied by the 9th section of the 2d article, might be usefully adapted to the regulation of this sort of political commerce, in which, at present, we cannot be gainers, for the United States have no constitutional power to export or banish offenders.

The power to pass uniform laws on the subject of bankruptcies, is contained in the same paragraph. It is held, however, from its nature, not to be completely exclusive.

Until it is exercised, the states are not forbidden to pass bankrupt laws, except so far as they impair the obligation of contracts. When congress enacts a general bankrupt law, the right of the states is suspended, though not extinguished. From the expiration or repeal of the bankrupt law, the ability of the state to exercise the power, qualified as above mentioned, revives. [13] And even while the act of congress is in force, the power of the state continues over such cases as the law does not embrace. Hence the power to pass insolvent laws remains with the state. Bankrupt laws are generally, perhaps properly, considered as confined to the mercantile class, who are more exposed to pecuniary vicissitudes than those who pursue other occupations. Yet as poverty may also assail the latter, it would be hard to exclude them from the humane protection of the state legislatures. But as states are prohibited from passing laws impairing the obligation of contracts, it has been contended that their power to pass insolvent laws is now questionable. The answer to this objection is, that without impairing the obligation of a contract, the remedy to enforce it may be modified as the wisdom of the legislature may direct. Confinement of the debtor may be a punishment for not performing his contract, or may be allowed as the means of inducing him to perform it. The state may withhold this mean and leave the contract in full force. Imprisonment is no part of the contract, and simply to release the prisoner does not impair its obligations. [14]

Congress shall have power to coin money, regulate the value thereof, and of foreign coin, and fix the standard of weights and measures. In a subsequent section of the same article, the separate states are prohibited from coining money and emitting bills of credit. [15] The other parts of this section seem proper objects for the exclusive power of congress. But until it shall be exercised, each state, it is presumed, retains the right to fix the standard of weights and measures within its own precincts.

A power to provide for the punishment of counterfeiting the securities and current coin of the United States, is incident to part of the antecedent section, and in itself purports the exclusion of state power. But whether the exclusive cognizance of such cases may be given to the tribunals of the United States, or may not under some circumstances be concurrently exercised by the state courts, belongs to another head, and will be hereafter considered.

The power to establish post offices and post roads, has a necessary connection with the promotion of commerce and the general welfare of the Union.

A regular system of free and speedy communication, is of vital importance to the mercantile interest, but on a wider scale we must also admit it to be of the first consequence to the general benefit. In time of peace, it tends to keep the people duly informed of their political interests; it assists the measures of government, and the private intercourse of individuals. During a war, the rapid communication of intelligence, by means of the post, and the greater facility of transferring bodies of men or munitions of war, to different places, by the aid of good roads, are evident advantages. If these establishments should in practice produce no revenue, the expense would be properly chargeable to the Union, and the proceeds of taxation in the common forms be justly applied to defray it. If, however, as has proved to be the case, the post office yields a revenue, which is with the other revenues of the United States applicable only to the general service, it is obvious, that no state ought to interfere by establishing a post office of its own. This is therefore an exclusive power so far as relates to the conveyance of letters, &c. In regard to post roads, it is unnecessary, and therefore would be unwarrantable in congress where a sufficient road already exists, to make another; and on the other hand, no state has a power to deny or obstruct the passage of the mail, or the passage of troops, or the property of the United States over its public roads.

The power given to congress, in respect to this subject, was brought into operation soon after the Constitution was adopted, and various provisions have at different times been enacted, founded on the principle of its being an exclusive power.

It has been made a constitutional question, whether congress has a right to open a new mail road through a state or states for general purposes, involving the public benefit, and the same doubt has been extended to the right of appropriating money in aid of canals through states. If we adhere to the words of the text, we are confined to post roads; but it appears to the author to be one of those implied powers which may fairly be considered as within the principles of the Constitution, and which there is no danger in allowing. The general welfare may imperiously require communications of either of these descriptions. A state is bound to consult only its own immediate interests, and not to incur expense for the benefit of other states. The United States are bound to uphold the general interest at the general expense. To restrain them to pointing out the utility of the measure, and calling on particular states to execute it, would be partially to recall the inefficiency of the old government and to violate the main principle of the present one. If any political evil could result from the procedure, it would present a strong argument against the allowance of the power; but good roads, and facile, aquatic communications, while they promote the prosperity of the country, cannot be seriously alleged to affect the sovereignty of the states, or the liberties of the people. The road ought, however, to be an open, not a close one. It is doubtful whether tolls for passage on it, can be constitutionally exacted.

In the succeeding section, the interests of science and the useful arts are laudably provided for, by empowering congress to secure for limited times, to authors and inventors, the exclusive right to their respective writings and discoveries.

At common law, it seems to have been a question whether the inventor of any new art or improvement had such a special property in it, as to entitle him to pursue another who made use of it after the inventor had made it public. But there was no doubt that if another person had fallen on the same invention, without a knowledge of the first, he would be entitled to the benefit of his own talents. It has however been deemed in many countries politic and wise, to secure to the first inventor a reward for the time and study employed in such pursuits. In England, the king undertook, on the score of royal prerogative, to grant exclusive privileges of making and selling articles of domestic manufacture, and of importing foreign articles, by which protection to such inventors was occasionally obtained. But this practice began to be abused, and such licenses or monopolies, often conferred as rewards on particular favorites, or used merely to promote the interest of the crown, had increased in the reign of Elizabeth and James I. to an alarming degree, [16] and therefore, by an act passed in the twenty-first year of the reign of the latter, all such grants are declared to be void; in the fifth section, however, a proviso is introduced, which is the foundation of the present system in that country relative to patents, by allowing them to be granted to the authors of any new inventions for a term not exceeding fourteen years.

In respect to what is termed literary property; the right which a person may be supposed to have in his own original compositions, — the same doubts as to the common law are entertained, and the protection of a statute has been likewise extended, [17] which at the same time disposed of the common law question, as to those who complied with its forms, by declaring that the author should have the benefit of it for fourteen years, and no longer, unless he was still living at the expiration of the first term, when it might be renewed for fourteen years more. But as the author might not avail himself of the benefit of the statute, the question remained unsettled till the year 1774, when a small majority of the twelve Judges decided against it. [18] This interesting question merits much consideration. At present it is sufficient to say, that as from the nature of our Constitution, no new rights can be considered as created by it, but its operation more properly is the organization and distribution of a conceded power in relation to rights already existing, we must regard these provisions as at least the evidence of opinion, that such a species of property, both in the works of authors and in the inventions of artists, had a legal existence.

In some of the states, prior to the adoption of the general Constitution, acts of the legislature in favor of meritorious discoveries and improvements, had been passed; but their efficacy being confined to the boundaries of the states, was of little value, and there can be no doubt that, as soon as congress legislated on the subject, (which was as early as the second session, 1790,) all the state provisions ceased; although in the act of 21 Feb. 1793, it is cautiously provided that the applicant for the benefit of the protection of the United States, shall surrender his right under any state law; of which his obtaining a patent shall he sufficient evidence.

To define and punish piracies and felonies committed on the high seas is an exclusive power.

The regulation of foreign commerce appertains to congress alone, and the punishment of offences committed on the high seas is an unavoidable incident to this power: as soon as the Constitution was adopted, the power of the states in this respect was at an end. But the principle of this exclusive jurisdiction might perhaps be further extended. After the territorial boundaries of a nation are left, the sea becomes the common property of all nations, and the rights and privileges relative thereto being regulated by the law of nations and treaties, properly belong to the national jurisdiction, and would be inconveniently retained by the states which, in this respect, form only parts of the nation.

It does not seem to have been necessary to define the crime of piracy. There is no act on which the universal sense of nations has been so fully and distinctly expressed, as there is no act which is so universally punished. The pirate is the enemy of all nations, and all nations are the enemy of the pirate.

Felony is a term derived from the common law of England, and when committed on the high seas, amounts to piracy. The power to define either may have been introduced to authorize congress to qualify and reduce the acts which should amount to either. It is coupled with the power to punish, and this power extends not merely to citizens of the United States, but to all others except the citizens or subjects of a foreign state sailing under its flag and committing acts which amount to piracy; but general piracy committed by persons on board of a vessel, acting in defiance of all law, and acknowledging obedience to no government, are punishable in our courts, and in the courts of all nations. [19]

By the high seas we are to understand not only the ocean out of sight of land, but waters on the sea coast beyond the boundaries of low water mark, although in a roadstead or bay, within the jurisdiction or limits of one of the states or of a foreign government. [20]

A power to define and to punish offences against the law of nations is contained in the same paragraph, but it is doubtful whether the power to punish ought to be considered as an exclusive one. The law of nations forms a part of the common law of every civilized country; violations of it may be committed as well on land as at sea, and while the jurisdiction of the separate states is admitted to be withdrawn from them in regard to acts committed on the sea, it does not seem to follow that it is superseded as to those on shore.

Such acts may be of various kinds, and although the most prominent subjects under this head are those which relate to the persons and privileges of ambassadors, yet in many other particulars, infringements of the law of nations may be proper subjects of state jurisdiction. But even if an outrage were committed on a diplomatic character, and he preferred the redress to be obtained from a state court to that afforded by the courts of the United States, it is not perceived that this clause would prohibit him from so doing; yet whether the power is exclusive or not, on which some further remarks will be made, the power to define and to punish this class of offences is with great propriety given to congress. The United States being alone responsible to foreign nations for all that affects their mutual intercourse, and tends to promote the general relations of good order and just demeanor, it rests with them alone to declare what shall constitute such crimes, and to prescribe suitable punishments.

When such laws are made, they become binding rules of decision as well on the state courts as on the courts of the United States; but if cases arise for which no such statutory provision has been made, both these descriptions of courts are thrown upon those general principles, which being enforced by other nations, those nations have a right to require us to apply and enforce in their favor, or for the benefit of their citizens and subjects.

The power of declaring war, with all its train of consequences, direct and indirect, forms the next branch of powers exclusively confided to congress.

The right of using force, or of making war, belongs to nations, so far as it is necessary for their defense and the support of their rights. But the evils of war are certain, and the event doubtful, and therefore both wisdom and humanity require, that every possible precaution should be used before a nation is plunged into it. In monarchies, the king generally possesses this power, and it is as often exercised for his own aggrandizement as for the good of the nation. Republics, though they cannot be wholly exonerated from the imputation of ambition, jealousies, causeless irritations, and other personal passions, enter into war more deliberately and reluctantly.

It is not easy to perceive where this power could, with us, be more prudently placed. But it must be remembered, that we may be involved in a war without a formal declaration of it. In the year 1800, we were engaged in a qualified, but public, war with France; [21] qualified, because it was only waged on the high seas — public, because the whole nation was involved in it. It was founded on the hostile measures authorized by congress against France, by reason of her unjust aggressions on our commerce — yet there was no declaration of war. In such a war we may also be involved by the conduct of the executive, without the participation of the legislature. The intercourse with foreign nations, the direction of the military and naval power, being confided to the president, his errors or misconduct may draw hostilities upon us. No other restraint appears to exist, than that of withholding the supplies to carry it on, which indeed congress can in no case grant beyond the term of two years. But in England, the king is, in this respect, equally dependent on the parliament, and its history shows that this dependence is not always adequate to prevent unpopular wars.

The several states are, by another clause, prohibited from engaging in war, unless actually invaded, or in such imminent danger as will not admit of delay.[58]

But although congress alone can subject us to the dubious results of formal war, a smaller portion of the government can restore us to peace. Hostilities may be terminated by a truce, which the president alone (it is conceived) may make. The duration of a truce is indefinite. It suspends all hostilities while it continues in force; but it does not revive treaties which were broken by the commencement of the war, or restore rights of any sort, which were suspended by it. It may be general or partial — it may extend to all places and to all the mutual forces of the belligerents, or it may be confined to particular places or particular armaments. When it ceases, it is unnecessary to repeat the declaration of war. But before its conventual termination, unless some fresh cause of complaint should have arisen, it would be inconsistent

---

58 *It is noteworthy to point out that the Sovereign States never surrendered the right to wage war. They delegated to the Federal government the sole right to wage war for the United States. The States did not reserve the right to wage a war of aggression, but, if attacked or in imminent danger of such an attack, a State has the right of self-defense. The right of a State to wage war was thereby attenuated to the point of acting only in self-defense (U.S. Constitution, Article I, Section 10, paragraph 3).*

with good faith to renew hostilities.

Treaties, by which peace is completely restored, may, as already shown, be made by the president and senate alone, without the concurrence, and against the will of the house of representatives.

It has been made a subject of doubt, whether the power to make war and peace, should not be the same, and why a smaller part of the government should be entrusted with the latter, than the former. Sufficient reasons may certainly be assigned for the distinction. Peace is seldom effected without preparatory discussions, often of length and difficulty, the conduct of which, of course, belongs only to the president and senate. War is always an evil; peace is the cure of that evil. War should always be avoided as long as possible, and although it may happen to be brought on us as before observed, without the previous assent of congress, yet a regular and formal war should never be entered into, without the united approbation of the whole legislature. But although a peace is seldom obnoxious and unacceptable to the public, yet its necessity or propriety may not always be apparent, and a public disclosure of the urgent motives that really exist in favor of it, may be prejudicial. The people have, in such case, a stronger motive for relying on the wisdom and justice of the president and senate, than in the case of ordinary treaties. They are less likely than a larger body to be influenced by partial views or occasional inflammation, and the very circumstance of the smallness of their numbers increases their responsibility to public opinion.

By the fifteenth and sixteenth paragraphs of the same important section, congress is empowered to provide for calling forth the militia to execute the laws of the Union, suppress insurrections, and repel invasions, but in respect to the two last mentioned objects, it is not to be understood as an exclusive power. There cannot at least be any doubt, that on the first emergency, each state enjoys a similar power, of which no act of congress can deprive them. For the principle of the Constitution is not to deny to the states the right of self-protection in such cases, but to co-operate with the collective force of the Union in aid of the state.

Uniformity in the organization and discipline of the militia, should extend through the Union. The imbecility of the confederation in this respect, together with the variety of the periods of service for which the militia were engaged, produced considerable inconvenience during the war of the revolution. Hence, congress is further empowered to provide for organizing, arming, and disciplining the militia, and for governing such part of them as may be employed in the service of the United States. This power cannot be considered as infringing the rights and privileges of the states, since, however necessary, it cannot effectually be vested elsewhere, and since it is accompanied with an express reservation to them, of the appointment of the officers, and of the authority of training the militia, according to the discipline, prescribed by congress. This subject will be hereafter resumed.

The last enumerated power is to, "exercise exclusive legislation in all cases whatever, over such district, not exceeding ten miles square, as may by cession of particular states, and the acceptance of congress, become the seat of the government of the United States, and to exercise like authority over all places purchased by the consent of the legislature of the state in which the same shall be, for the erection of forts, magazines, arsenals, dock-yards, and other needful buildings."

A provision of this kind, is peculiar to the United States, [22] and the reasons in favor of it, are cogent.

If the general government held its sessions within the limits, and under the jurisdiction of a state, it would be dependent on that state for protection and safety. If it should happen, that at any time, unkind opinions, in respect to if, existed on the part of the state, or, if the state government were deficient in firmness and power, the general legislature might be subjected to insult and disgrace, in the midst of its most important functions. It would thus be dishonored in the eyes of foreign powers, and pitied or despised at home. Nor is this an imaginary or improbable event. At the close of the war of the revolution, the congress, then sitting at Philadelphia, was surrounded and insulted by a small, but insolent body of mutineers of the continental army. It applied to the executive authority of Pennsylvania for defense; but under the ill conceived constitution of the state at that time, the executive power was vested in a council, consisting of thirteen members; and they possessed or exhibited so little energy, and such apparent intimidation, that the congress indignantly removed to New Jersey, whose inhabitants welcomed it with promises of defending it. It remained for some time at Princeton, without being again insulted, till, for the sake of greater convenience, it adjourned to Annapolis. The general dissatisfaction with the proceedings of the executive authority of Pennsylvania, and the degrading spectacle of a fugitive congress, suggested the remedial provisions now under consideration.

It has been carried into effect, by the cession and acceptance of a tract of land on the river Potomac, partly from the state of Virginia, and partly from the state of Maryland. The inhabitants generally were satisfied. But some consequences, that perhaps were not fully foreseen, have flowed from it. The inhabitants of the District of Columbia, are no longer in all respects citizens of a state, although they are unquestionably, to a certain extent, citizens of the United States. As such, they are entitled to the benefit of all commercial or political treaties with foreign powers, and to the protection of the Union at home. But they have no representatives in the senate; they cannot partake in the election of members of the house of representatives, or of electors of president and vice president. The judiciary power between citizens of different states, does not extend to them, [23] in which respect, they are more unfavorably situate than aliens; but suitable courts of justice, and certain adequate provisions for its local government, have been made by congress. The immediate residence of government, has greatly contributed to its prosperity, and its political anomaly has produced no general inconvenience. Under a subsequent head, some remarks will be made on the judicial relations affecting this, and other separated districts.

The enumeration closes with a declaration of the powers of congress, to, "make all laws which shall be necessary and proper for carrying into execution the foregoing powers, and all others vested by the Constitution in the government of the United States, or in any department or officer thereof."

It is impossible not to perceive in this, as in so many other instances, the circumspection that confined the legislature to its proper bounds; the wisdom that, within those bounds, left nothing unsupplied.

Without this clause, the specific enumeration might have been construed by a morbid jealousy, to imply, that congress possessed no other powers of legislation; and some parts of the executive duties might have doubtfully rested only on the general description in the Constitution. Even the functions of the judicial tribunals require legislative development and assistance. All necessary power, and no power that is not necessary, is contained in this final provision.

CHAPTER NOTES
IX

1. See the case of Hylton v. The United States, 3d Dall. 171.

2. Gibbons v. Ogden, 9th Wheaton, p. 1, &c.

3. See 7 Coke's Rep. 7.

4. 7 Coke's Rep. 6.

5. See Wooddeson, vol. i. 232, and many of the British treaties evince the truth of his position. In 1783, the cessions of Tobago, East Florida, &c.; the numerous transfers among the European monarchs since the year 1795, form striking instances of the general adoption of the principle. Time indeed is sometimes allowed to the people to withdraw themselves and their property, but age or other causes may render this impossible. In Great Britain such treaties are often confirmed by acts of parliament, but the principle is the same. Their colonies are not represented in parliament.

6. The words of the law are these: —
Whensoever any citizen of this commonwealth shall by deed in writing under his hand and seal, executed in the presence of and subscribed by three witnesses, and by them or two of them proved in the general court, any district court, or the court of the county or corporation where he resides, or by open verbal declaration made in either of said courts to be by them entered of record, declare that he relinquishes the character of a citizen, and shall depart out of this commonwealth, such person shall from the time of his departure be considered as having exercised his right of expatriation and shall thenceforth be deemed no citizen." — Passed 23d December, 1792.

7. 3 Dallas, 133. The author apprehends that no principle can be more clear than that a state cannot discharge a citizen from his allegiance to the United states.

8. *United States v. Williams*, 4 Hall's Law Journal, 401.

9. *United States v. Gillies*, I Peters 120 — See 2 Cranch, 126.
During the late war President Madison directed one Clark, a citizen of the United States who had removed to Canada, and was afterwards taken within our lines and sentenced to death by a court martial as a spy — to be delivered to the civil authority, thereby disclaiming military power over him as an alien enemy.

10. Isaac Williams, whose case has been noticed, expressly renounced his allegiance to this country when he was naturalized in France. In the opinion of the chief justice, this circumstance made no difference.

11. The legislature of Pennsylvania on the 29th of March, 1783, expunged from the oath, the part which required a renunciation of allegiance to the King of Great Britain, declaring that it was wholly useless.

12. It is proper, however, to observe, that a contrary opinion has been given in the state of New York by a judge of great learning and acuteness, Washburn's case, 4 Johnson, Ch. 106, to which is opposed the later decision of a man of equal character and talent, Chief Justice Tilghman, in the case of Edward Short on a habeas corpus, Aug. 20, 1824.

13. 4 Wheaton, 122.

14. ibid. 200.

15. § 10.

16. Coke's Inst. vol. iii. 181.

17. 8 Ann. c. 19. 15 Geo. 3. c. 53.

18. 4 Burrow, 2417.

19. 5 Wheaton, 151, 417.

20. 1 Gallison, 124. 5 Wheaton, 204, 206.

21. 4 Dallas, 37.

22. In England, the Royal Palace, with an extent of twelve miles round it, has a peculiar jurisdiction in regard to some legal controversies; but any suits brought in the Marshalsea or Palace Courts, (as they are styled,) may be, and now generally are, removed at once to the King's Bench or Common Pleas. For all the purposes of legislation, there is no distinction between the "verge of the court," and the kingdom at large.

23. 2 Cranch, 452.

CHAPTER X.

OF THE RESTRICTIONS ON THE POWERS OF CONGRESS — AND ON THE EXECUTIVE AND JUDICIAL AUTHORITIES — RESTRICTIONS ON THE POWERS OF STATES AND SECURITY TO THE RIGHTS OF INDIVIDUALS.

THE restrictions on the powers of congress contained in the original text are few. The general principle on which it is constructed being declared and manifest throughout, it follows that to no purpose inconsistent with or extending beyond that principle, can its power of legislation be carried. Yet it was expedient in some instances to introduce positive exceptions; in some, to qualify powers enumerated or implied, and in others to secure by explicit declarations both the republican foundation and the equality of the states in all points within the sphere of the general government.

The first class of these restrictions relates to commerce.

"No tax or duty shall be laid on articles exported from any state."

It has been repeatedly observed, that the leading principle of the whole Constitution is uniformity in respect to the several states, as far as it can be obtained. The natural or artificial products of states are different — to lay a general duty on the exports of rice or cotton, or tobacco, would affect only the southern states; on flour or grain, principally the central states, and on the domestic manufactures would operate chiefly on the northern and eastern states engaged in them -yet without this restriction perhaps it might have been done.

A restriction both as to exports and imports is subsequently extended to the states themselves, except what may be absolutely necessary to execute their own inspection laws; and, to prevent evasion under color of only securing the right of inspection, it is provided that the net produce of all duties and imposts laid by any state on imports or exports, shall be for the use of the treasury of the United States, and that all such laws shall be subject to the revision and control of congress.

On the same principle it is provided in general terms, that, "no preference shall be given by any regulations of commerce or revenue to the ports of one state over those of another, nor shall vessels bound from one state be obliged to enter, clear, or pay duties in another." A vessel bound to or from Philadelphia, shall not be obliged to enter or pay duties in the state of Delaware or New Jersey. It is not however probable that congress, although unrestrained, would make such regulations.

These are all the restrictions immediately relating to commerce, but one of some importance was omitted. The danger of introducing contagious diseases, has suggested to commercial countries the propriety of interposing the utmost care in regard to the admission of vessels from suspected places. In the Mediterranean, where on account of the frequency of the plague, the practice began, it was required that such vessels should ride at anchor forty days without intercourse with the shore. Hence the term quarantine has been introduced, although the limitation of time is varied according to circumstances. The state or port at which the vessel immediately arrives being the first in danger, has the greatest interest in taking proper precautions according to its situations and means of enforcing them. But the utility of such precautions escaped notice in framing the Constitution; and Congress, with a fair construction of its implied powers, has made suitable provisions to enable the states to protect the health of their inhabitants, although by so doing, they may, in some degree, be considered as partaking of the power to regulate commerce.

An important clause with which this section commences, is partly of a commercial, and partly of a political and moral kind. It was foreseen, that the general power to regulate commerce would include a traffic now justly reprobated by most Christian nations, but some interests and opinions were to be respected, and while the power to abolish the slave trade entirely was indirectly conceded, the exercise of it till the year 1808, otherwise than by laying a tax or duty of ten dollars on each person imported, was prohibited. Congress did not fail to avail itself of the power, as soon as it became lawful to execute it.

The restrictions in regard to taxation and public moneys have already been mentioned.

Reasons will be given hereafter for considering many of the restrictions, contained in the amendments to the Constitution, as extending to the states as well as to the United States, but the nature of the writ of *habeas corpus* seems peculiarly to call for this construction. It is the great remedy of the citizen or subject against arbitrary or illegal imprisonment; it is the mode by which the judicial power speedily and effectually protects the personal liberty of every individual, and repels the injustice of unconstitutional laws or despotic governors. After erecting the distinct government which we are considering, and after declaring what should constitute the supreme law in every state in the Union, fearful minds might entertain jealousies of this great and all-controlling power, if some protection against its energies when misdirected, was not provided by itself.

The national code in which the writ of *habeas corpus* was originally found, is not expressly or directly incorporated into the Constitution.

If this provision bad been omitted, the existing powers under the state governments, none of whom are without it, might be questioned, and a person imprisoned on a mandate of the president or other officer, under color of lawful authority derived from the United States, might be denied relief. But the judicial authority, whether vested in a state judge, or a judge of the United States, is an integral and identified capacity; and if congress never made any provision for issuing writs of *habeas corpus*, either the state judges must issue them, or the individual be without redress. The Constitution seems to have secured this benefit to the citizen by the description of the writ, and in an unqualified manner admitting its efficacy, while it declares that, "it shall not be suspended unless when, in case of rebellion or invasion, the public safety shall require it." This writ is believed to be known only in countries governed by the common law, as it is established in England; but in that country the benefit of it may at any time be withheld by the authority of parliament, whereas we see that in this country it cannot be suspended even in cases of rebellion or invasion, unless the public safety shall require it. Of this necessity the Constitution probably intends, that the legislature of the United States shall be the judges.[59] Charged as they are with the preservation of the United States from both those evils, and superseding the powers of the several states in the prosecution of the measures they may find it expedient to adopt, it seems not unreasonable that this con-

---

59 *Lincoln suspended the writ of* habeas corpus *even though English Law allowed suspension only by Parliament and in face of a written decision by Chief Justice Taney declaring that only Congress could suspend it. Prior to Chief Justice Taney's decision, Chief Justice John Marshall declared, "if ... the public safety should require the suspension of [habeas corpus] it is for the legislature to say so." Lincoln's acts were the acts of a dictator, in plain violation of Constitutional restraints on his acts.* [John Marshall cited in, DiLorenzo, Thomas J., *The Real Lincoln*, 136.]

trol over the writ of *habeas corpus*, which ought only to be exercised on extraordinary occasions, should rest with them. It is at any rate certain, that congress, which has authorized the courts and judges of the United States to issue writs of *habeas corpus* in cases within their jurisdiction, can alone suspend their power, and that no state can prevent those courts and judges from exercising their regular functions, which are, however, confined to cases of imprisonment professed to be under the authority of the United States. But the state courts and judges possess the right of determining on the legality of imprisonment under either authority. [1]

"No bill of attainder, nor ex post facto law shall be passed."

Bills of attainder are those by which a person without a judicial trial, is declared by the legislature to be guilty of some particular crime. The definition itself shows the atrocity of the act. Such laws are never passed but in times of wild commotion or arbitrary misrule.

Ex post facto laws are often supposed to signify all laws having a retrospective operation, but the technical meaning of them is more confined. An *ex post facto* law is when an action is declared to be a crime, which at the time it was done was innocent, or when it aggravates a crime, and declares it to be greater than it was when committed, or when it increases the punishment, or directs that different or less evidence shall be sufficient to convict the offender; [60] but if it softens the rigor of the ancient law, it is not within the prohibition. [2] The Constitution does not prevent congress from passing retrospective laws in civil cases. Why this was omitted when the states in the same instrument are restrained from passing laws impairing the obligations of contracts, will be hereafter explained.

"No title of nobility, shall be granted by the United States, or by any individual state." Of this there could have been but little danger. The independent spirit of republicans leads them to contemn [to regard with disdain or contempt] the vanity of hereditary distinctions, but the residue of the clause is more important. "No person holding any office of trust or profit under the United States shall, without the consent of congress, accept of any present, emolument, office, or title

---

60 *Post-war Republicans in Congress used* ex post facto *legislation to disenfranchise Southerners, confiscate their land and property, and force the people of the South to accept unconstitutional changes in the form and function of the Federal government. Congress's establishment of illegitimate puppet governments in Southern States was a direct violation of the Constitutional requirement to maintain in each state "Republican Form of Government." See, Article IV, Section 4, U.S. Constitution.*

of any kind whatever, from any king, prince, or foreign state."

There cannot be too much jealousy in respect to foreign influence. The treasures of Persia were successfully distributed in Athens; and it is now known that in England a profligate prince and many of his venal courtiers were bribed into measures injurious to the nation by the gold of Louis XIV. [3]

A salutary amendment, extending the prohibition to all citizens of the United States, and disfranchising those who infringe it, has been adopted by some of the states; but not yet by a sufficient number. The clause in the text is defective in not providing a specific penalty for a breach of it. Disfranchisement, or a deprivation of all the rights of a citizen, seems the most appropriate punishment that could be applied, since it renders the seduction useless to those who were the authors of it, and disgraceful to the person seduced.

Of the amendments already adopted, (for which see the appendix,) the eight first in order fall within the class of restrictions on the legislative power, some of which would have been implied, some are original, and all are highly valuable. Some are also to be considered as restrictions on the judicial power.

The constitutions of some of the states contain bills of rights; others do not. A declaration of rights, therefore, properly finds a place in the general Constitution, where it equalizes all and binds all.

Each state is obliged, while it remains a member of the Union, to preserve the republican form of government in all its strength and purity. The people of each state, by the amended constitution, pledge themselves to each other for the sacred preservation of certain detailed principles, without which the republican form would be impure and weak.

They will now be viewed in succession.

The first amendment prohibits congress from passing, "any law respecting an establishment of religion, or preventing the free exercise of it." It would be difficult to conceive on what possible construction of the Constitution such a power could ever be claimed by congress. The time has long passed by when enlightened men in this country entertained the opinion that the general welfare of a nation could be promoted by religious intolerance, and under no other clause could a pretense for it be found. Individual states whose legislatures are not restrained by their own constitutions, have been occasionally found to make some distinctions; but when we advert to those parts of the Constitution of the United States, which so strongly enforce the equality of all our citizens, we may reasonably doubt whether the denial of the smallest civic right under this pretense can be reconciled to it. In most of the governments of Europe, some one religious system enjoys a preference, enforced with more or less severity, according to circumstances. Opinions and modes of worship differing from those which form the established religion, are sometimes expressly forbidden, sometimes punished, and in the mildest cases, only tolerated without patronage or encouragement. Thus a human government interposes between the Creator and his creature, intercepts the devotion of the latter, or condescends to permit it only under political regulations. From injustice so gross, and impiety so manifest, multitudes sought an asylum in America, and hence she ought to be the hospitable and benign receiver of every variety of religious opinion. It is true, that in her early provincial stage, the equality of those rights does not seem to have been universally admitted. Those who claimed religious freedom for themselves, did not immediately perceive that others were also entitled to it; but the history of the stern exclusion or reluctant admission of other sects in several of the provinces, would be an improper digression in this work. In tracing the annals of some of the provinces, it is pleasing to observe that in the very outset, their enlightened founders publicly recognized the perfect freedom of conscience. There was indeed sometimes an inconsistency, perhaps not adverted to in the occlusion of public offices to all but Christians, which was the case in Pennsylvania, but it was then of little practical importance. In the constitution adopted by that state in 1776, the same inconsistency, though expressed in language somewhat different, was retained, but in her present constitution, nothing abridges, nothing qualifies, nothing defeats, the full effect of the original declaration. Both the elector and the elected are entitled, whatever their religious tenets may be, to the fullest enjoyment of political rights, provided in the latter description, the party publicly declares his belief in the being of a God, and a future state of rewards and punishments. This qualification is not expressly required of an elector, and perhaps was introduced in respect to those elected, chiefly for the purpose of more particularly explaining the sense of a preceding section. It is indeed to such a degree doubtful whether any can be found so weak and depraved as to disbelieve these cardinal points of all religions, that it can scarcely be supposed to have been introduced for any other purpose. [4]

Just and liberal principles on this subject, throw a luster round the Constitution in which they are found, and while they dignify the nation, promote its internal peace and harmony. No predominant religion overpowers another, the votaries of which are few and humble; no lordly hierarchy excites odium or terror; legal persecution is unknown, and freedom of discussion, while it tends to promote the knowledge, contributes to increase the fervor of piety.

The freedom of speech and of the press forms part of the same article, and in part relates to the same subject; it embraces all matters of religious, moral, political, or physical discussion. Tacitus, in gloomy meditation on the imperial despotism of Rome, exclaims, "How rare are those happy times when men may think what they please and say what they think." Under the denial of such rights, life is indeed of little value. The foundation of a free government begins to be undermined when freedom of speech on political subjects is restrained; it is destroyed when freedom of speech is wholly denied. The press is a vehicle of the freedom of speech. The art of printing illuminates the world, by a rapid dissemination of what would otherwise be slowly communicated and partially understood. This may easily be conceived, if we were to figure to ourselves the total suppression of printing for even a short time in this country. Our newspapers are now more numerous than such publications are in an equal amount of population in any other part of the world. Wherever a new settlement is formed, and every year presents many such, a printing press is established as soon as a sufficient number of inhabitants is collected. Information is the moral food, for which the active American intellect ever hungers.

But the liberty of speech and of the press may be abused, and so may every human institution. It is not, however, to be supposed that it may be abused with impunity. Remedies will always be found while the protection of individual rights and the reasonable safeguards of society itself form parts of the principles of our government.[61] A previous superintendency of the press, an arbitrary power to direct or

61 *The Federal government first attempt to suppress free speech and freedom of the press was with the passage of the Sedition Act of 1798. Congress passed the law, the president enforced it and the Federal Supreme Court upheld it! The recourse was via nullification and eventual removal of the Federalist Party which had enacted the law and the Federalist President who enforced it — but the Supreme Court who upheld it remained in place! The Act was the occasion for the Kentucky and Virginia Resolutions of 1798 authored by Thomas Jefferson and James Madison. No section of the Constitution is self-enforcing! States' Rights was, but no longer is, the ultimate defender of liberty.*

prohibit its publications are withheld, but the punishment of dangerous or offensive publications, which on a fair and impartial trial are found to have a pernicious tendency, is necessary for the peace and order of government and religion, which are the solid foundations of civil liberty.

The right of the people peaceably to assemble and petition government for a redress of grievances concludes the article.

Of this right in the abstract there cannot be a doubt. To withhold from the injured, the privilege of complaint, and to debar the rulers from the benefit of information that may apprize them of their errors, is mutually unjust. It may, however, be urged, that history shows how those meetings and petitions have been abused, and we may be turned to an English statute, which, though ill observed, is said to be still in force, [5] and which is understood to have been founded on the mischiefs and disorders experienced from large and tumultuous assemblies, presenting petitions for the redress of grievances in the reign of Charles I. But besides the well known irrelevancy of the argument from the abuse of any thing against its use, we must remember that by requiring the assembly to be peaceable, the usual remedies of the law are retained, if the right is illegally exercised.

The preceding article expressly refers to the powers of congress alone, but some of those which follow are to be more generally construed, and considered as applying to the state legislatures as well as that of the Union. The important principles contained in them are now incorporated by adoption into the instrument itself; they form parts of the declared rights of the people, of which neither the state powers nor those of the Union can ever deprive them.[62]

A subsequent article declares that, "powers not delegated to congress by the Constitution, nor prohibited by it to the states, are reserved to the states respectively, or to the people." What we are about to consider are certainly not delegated to congress, nor are they noticed in the prohibitions to states; they are therefore reserved either to the states or to the people. Their high nature, their necessity to the general security and happiness will be distinctly perceived.

In the second article, it is declared, that a well regulated militia is necessary to the security of a free state; a proposition from which few

---

62 *The United States Supreme Court in Barron v. Baltimore, 32 U.S. 243, (1833), ruled that the limitations imposed by the Bill of Rights "contain no expression indicating an intention to apply them to the state governments." Note this case was decided after the publication of Rawle's text.*

will dissent. Although in actual war, the services of regular troops are confessedly more valuable; yet, while peace prevails, and in the commencement of a war before a regular force can be raised, the militia form the palladium of the country. They are ready to repel invasion, to suppress insurrection, and preserve the good order and peace of government. That they should be well regulated, is judiciously added. A disorderly militia is disgraceful to itself, and dangerous not to the enemy, but to its own country. The duty of the state government is, to adopt such regulations as will tend to make good soldiers with the least interruptions of the ordinary and useful occupations of civil life. In this all the Union has a strong and visible interest.

The corollary, from the first position, is, that, "the right of the people to keep and bear arms shall not be infringed."

The prohibition is general. No clause in the Constitution could by any rule of construction be conceived to give to congress a power to disarm the people. Such a flagitious attempt could only be made under some general pretense by a state legislature. But if in any blind pursuit of inordinate power, either should attempt it, this amendment may be appealed to as a restraint on both.

In most of the countries of Europe, this right does not seem to be denied, although it is allowed more, or less sparingly, according to circumstances. In England, a country which boasts so much of its freedom, the right was secured to Protestant subjects only, on the revolution of 1688; and it is cautiously described to be that of bearing arms for their defense, "suitable to their conditions, and as allowed by law." [6] An arbitrary code for the preservation of game in that country has long disgraced them. A very small proportion of the people being permitted to kill it, though for their own subsistence; a gun or other instrument, used for that purpose by an unqualified person, may be seized and forfeited. Blackstone, in whom we regret that we cannot always trace the expanded principles of rational liberty, observes however, on this subject, that the prevention of popular insurrections and resistance to government by disarming the people, is oftener meant than avowed, by the makers of forest and game laws. [7] [63]

This right ought not, however, in any government, to be abused to the disturbance of the public peace.

---

63 *Rawle makes clear the Second Amendment is not a "squirrel hunting" amendment. The right to bear arms is necessary to protect liberty. Its existence is a major deterrent to power hungry politicians and Deep State elites.*

An assemblage of persons with arms, for an unlawful purpose, is an indictable offence, and even the carrying of arms abroad by a single, individual, attended with circumstances giving just reason to fear that he purposes to make an unlawful use of them, would be sufficient cause to require him to give surety of the peace. If he refused he would be liable to imprisonments. [8]

"No soldier shall in time of peace be quartered in any house without the consent of the owner," (here the restriction is general,) "nor in time of war, but in a manner to be prescribed by law;" and this must be construed a law of the United States when the war is general, or of the state when in the authorized exercise of the right of self-defense on the sudden emergencies adverted to in the Constitution, immediate state operations have become necessary. In the former case, the sole conduct of the war is given to the general government, and it ought not to be dependent on, or controlled by the state governments in its modes of proceeding. In the latter, the state, relying on its own energies, is entitled to the benefit of the same principle. The practice would be needlessly burthensome to the people in time of peace, and by a government having improper views, it might be rendered an in direct and odious mean of compelling submission to improper measures. During a war, when it becomes necessary to garrison a town, or station a body of troops for a time in a particular place, the common interest will naturally supersede minor objections.

By the general term soldier, we are to understand as, well the militia in actual service as regular troops.

The following article declares, that, "the right of the people to be secure in their houses, papers, and effects, against unreasonable searches and seizures, shall not be violated, and no warrants shall issue but upon probable cause, supported by oath or affirmation, particularly describing the place to be searched, and the persons or things to be seized."

Here again we find the general terms which prohibit all violations of these personal rights, and of course extend both to the state and the United States.

The term unreasonable is used to indicate that the sanction of a legal warrant is to be obtained, before such searches or seizures are made, but when upon probable cause, supported by oath or affirmation, such a warrant is issued, not only may other effects, but the papers of the accused be taken into the custody of the law.

The following part of the 6th article has more immediate reference to the judicial proceedings of the United States, and may therefore be considered as restraints only on the legislation of the United States.

"In all criminal prosecutions, the accused shall enjoy the right of a speedy and public trial by an impartial jury of the state and district wherein the crime shall have been committed, which district shall have been previously ascertained by law." For the better understanding of this provision, it is proper to explain that it had already been provided in the Constitution, [9] that the trials of offences should be had in the state where they were committed; but, in organizing the judiciary system, it had appeared to congress proper to form judicial districts, and it was found inconvenient to make them always commensurate with the boundaries of states. Thus two districts bad been formed out of the state of Massachusetts, and two out of Virginia. [10] By virtue of this amendment, an offence committed in that part of Massachusetts which lay eastward of New Hampshire could only be tried in the district of Maine. It is a wise and merciful measure. It would have been highly oppressive to carry a mail from Norfolk, in Virginia, to take his trial at Harrodsburg in Kentucky.

Another part of the sixth article is calculated to secure to the accused a protection which, to those familiar only with the habits of this country, would appear superfluous. The accused is to be, "informed of the nature and cause of the accusation, to be confronted with the witnesses against him; to have compulsory process for obtaining witnesses in his favor, and to have the assistance of counsel in his defense."

It seems monstrous that in any country the testimony on which a person might be convicted should be taken in his absence. Yet it is certain, that in some places, the testimony on which a person might be convicted of the greatest crimes was often taken without his being present, sometimes even without his knowing who the witnesses were. The evidence thus collected was embodied in the accusation, and he was required to defend himself against invisible enemies. This severity has indeed been mitigated in modern times, but it is believed to be not yet totally abolished.

A person accused ought to have all the aid of the law to his defense; those on whose testimony he must rely, may, from intimidation or corruption, be unwilling to assist him. The public is considered as always having it in their power to compel the appearance of witnesses against him. It is just that he should be armed in the like manner. No judge can now refuse to issue process against those whom the accused shall nominate to him — and to compel them, to enter into recognizance to appear and testify on the trial. Circumstances may even render it necessary that he should go further. If there is a probability that the witness will leave the state or district before the trial comes on, it seems to be the right of the accused to demand security for his appearance.

But with all these humane provisions, something more is wanting. The most innocent man, pressed by the awful solemnities of a public accusation and trial, may be incapable of supporting his own cause. He may be utterly unfit to cross-examine the witnesses against him, to point out the defects of their testimony, and to counteract it by properly introducing and applying his own. Hence the importance, we might say, the right, of having the aid of men educated and accustomed to manage criminal trials, to whose, knowledge and skill be may safely commit the conduct of his defense. Will it be believed, that, even at this day, in England, a person indicted of any capital crime (unless in the case of high treason by express statute) is not allowed the benefit of counsel, except to address the judge on a question of law? Those observations on the facts of the case, which, in the hands of able and experienced advocates, might secure the acquittal of an innocent man, are wholly prohibited. The trembling prisoner may make a fruitless effort himself, and he frequently has the consolation to be told, that the court is his counsel, and will call the attention of the jury to whatever may operate in his favor. An empty fiction, which often deludes him who relies on it. Two benevolent efforts have recently been made in the house of commons to procure this right to such defendants, but, being opposed by the whole force of the ministerial party, they both failed.

The protection of the individual against all unnecessary severity in the prosecution of justice, characterizes the greatest part of the fifth, and the whole of the eighth amendment.

The latter declares, that, "excessive bail shall not be required, nor excessive fines imposed, nor cruel and unusual punishments inflicted."

During the arbitrary reigns of the Stuarts in Britain, particularly of the two last, one frequent mode of oppressing those who were obnoxious to the court, was to cause criminal proceedings to be instituted against them, to demand bail in extravagant sums, and on their falling to procure it, to commit them to prison.

When the revolution took place, among other provisions demanded by the people, and readily assented to by William III. was the clause which has been transcribed into this amendment. If excessive bail is demanded by one magistrate, another may moderate it on a habeas corpus, issued to the keeper of the prison in whose custody the party is. This power is not, however, to be abused, by reducing, the bail below a reasonable sum. In such a case, the latter magistrate would himself be liable to a fine, if the criminal should not appear at the appointed time.

Excessive fines constitute one mode of inflicting cruel punishments.

This restriction applies equally to the legislative and to the judicial authority. In respect to the former, however, it is rather to be considered in the light of a recommendation than as a condition on which the constitutionality of the law depends. The judicial authority would not undertake to pronounce a law void, because the fine it imposed appeared to them excessive; and, therefore, if the legislature should commit, and persist in, gross errors in this respect, the ultimate remedy must be sought among the checks on the legislative power, which will hereafter be brought into view.

The prohibition of unusual punishments applies alike, under the qualifications already noticed, to the legislative and to the judicial power.

The laws of a free country seldom leave the sort of punishment to be inflicted to the discretion of the judge, although the measure or extent of it, as for instance the quantum of a limited fine, or the duration of a term of imprisonment, which, by the law is not to be exceeded, is often submitted to him. The peculiar circumstances of each case, the contrition or general good character of the offender, may suggest and justify a moderation of the full extent of the punishment. But a law which subjects an offender to any sort of punishment, is unknown to our civil code. If the law is silent in respect to the mode of punishment which is sometimes the case when an act is prohibited in general terms, without saying more, the court is understood to be confined to the usual moderate punishment of fine and imprisonment, or one of them. If a fine alone is imposed, imprisonment may be an adjunct, to enforce the payment of it.

The obligation on the legislature not to pass laws inflicting unusual punishments must be considered as subject to some qualification. The established forms of punishment may have proved ineffectual to prevent the commission of some kinds of offences. We may instance (consider) the practice of dueling, an offence against God and society, which no law has yet been found sufficient to prevent. It would be no violation of the Constitution if congress, within the sphere of their separate legislation, could by the invention of some new punishment, striking at the false honor which leads folly to the field, put an end to a custom so inhuman and absurd.

At common law there are two modes of instituting prosecutions; one of which is by an information filed by the officer who represents the public, on his own judgment and discretion, which, if unadvisedly or corruptly done, may subject the individual to causeless trouble and expense. The other is by an indictment which is prepared by the same officer, and sent to a grand jury, or it may be done by the grand jury themselves. In both of these cases, witnesses are carefully examined on the part of the public, and the accused is not put on his trial unless at least twelve grand jurymen, on their oaths or affirmations, find that there is sufficient cause for it. In the fifth article it is expressly declared, that, "no person, except in cases arising in the land or naval forces, or in the militia when in actual service in time of war or public danger, shall be held to answer for a capital or otherwise infamous crime, unless on a presentment or indictment of a grand jury, and in no case shall he be compelled to be a witness against himself."

That no one shall be, "subject for the same offence, to be twice put in jeopardy of life or limb," which is also provided, is perhaps too narrow — no one, after a full trial and a fair acquittal, ought to be subjected to another trial for the same offence, whether it be great or small, and such indeed is the settled rule of law. The plea of a former acquittal, is a complete bar to every subsequent prosecution for the same offence. It follows from all the antecedent precautions, that, "no one can be deprived of life, liberty, or property, without due process of law;" and the repetition of this declaration, is only valuable, as it exhibits the summary of the whole, and the anxiety that it should never be forgotten.[64]

But one part of the clause, connected with the last mentioned, requires more particular explanation.

In some countries when the public interest may occasionally

64 *The Federal government in its unconstitutional War to Prevent Southern Independence took and destroyed private property without just compensation. Said "taking" continued well after the end of the War.* See, Kennedy & Kennedy, *Punished With Poverty* (Shotwell Publishing Co., Columbia, SC: 2017).

require that private property should be appropriated to public purposes, the sovereign makes use of it without ceremony. In others, it cannot be taken from the individual on any terms without his own consent. A middle line is the correct course. A perverse and obstinate man, might otherwise impede or wholly prevent measures of the most cogent necessity for the public benefit, in which his own would be included. The people by declaring, that, "private property shall not be taken for public use, without just compensation," have agreed that in such cases and on such terms it may be taken. Of the necessity, the legislature is the only judge; it does not rest with the judicial power to determine whether the public exigence was such as to require it: great inconveniences might ensue from their assuming such a right. For example, a particular piece of ground might appear to the legislature, a suitable site for a fort in time of danger, and if they proceeded in a legal manner to vest the right to the ground in the public, it would not be competent for the judiciary to decide, that a better spot might have been chosen, or that there was no necessity for any fort.

In this manner, the property of an individual may be legally transferred against his will to the state, but the legislature has no power to transfer the property of A. to B. although it may appear more beneficial to the state that B. should have it. [11] The just compensation spoken of, should be ascertained by a jury impartially selected, and should be paid in money, the universal representative and common standard of value. [12]

Among these just and humane provisions, we observe, that trial by jury is expressly secured in all prosecutions for offences committed on land. Those which may have been committed on the high seas, would properly fall within the admiralty jurisdiction, and might, consistently with its nature, be decided without the intervention of a jury. But in conferring on congress the power to define and to punish such offences, the right to direct the mode of trial is granted as a necessary incident.

Offences committed on the high seas, being as already observed, [13] within the cognizance of all nations, and the offender liable to prosecution by the power which first apprehends him, he may consequently be subjected to a mode of trial in which a jury is unknown. Reasons of general policy may therefore possibly suggest the withholding the absolute right to trial by jury in such cases, and hence, it is omitted, not only in the original text but in the amendments. It is properly confided to congress, whose legislation on the subject, may, as good reasons occasionally are presented, recall, abridge, or modify the grant.

In respect to civil controversies, doubts arose in some of the state conventions, whether the original text was sufficiently explicit. It did not, indeed, abolish trial by jury in any case, but it was apprehended that a positive declaration in favor of it, in civil controversies, also was expedient.

Hence by the 7th amendment, it is provided, that, "in trials at common law, when the value in controversy exceeds twenty dollars, the right of trial by jury shall be preserved, and no fact, tried by a jury shall be otherwise re-examined in any court of the United States, than according to the rules of the common law."

By the first part of it, congress is disabled from ever taking it away; and by the second, neither a law can be passed by them, nor a practice adopted by the courts, to re-examine facts tried by a jury, otherwise than according to well known and long established principles.

The word "appellate," applied in the original instrument to the jurisdiction of the supreme court, was by some deemed ambiguous and inconsistent with technical phraseology; an appeal is not the mode of re-examining the decisions of common law courts, which can only be done on a writ of error, by which the record of an inferior court is brought before the superior one; and no facts can be inquired into, which do not appear on the record. New trials may be granted, if sufficient cause is shown, by the court in which the verdict is given, or, if the judgment is reversed in the court above, a venire de novo, which is a direction to the inferior court to summon another jury is issued, it the case requires it, but in no other manner can the facts be re-examined. An appeal is the process of re-examination in courts of admiralty and chancery jurisdiction from which trial by jury is systematically excluded, and in respect to which, no alteration is intended.

By this very proper amendment, all ambiguity is, removed, and all doubt is satisfied. The reference to the common law, precludes the necessity of fuller detail. The trial by jury is for ever secured on its ancient basis, and cannot be multiplied beyond it.

Here we close this part of our view of the Constitution. In the restrictions on the legislative power, we perceive two great principles — the security of the people's rights, and the preservation of the great national system. We have noticed those parts which necessarily exclude the action of the states on the same subject; but it will also be proper to advert to those express restrictions on the states, which amount to the diminution or relinquishment of so much of the state sovereignty, as the people thought it expedient to transfer to the United States.

"No state shall enter into any treaty, alliance, or confederation, nor into any agreement or compact with another state, or with a foreign power." If literally construed, this restriction would be total and absolute, and yet, as between states, some compacts certainly may be made. Thus when a large river forms a boundary between two states, a compact in regard to the exercise of jurisdiction on the river, or in respect to its fisheries, or its islands, would be lawful. And perhaps the true construction of this clause is, that political compacts in any form are alone intended.

If a state has received a particular injury from a foreign power, it is not to give way to the natural impulse of granting letters of marque and reprisal, for this would invade an essential attribute of the general government.

The power to coin money, emit bills of credit, and make any thing but gold and silver a tender in the payment of debts, is likewise withdrawn from them, although not withheld from the United States.

The restrictions of passing bills of attainder and ex post facto laws, and granting titles of nobility, is common to both, but the express prohibition of passing laws impairing the obligation of contracts is confined to the separate states, and it may, as already noticed, be inquired why it was not extended to the United States. Before an answer is given, an explanation of the sense in which the term contract is here to be expounded, drawn from the highest authority, will be useful.

By contracts we are to understand every executed agreement, whether between individuals or between individuals and a state, by which a right is vested, and every executory agreement which confers a right of action, or creates a binding obligation in relation to subjects of a valuable nature, such as may be asserted in a court of justice; but it does not comprehend the political relations of a government and its citizens; civil institutions which must be liable to change with circumstances, and to be modified by ordinary legislation, those which deeply concern the public, and which to preserve good government, the public judgment must control. [14]

The plenitude of power possessed by a state legislature, to which every thing that is not reserved is granted, and the temptations to an erroneous exercise of this power which sometimes occur, render express restrictions, if not absolutely necessary, at least very useful; but the legislature of the United States can have no such power, unless it is expressly granted to them.[65]

A system of bankruptcy impairs the obligation of contracts, when it releases the party from the necessity of performing them; but congress is expressly invested with this power in regard to bankruptcy. It is an enumerated, and not an implied one, and in no other form, can the obligation of contracts be impaired by them. A system of bankruptcy is practically limited to two objects, the relief of honest insolvency and the equal distribution of the remnants of property among the creditors. The United States therefore, possess no vague and indefinite power, that may be exercised to the prejudice of individuals among themselves, or the exaltation of the public authority over private rights.

The remaining restrictions have already been generally noticed, but will here be transcribed to close the subject.

"No state shall, without the consent of the congress, lay any imposts or duties on imports or exports, except what may be absolutely necessary for executing its inspection laws, and the net produce of all duties and imposts, laid by any state on imports or exports, shall be for the use of the treasury of the United States, and all such laws shall be subject to the revision and control of the congress. No state shall, without the consent of congress, lay any duty of tonnage, keep troops or ships of war in time of peace, or engage in war unless actually invaded, or in such imminent danger as will not admit of delay."[66]

---

65 *Able Upsher, in* The Federal Government: Its True Nature and Character, *states " ... in the State constitutions every power is granted which is not denied; in the Federal Constitution, every power is denied which is not granted." The powers exercised by the States are original that is, they are from the people, whereas the powers exercised by the Federal government are secondary — that is, they are delegated from the original powers of the States. The Sovereign States obtain their powers from the people who created the State government. The States, acting as the agent of their people (the sovereign community, as per John C. Calhoun), delegate a portion of their sovereign power to form the Federal government. Thus, State powers are original whereas Federal powers are secondary — that is, derived from the States.*

66 *The Sovereign States delegated to their agent, the Federal government, the authority to engage in aggressive war against foreign nations but these same Sovereign States reserved the right to engage in defensive war if necessary, to protect their State's citizens and immediate action is required. This is another recognition of States Rights as reserved by Sovereign States in the Constitutionally limited Republic of Sovereign States. See, Article I, Section 10, paragraph 4, U.S. Constitution.*

CHAPTER NOTES
X

1. See among other instances, the case of Commonwealth v. Smith, before Chief Justice Tilghman, 1809.

2. 3 Dallas, 386. Calder v. Bull.

3. See Dalrymple's Memoirs, vol. 2, Mazure's late History of the Revolution of 1688, &c.

4. There are now but two states in the Union whose constitutions contain exclusive provisions in regard to religious opinions. In Maryland, no one who does not believe in the Christian religion can be admitted to an office of trust or profit. In North Carolina, the same exclusion is extended to all who deny the truth of the protestant religion. But in every other respect than the capacity to hold such offices, all stand on the same footing in both states.

5. 1 Bl. 143. 4 Bl. 147. Lord Mansfield on the Trial of Lord George Gordon.

6. 1 Will. & Mary, c. 2.

7. 2 Bl. 412.

8. 3 Coke's Inst. 160. Hawkins, b. 1. c. 60.

9. Art. 3. § 9.

10. Other subdivisions have since taken place in other states: the general principle is now adverted to.

11. *Vanhorn's lessee v. Dorrance*, 2 Dall. 384.

12. *Vanhorn's lessee v. Dorrance*, 2 Dall. 384.

13. P. 102.

14. 6 Cranch, p. 136. 4 Wheaton, p. 627.

SECTION IV
CHAPTERS XI-XX

In the following ten chapters, Rawle reviews the act of treason against the United States and the function and power of the president of the United States. The function and duties of the president are found in Article II of the United States Constitution.

CHAPTER XI.

OF TREASON AGAINST THE UNITED STATES.

THE importance of this subject merits a separate chapter.

It was highly proper, perhaps absolutely necessary, that a crime, the commission of which must owe its existence to the formation of the government, should be both recognized and defined in the Constitution.

Although it is a general principle that all governments must be understood to contain within themselves the materials for their own preservation, and it could not be supposed that the national government now created was to depend on the individual states for protection against traitors, yet to have left the power of self-defense to inference and to argument, would have been unwise.

The unity of the government in its limited character required from the judicial authority, which appertained to it, a concurrent aid, simple and uniform in its nature, and adequate in its effect. To leave this offence liable to prosecution in the state courts only, would have been to hazard the consequences of a variety of opinions and discordances of adjudication, and, perhaps, occasionally, to the inconvenience of encountering some political reluctance or dissatisfaction on the part of the states. For although, as will be hereafter more fully shown, the judicial power is, in its nature, superior to the bias of party or personal motives; yet it is prudent, whenever it is practicable, to guard against the possible relaxation of this exalted principle. It was also recollected that in the proceedings preparatory to the trial, much is to be done by inferior officers, among whom such independence is not always to be found.

The United States, therefore, justly reserved to themselves the right to punish this high offence, and the state courts, since the adoption of the Constitution, have abstained from intermeddling with prosecutions on account of it.[1]

But something more than the recognition of the crime, and the provision of exclusive tribunals for its punishment, was requisite for the security of the people. It is of all offences that which it is the most necessary to define with precision.

The natural inclination of those who possess power, is to increase it. History shows that to enlarge the description of treason has often been resorted to as one of the means of increasing power. To have left to the legislature an unlimited right to declare what should amount to this crime would have been less consistent with public safety, than to fix, by common consent, its plain definition and exact limits. It is, so far, withheld from the power of those who, under the influence of sudden resentment or ambitious views, might unreasonably extend its character; while, on the other hand, except by the voice of the people at large, acting through the medium of a change of the Constitution itself, it cannot be contracted to a narrower compass, which might weaken the safeguards of the general system.

In giving the definition, general principles only can be adopted; it rests with the judicial power to determine whether the acts that may be committed, fall within these principles.

Treason is the attempt of one or more individuals, who are citizens or subjects of a government, to subvert and destroy it. The intention must be that this end shall be effected by force, in some stage of the proceeding, but the offence may be complete before any force is actually used.

It is one of those crimes which may not be accomplished by a single act; but, on the contrary, is in its very nature progressive yet continuous. Robbery, murder, and many other crimes, are or may be effectuated in a short space of time; and when the body is deprived of life or the goods are taken from the spot, the perpetration of the guilt is full and entire: but the attempt to subvert a government is not a momentary act; combinations are formed, unlawful schemes devised and pursued; opposition is commenced and carried on, and the crime is ever the same; the protraction of time may increase the terror and the injury, but in a legal view they do not enhance the guilt: in its outset it is deemed the highest crime that can be committed, and of course, no subsequent circumstances can raise it higher.

But, from the different nature of governments, there is a difference in the manifestations of treason in a monarchy and in a republic. In the former, it is considered as an offence against the supreme executive magistrate; in the latter it is an offence against the body of the people. Hence, to slay or to endeavor to slay the king, is, in itself, high-treason, although it may be the uncounseled thought and unassisted act of a single individual; but in a republic, not the life of a monarch, but the life of the republic is at stake. There must in the latter case be a combination with others; for no man could be supposed capable of intending singly and alone to subvert a government formed on the authority of the people. But those with whom he combines may not, themselves, be guilty of treason. The citizen who unites himself with a hostile nation, waging war against his country, is guilty of a crime of which the foreign army is innocent; with him it is treason, with his associates it is, in the code of nations, legitimate warfare. If he should be made prisoner and proceeded against as a traitor, it is against the usage of nations for those who have accepted his co-operation to object to the course which the laws of his own country impose on him.

Treason is declared to consist only in levying war against the United States, or in adhering to their enemies, giving them aid and comfort. The term levying war is understood to have been taken from the English statute of 25th Edward III., and receives the same construction with us which is given to it in that country.

The war which is spoken of embraces, as before observed, both hostilities from abroad and internal rebellion.

An insurrection, the object of which was to suppress an office of excise established under a law of the United States, and the marching with a party in arms to the house of the excise officer, and committing acts of violence and outrage there, with a view by force and intimidation to prevent the execution of the law, has been held to amount to a levying of war against the United States. [2] A conspiracy to subvert by force the government of the United States, violently to dismember the Union, to coerce repeal of a general law, or to revolutionize a territorial government by force, if carried into effect, by embodying and assembling a military body in a military posture, is an overt act of levying war; and not only those who bear arms, but those who perform the various and essential parts which must be assigned to different persons, for the purpose of prosecuting the war, are guilty of the crime. [3]

Similar acts committed against the laws or government of a particular state, are punishable according to the laws of that state, but do not amount to treason against the United States; and on the other hand, in case of a war between the United States and a foreign nation, adhering to such foreign nation, and giving them aid and comfort in the prosecution of the war, amounts to treason against the United States, and not against the state of which the party is a citizen. [4] The restrictions are dictated by a spirit of humanity. "No person shall be convicted of this crime, unless on the testimony of two witnesses to the same overt act, or on confession in open court." A confession out of court, although before a magistrate, is not sufficient; but after the overt act of treason is proved by two witnesses, it may be given in evidence by way of corroboration. [5] The testimony of the two witnesses must be to the same overt act, and not, as in England it may be, to two different acts of the same species of treason.

It is not within the scope of this work to notice all the legislative provisions which have since been made in respect to trials for treason; it is sufficient to say, that they pursue the same liberal and humane spirit for the purpose of affording to the accused the utmost latitude of defense, but in case of his conviction, congress, which has the power to declare the punishments has imposed that of death. But the forfeiture of life is not, with us, aggravated by refined and useless cruelty. Who can read without horror the punishments of Ravaillac and Damiens, or the sentences, in modern times deemed too barbarous to be enforced, against traitors in England?

The restriction on congress in respect to the punishment is, that, "no attainder of treason shall work corruption of blood, or forfeiture, except during the life of the person attainted."

Corruption of blood is derived from the common law of England, and signifies that an attainted person can neither inherit land from his ancestors, nor retain what he is in possession of, nor transmit it by descent to his heirs, nor shall any person make title by descent through him, though from a more remote ancestor.

In respect to the forfeiture, the meaning seems to be, that congress shall not impose a forfeiture beyond the term of the offender's life, but it may be abolished altogether, and in this sense, it has been understood and acted on in the law, for the punishment of certain crimes against the United States, passed on the 30th of April, 1790, the language of which is as follows: "no conviction or judgment for any of the offences aforesaid, (in which are included treason, murder, robbery, piracy, and other crimes,) shall work corruption of blood or any forfeiture of estate."

But a future legislature is neither bound to enforce this humane part of the act, nor to continue other parts which bear the cast of some severity.

The immediate forfeiture of the possessions of an offender, although its hardship in capital cases is felt, not by himself, but by his family reduced to want, has been vindicated on the supposition, that it would tend to set the paternal feelings in motion on the side of the commonwealth; *acerbum*, says Cicero in a letter to Brutus, *parentum scelera filiorum poenis lui, sed hoc preclare legibus comparatum est, ut caritas liberorum amicitiores parentes reipublicæ redderet.*

And such considerations may have some effect; but the depravity that leads to the hazard of life, seldom refrains from the commission of crime by adverting to the sufferings of children. The bad citizen is most commonly a bad parent.

The affliction felt by such near relations, both for the guilt and the loss of the parent, is unreasonably aggravated by their being thus subjected to partake, though in a different form, of the punishment inflicted, when, in common with their fellow citizens, they may have sincerely abhorred the crime.

But while in this particular, opinion has been divided, all seem to have condemned, and many to have been at a loss to account for the extension of this penal principle to the destruction of the power to inherit through the person attainted.

We cannot be reconciled to it, by being told that property being the creature of society, we have no right to complain of the manner in which it is regulated, [6] for, on such grounds, the most unjust laws might be defended.

But we may account for its origin from a former state of society, which has been greatly altered in modern times. It is an ancient feudal principle, that where there is no inheritable blood, the land shall escheat to the lord of the fee. Applying, or rather perverting the doctrine of present forfeiture to the incapacity of taking by descent, was the first and very easy step in a process, by which all that would have vested in the criminal, became the property of the lord. The avidity of the lord, which was thus gratified, cast about for still more prey and as the attainder of the offender removed him from being the immediate object of a descent, the principle, it was found, could also be successfully applied to his being the channel through which others might inherit. If the grandfather, after the attainder of the son for treason or felony, died seized of land and intestate, the grandson could not inherit, because he could not be his heir, as he was not the heir of his own father. By a fiction engrafted on the substantial punishment of the father, the grandfather was considered as dying without heirs, and his lands also escheated to the lord.

Thus the doctrine is resolved into an odious fiction, founded on a compound of cruelty and avarice, springing from a perversion of the system of tenures, and at variance with the liberal principles of modern times and the very elements of justice.

Had it been prohibited by the Constitution in regard to all offences whatever, it would have merited public approbation.

CHAPTER NOTES
XI

1. If this provision had not been made, the state courts would not have refused to sustain such prosecutions. See post ch. xxix.

2. *United States v. Vigol*, 2 Dallas, 346. *United States v. Mitchell*, ib. 348.

3. 4 Cranch, 470. United States v. Burr et al.

4. Lynch's case in New York, 11 Johnson, 553.

5. *United States v. Fries*, printed report of the trial, p. 171.

6. Considerations on the law of forfeitures, attributed to Charles Yorke.

CHAPTER XII.

OF THE EXECUTIVE POWER.

IN the formation of a republic there is perhaps no part more difficult than the right constitution of the executive authority. The three qualities of promptness, vigor, and responsibility, ought to be combined in it. In the two other branches, more deliberation is necessary. Whether to make laws or to expound them, the motions should, in general, be slow and cautious. The acts of either, when constitutionally consummate, are obligatory on those, whose duty, it is to enforce them. The office of executing a law, excludes the right to judge of it, and of course does not require that the executive power should concur in opinion on its utility. When the meaning and intention of the legislature are ascertained, and the law itself is constitutional, delay in the execution of it is culpable. The public, which may blame the legislator, requires of the executive officer to carry it into effect, because to subvert the order of government, is one of the greatest evils that can befall it. Every individual is bound to obey the law, however objectionable it may appear to him: the executive power is bound not only to obey, but to execute it. To hesitate, to delay, perhaps to lose the proper moment of action, would approach to entire disobedience. A prompt submission to the law, and an immediate preparation to enforce it, are therefore absolutely necessary in relation to the authority from which the law has emanated. But we must also consider this quality in respect to its effect. The operation of a law, whenever the time of acting upon it has arrived, should be immediate and decisive. The law is a power of which the force and existence should never be unfelt or forgotten. Like the pillar which led the Israelites through the wilderness, it should always be in sight. The commonwealth in which its pre-eminence is not constantly present to the mind, is in danger. But the sensation of its continued presence, and uncontrollable power, will be greatly weakened, if time is suffered to elapse without necessity, after its action ought to take place.

On general political principles therefore, as delay is reprehensible, promptness is a duty, the non-performance of which may enable transgressors to escape. For this reason, it is both wise and humane that the execution of laws should be speedy; that is, that no unreasonable interval should be allowed between the violation of the law and the adoption of such measures as may be necessary to enforce it.

For this purpose the executive must also be endowed with sufficient energy. It has been justly said that a feeble executive implies a feeble execution of the government. A feeble execution is but another phrase for a bad execution; and a government ill executed, whatever it may be in theory, must in practice, be a bad government. [1] It is in fact only by the execution of the Constitution and the laws, that the true value of either is known. If they are left as dead letters, they confer no benefit, and avert no evil. Principles without practice are like the intentions of an individual without acts. An energy of action, duly proportioned to the exigencies that arise, must be seated in the executive power. The proportion of the power to the occasions that are expected to require its use, should be as exact as possible. If it falls short, the evils we have already adverted to will ensue; if it exceeds them, the liberty of the people is endangered. It is difficult to adopt general expressions exactly descriptive of the proper extent and limitation of this power. Perhaps those we find in the Constitution are as competent as any that could be applied. "The president shall take care that the laws [of the United States] shall be faithfully executed." The simplicity of the language accords with the general character of the instrument. It declares what is his duty, and it gives him no power beyond it. The Constitution, treaties, and acts of congress, are declared to be the supreme law of the land. He is bound to enforce them; if he attempts to carry his power further, he violates the Constitution.[67]

But although an exact specification of the manner in which the executive power shall be exercised, is not, and could not be introduced into, the Constitution, although it would be at once unnecessary and impossible to define all the modes in which it may be executed, yet the auxiliary means are not wholly omitted, and will be noticed after we have considered the composition of the executive.

---

67 *Hamilton, in Federalist No. 33, states that all acts of the Federal government must be in accord with the Constitution. If any portion of the Federal government acts beyond its delegated authority, its acts are unconstitutional. Hamilton states "... it will not follow ... that the acts of the larger society [Federal] which are not pursuant to its constitutional powers, but which are invasions of the residuary authorities of the smaller societies [States], will become the supreme law of the land. These will be merely acts of usurpation, and will deserve to be treated as such. ... It will not ... have escaped observation, that it [the Constitution] expressly confines this supremacy to laws made pursuant to the Constitution."*

In some republics, the fear of evil from a single head, has led to the creation of councils and other subdivisions of the executive power, and the consequent imbecility and distractions of those governments have probably contributed to lead most of the nations of Europe to the preference given to monarchies. It was falsely conceived that to vest the executive power in a single person, was inconsistent with the nature of a republic, or it was supposed that a republic so constituted could not long retain its freedom, against the ambitious views, and alarming domination of a single magistrate. But in America, neither the fervor of republican principles, nor the odium of monarchy, then in hostile array against us, overpowered the calm and deliberate exercise of a sound judgment in this respect, and in every state but one, the unity of the executive power was adopted as a principle. Pennsylvania alone, whose original constitution has since been altered by the people, created an executive council, formed of a member from each county, and we have heretofore noticed its feebleness and inefficiency on a distressing occasion. [2]

The experience of nearly half a century in respect to these state governments; the experience of upwards of a third of a century in respect to the United States government, evince that under proper regulations no abuse of such powers is to be feared. Limited and restrained as the president is, creature of the people, and subject to the law, with all power to do right, he possesses none to do wrong; his general responsibility by being undivided, is complete, his liability to impeachment, by accusers, in whose appointment he has no share, before a court which he does not create, both emanating from the same source to which he owes his own existence; his term of office exactly limited, his official power entirely gone the moment that of his successor commences, or the moment when the senate shall pass on him a sentence of deprivation of office; his only safety consists in doing what is right; his speedy and certain destitution would follow a contrary conduct.

CHAPTER NOTES
XII

1. Fed. No. 70.

2. P. 108.

CHAPTER XIII.

OF THE MEANS PROVIDED FOR THE PERFORMANCE OF THE EXECUTIVE DUTIES.

AMONG the means provided to enable the president to perform his public duties, the command of the military force will first be considered.

The principal clauses in the Constitution which affect the subject are the following: —

"The Congress shall have power to raise and support armies, to provide and maintain a navy, to make rules for the government and regulation of the army, the navy, and also of the militia, when the latter are in the service of the United States."

"The president shall be commander in chief of the army and navy, and of the militia of the several states when called into the actual service of the United States."

These are the modes of action expressly provided for the executive magistrate, whenever his functions assume a military cast. In relation to those of a nature merely civil, the Constitution is silent, because particular description would not be equally practicable, and hence as before observed, congress is empowered to, "pass such laws as may be requisite and proper for carrying into execution the powers vested in the officers of government."

Subordinate offices are therefore created by congress when necessary, whose functions are either expressly defined, or implied from the nature of the office, or left wholly or in part to the direction of the president.

But the military power is at present to be considered, and this, it appears, consists of two classes; first, those who are regularly retained on stipulated compensations to serve in the army or navy, and secondly, the militia who are called forth as occasion may require, but when in service are subject to the same regulations as regular troops.

On the nature and character of the first, little needs at present to be said. The caution that no appropriation of money for the support of an army for a longer term than two years has been mentioned. The manner of employment may be directed by congress, or confided to the president. Congress, which may direct when and where forts shall be built, may also prescribe that they shall be garrisoned either with specific numbers, or with such a number as the president may think proper. So in times of peace, troops may be stationed by congress in particular parts of the United States, having a view either to their health and easy subsistence, or to the security of distant and frontier stations; but during the emergencies of a war, when the defense of the country is cast on the president, and dangers not foreseen may require measures of defense not provided for, the president would certainly be justified in preferring the execution of his constitutional duties, to the literal obedience of a law, the original object of which was of less vital importance than that created by subsequent exigencies, and there can be no doubt, that this necessary power would extend to the erecting of new fortresses, and to the abandoning of those erected by order of congress, as well as to the concentration, division or other local employment of the troops, which in his judgment or that of the officers under his command, became expedient from circumstances. This would not be a violation of the rules laid down in the preceding pages, since the obligation of the law is lost in the succession of causes that prevent its operation, and the Constitution itself may be considered as thus superseding it.

The power of the president over the militia depends on the same principle; the necessary supply of the means to enable him to perform his executive duties.

In a people permitted and accustomed to bear arms, we have the rudiments of a militia, which properly consists of armed citizens, divided into military bands, and instructed at least in part in the use of arms for the purposes of war.[68] Their civil occupations are not relinquished, except while they are actually in the field, and the inconvenience of withdrawing them from their accustomed labors, abridges the time required for military instruction. Militia therefore never amount to perfect soldiers, unless the public exigencies shall have kept them so long together as to absorb the civil, in the military character.

The human mind is of a nature so flexible, that it may by persever-

---

68 *Rawle explains why it is so important for a free people to maintain the right to bear arms. The writings of the Anti-Federalists of Pennsylvania also demonstrate why maintaining the right to bear arms is important for a free people. "That the people have a right to bear arms for the defense of themselves and their own state, or the United States ... and no law shall be passed for disarming the people or any of them. ..." Free people have the right of self-protection.*

ance, be disciplined to results, which at first view would be deemed almost impossible. The fear of death is certainly one of the earliest, and most natural passions; yet in a well regulated army, it gives way to the fear of disgrace; and the soldier becomes more apprehensive of the displeasure of his commanders, than of the fire of the enemy. Another sort of mechanism also contributes to actuate a disciplined army; it is the voluntary and entire surrender of its own judgment to that of the commander. Obedience would be slow and uncertain, if the soldier was to allow himself to reflect on the propriety of the orders given: he is habituated to deem them right, merely because they are orders, and from the common soldier to the highest subordinate officer, no other rule is known than that of implicit obedience. The confidence thus reposed is not of a personal nature; it does not depend merely on the character of the individual in command. If the commander should fall during an engagement, it is immediately transferred to his successor, who on his part, at once assumes the suspended faculty of deciding what is proper to be done, in lieu of the implicit obedience without inquiry, under which till that moment he had acted. This at first view appears inconsistent with individual freedom and independence, and hence it is that militia are systematically less tractable than regular troops. Devoted patriotism and personal courage, although they frequently produce feats of exalted men, are insufficient for the combinations of an army. The conquests of the Macedonian Alexander may easily be accounted for on this ground; he had received from his father Philip the first regular army of which we have an account in history, and with these he fearlessly advanced into distant countries, and successively defeated immense multitudes of the Persian and Indian militia, among whom there were doubtless much individual bravery, and strong desires of defending their country. [1]

But notwithstanding their inferiority to soldiers schooled and practiced in the field, gallant actions have been performed by our militia collectively. The capture of an entire army under General Burgoyne in 1777, and the celebrated defense of New Orleans in 1814, were chiefly effected by militia.

But however inferior in military estimate to armies regularly trained, the militia constitutes one of the great bulwarks of the nation, and nothing which tends to improve and support it should be neglected.

The power given to congress over it is from its nature exclusive, to the extent that it is carried in the Constitution.

During the late war, a construction of this part of the Constitution was given in a highly respectable state, which excited no small uneasiness at the time, and ought not to be passed over in silence. The act of congress declaring war took place on the 18th of June, 1812, and the president was expressly authorized by the act to use the whole land and naval forces to carry it into effect. Orders were soon afterwards issued by him for calling out certain portions of the militia from each state. The opinions of the judges of the supreme judicial court of Massachusetts were required by the governor, and three of them in the absence of the others, declared their sentiments that the commander in chief of the militia of a state had a right to decide whether or not the exigencies to warrant the call existed. Of course, that whatever were the declarations of congress, or the course pursued by the president, if the governor of a state thought differently; if he thought there was no war, no insurrection, no invasion, he was not obliged to obey such requisitions. The governor expressed the same opinion in a message to the legislature; and a line of conduct was adopted, greatly tending to impair the energies of the country, and encourage the hopes of the enemy.

The apprehension professed was, that if congress by determining that those special cases existed, could at any time call forth the whole of the militia and subject them to the command of the president, it might produce a "military consolidation of the states," without any constitutional remedy. And that under the act of February 28th, 1795, the militia of the several states would be in fact at his command at any time when he thought proper, whether the exigency existed or not. [2]

But whatever weight might have been found in such objections against adopting the Constitution, they ceased when it was adopted. It was then the choice of the people to repose this confidence in congress to enable them to provide for the common defense and general welfare. If it had been thought necessary to impose any check or control; if in opposition to the whole spirit of the instrument, it had been deemed expedient to disunite the system, by requiring the concurrence of the states, it could undoubtedly have been so expressed, and in this respect at least we should not have advanced a step beyond the imbecility of the old government. Nothing would be more likely to enfeeble the Union than to have subjected the right of exercising these powers to the governors, or even the legislatures of the different states, some of which might hold one opinion, and some insist upon another; and it is by no means clear that the people did not apprehend a greater danger of abuse of confidence from the governor and legislature of a state, than from the government of the United States.

The act of February 28th, 1795, certainly vests in the president alone the power to call out and employ the militia, without waiting for, or pointing out any particular mode by which the evidence of the necessity for it shall be furnished. The former act had required that before the militia was called out to suppress an insurrection, a certificate should be given to the president by an associate judge of the supreme court, or the judge of the district court, that the laws of the United States were opposed by combinations too powerful to be suppressed by the ordinary course of judicial proceedings, &c. But besides the incongruity of thus requiring members of the judicial authority to decide in this manner upon facts, it was shifting a responsibility from the proper officer, the president, and throwing it upon those who were less amenable, if amenable at all, in such a case. The second act, therefore, very properly leaves it with the president to determine on the exigency which shall authorize the measure. Power so serious and important, it was believed would not be lightly or prematurely exercised by him. He who is charged with executing the laws of the Union, is naturally the best apprized [informed] of resistance to them, and for his own justification he will take care to be prepared with adequate proof of the fact.

In respect to foreign invasion, its public notoriety, when it actually takes place, renders no form of evidence necessary, and his power on such an occasion to call forth the militia, not merely of the state invaded, but from other parts, to assist in repelling an enemy, who, by the terms and spirit of our Constitution, is the enemy of the whole, is surely too salutary to be denied. Of the danger of an invasion before it happens, no one can be a better judge than he, who, being charged with all our foreign relations, must be the best informed of the proceedings of foreign powers. But in the case of war actually declared by law, it is difficult to conceive even a plausible doubt. The law itself constitutes the fact, and unless it should be seriously contended that congress was bound, before it declared war, to obtain the consent of the several states, there can be no pretense for saying that the commanders in chief of the militia in the several states were not required or authorized by the Constitution to obey his military orders.

It fortunately happened that no military operations of a serious character occurred in that part of the country during the war. If an invasion in much force had taken place, the probability is, that with a paternal disregard of these unconstitutional opinions, the president would have employed the force of the Union to repel it, and the temporary exhibition of local jealousy, would have been lost in the sense of the necessity of a common exertion, and the gratitude for the aid which produced a successful defense.

As it is the only instance in which a construction hostile to the full exercise of the president's authority has been distinctly avowed, and as it presents the opportunity of shortly elucidating this part of the Constitution, the author has felt it a duty to take some notice of it, though without the smallest intention to revive heats, now happily extinguished.

The governors of the several states are commanders in chief of their militia, except when they shall be called into the actual service of the United States. In fixing the moment when this power over them ceases, and that of the president commences, the language used in some of the state constitutions, and in the Constitution of the United States, is the same. The calling into actual service, and not the actual commencement of the service, is the period alluded to, and it would in some degree impair the energetic power, which in times of public danger is to be exercised by the president, if he possessed no right to enforce obedience to the call. It may therefore be doubted, whether an act of Congress postponing the commencement of the president's authority till the militia shall have obeyed the call, is perfectly consistent with the Constitution. The legislature can no more abridge, than it can enlarge the executive powers, under the Constitution. This question was discussed, but not directly decided in the case of Houston v. Moore. [3]

The president during the war had called upon the state of Pennsylvania, (as well as on other states,) for a portion of the militia. A person who was drafted for that purpose, disobeyed the summons and was fined by a court martial held under the authority of an act of assembly of Pennsylvania.

The main question was, whether the court martial ought to have been convened under the authority of the United States, or of the state. The acts of congress of 28th February, 1776, and of the 10th April, 1814, were much considered. It was held that congress not having legislated on the subject of holding courts martial in such cases, an act of the state legislature to that effect was constitutional. The 10th section of the latter provides for the expense of marching the militia to the place of rendezvous. Immediately on arriving there, they are undoubtedly in actual service, and if in their way to it they are under any military command whatever, it must be that of the president.

Circumstances may render it necessary for the president to appoint another place of rendezvous, before that previously appointed has been reached, and military operations may, from a change of the enemy's position, become necessary even on the march; surely in any such case, the military power of the president alone ought to be exercised over them. Considerations of economy in respect to their pay ought in such cases to be disregarded.

A case which in 1818 was decided in the supreme court of Pennsylvania, supports most of these principles, and is not at variance with any of them. That highly respectable court adopted the following construction of the Constitution and the powers of congress under it.

The president has a right to issue his orders for calling out the militia, not through the medium of the governor only, but directly to any officer he thinks proper.

If he makes a requisition on the governor in the first instance, and the latter declines to comply with it, the president may issue his command to any officer of the militia.

The governor is not justified in disobeying the requisition, because he differs in opinion as to the necessity of calling forth the militia.

The governor without the authority of congress, or of the state legislature, has no right to direct courts martial affecting those who disobey the call of the president.

A person enrolled, drafted, and regularly notified when and where to attend for muster and inspection, is liable to a penalty on the judgment of a court martial constituted under the authority of the United States — although such person, before he appears at the place of rendezvous, may not be justly considered as in actual service. The calling forth must precede the actual service. It would render the Constitution a dead letter, to suppose that he who is enrolled and drafted, but refuses to appear, shall be exempted from punishment because he has refused.

It is no infringement of the rights of citizens to proceed to the trial of delinquent militia-men by courts martial. [4]

The regular troops of the United States are under the immediate command of the president from the time of their enlistment; they may be marched to, or stationed at any part of the United States, at his discretion, unless prevented by some special legislative act: And although the genius of a republic and the peculiar character of our country would indicate that their employment should be only in its defense, yet since a defensive war is sometimes best carried on by invading the territory of the aggressor, the president may cause them to be marched out of the United States to effect this purpose, and there can be no doubt, that in such a case, he would possess the same power over the militia.

It may perhaps be made a question, whether for the suppression of insurrection, and in cases of a similar nature, the president can employ the regular troops in aid of the civil authority. The acts of congress are silent on the subject, and no power given by them would be valid unless it could be supported by the principles of the Constitution. It must be admitted to be a question of great delicacy and importance. No power is so likely to be abused as the command of a regular army — no measure would be, more dangerous to civil liberty than an habitual recurrence to military force in other cases than actual war; yet on the other hand, in times of dangerous commotion, when law is prostrated and the civil power is felt to be inadequate, the public good would appear to justify the most prompt and efficient remedy.

Soldiers do not cease to be citizens by being incorporated into a regular army, and it is the duty of every citizen in cases of this sort, to render his best services to his country. It can be no objection to the fulfilment of this duty, that it is rendered more efficacious by previous discipline, and by being performed in a regular and not a desultory manner. It is, however, always to be kept in mind, that the military should be subordinate to the civil power. The orders for the employment of this force on such occasions must emanate from the president in his civil capacity, or from civil officers of the United States, possessing the authority of conservators of the peace, if any such there be.

That the exercise of this power should be attended with great caution, no one will deny; real necessity alone will justify its being exercised at all. There can be no doubt that, if it occasioned the loss of human life, the whole measure would be liable to severe judicial scrutiny.[69]

CHAPTER NOTES
XIII

1. How well this is explained by Adam Smith in his *Wealth of Nations*, vol. 3. p. 56.
2. See 8 Mass. Reports, 551. Niles' Reg. vol. 3, 116.
3. 8 Wheaton, p. 1, and 3 Serg. & Rawle, 169.
4. 3 Sergeant & Rawle, 590. *Duffield v. Smith.*

---

69 *The Constitution gives the president the authority to call out a States' militia. The state, upon receiving the call, must comply as long as it remains in the Union. It could attempt to remain in the Union by nullifying the president's call but the other states acting via the amending process may decide to expel the nullifying state. This is certainly a more reasonable and humane alternative than conducting an armed invasion of the nullifying state and compelling its people to submit to federal military or puppet, state government rule. There is a price to be paid by each state for membership in the Union but, if a sovereign state is no longer willing to pay the price, it should be free to leave the Union. If you can't leave, then you are not free.*

CHAPTER XIV.

OF THE APPOINTMENT TO OFFICES.

IN addition to the power over the army, navy, and militia, already noticed, the president has a qualified power of appointing the executive and judicial officers. The former of these are held during his pleasure; the latter during good behavior. In respect to both, the commissions are granted by the president, but they specify that it is by and with the advice and consent of the senate. It was deemed expedient that the approbation of the senate should be given, unless a vacancy happened during its recess, in which case commissions are granted which expire at the end of the next session.

It may, however, be questioned, whether this restraint on the power of the president fully corresponds with the confidence which is otherwise reposed in him, and whether it does not in some degree affect the responsibility to public opinion which would accompany an unlimited power of appointments.

If it were left entirely to himself to select such agents as he might deem qualified for public duties, he would of course be scrupulous in his choice; but if a senate, either actuated by party motives, or for want of information of the fitness of the individual, rejects the nomination, not only may the public interests suffer in the immediate case, but the president be impelled to inadequate substitutions. It is true, that the converse of this proposition may also be admitted. Improper nominations, proceeding from personal or party influence, may be properly rejected by a virtuous and inflexible senate; but in the latter case, if it ever should be our misfortune to have a man so actuated, in possession of this high office, we may see him immediately after the rising of the senate, dismiss the incumbent, or in case of their rejecting one nomination, withholding another, and availing himself of the power to appoint during the recess. It would, therefore, appear upon the whole, that with the possibility of an evasion which would render the constitutional provision so entirely nugatory, it would have been more beneficial to have left this power in the president without restraint, and the more so, as the consent of the senate is not required for the dismission of the officer.

It would be improper to pass over the construction given by the senate to the power of appointing during their recess. It has been held by that venerable body, that if new offices are created by congress, the president cannot after the adjournment of the senate, make appointments to fill them. The vacancies do not happen during the recess of the senate. [1]

The text is not very explicit as to the officers whose appointments require the consent of the senate: it enumerates, "ambassadors, other public ministers, and consuls, judges of the supreme court, and all other officers of the United States, whose appointments are not therein otherwise provided for, and which shall be established by law; but the congress may by law vest the appointment of such inferior officers as they think proper in the president alone, in the courts of law, or in the heads of departments." The term "inferior" is somewhat vague, and it is perhaps left to congress to determine how to apply it; if they do not otherwise direct, the consent of the senate is necessary under the qualifications described.

A proper selection and appointment of subordinate officers, is one of the strongest marks of a powerful mind. It is a duty of the president to acquire, as far as possible, an intimate knowledge of the capacities and characters of his fellow citizens; to disregard the importunities of friends; the hints or menaces of enemies; the bias of party, and the hope of popularity. The latter is sometimes the refuge of feeble-minded men, but its gleam is transient if it is obtained by a dereliction of honest duty and sound discretion. Popular favor is best secured by carefully ascertaining and strictly pursuing the true interests of the people. The president himself is elected on the supposition that he is the most capable citizen to understand and promote those interests, and in every appointment he ought to consider himself as executing a public trust of the same nature.

Neither should the fear of giving offence to the public, or pain to the individual, deter him from the immediate exercise of his power of removal on proof of incapacity or infidelity in the subordinate officer. The public, uninformed of the necessity, may be surprised, and at first dissatisfied; but public approbation ultimately accompanies the fearless and upright discharge of duty. On the other hand, hasty and capricious dismissions from office are equally reprehensible. Although the officer may be dependent on the pleasure of the president, a sound discretion is expected to regulate that pleasure. The motives to attain a degree of excellence in the knowledge and performance of official duties are greatly abated, if the tenure is rendered altogether uncertain; and if he who by industry, capacity, and fidelity, has proved himself a useful servant of the public, is causelessly removed, the public will have much reason to complain.

A mode of proceeding is interwoven with the military organization of great benefit to the sound constitution of the army. Although the president is unquestionably authorized to deprive any military officer of his commission at pleasure, yet the established practice is, to allow the individual, whose conduct has given dissatisfaction, an opportunity of explaining and vindicating it, by means of a regular tribunal, before he, is dismissed, suspended, or even reproved. The same usage prevails in the navy. Thus a sort, of tenure during good behavior is produced, the effect of which, with men of integrity, is eminently useful. In the diversified employments of civil life, no similar institution could be systematically adopted, and a full analogy, therefore, cannot exist; but if we sometimes see in the revolutions of party, as well in other countries as in this, whole hosts of meritorious officers suddenly swept away, and their places filled by men without superior qualifications, we may regret that the principle is lost sight of, and that no remedy can be applied.

Four executive departments have been created by congress at different times. The department of state — of the treasury — of war — and of the navy — over each of which a principal officer, denominated the secretary, presides.[70] Through one of these organs, the directions of the president are communicated, in all matters relative to their respective departments. But it has been decided that the president is not confined in his executive functions to the use of a particular department. Thus in a case where it was objected that an order from the secretary of state ought not to be considered as an act of the president; it was held that reference must be had to this department for the official acts of the president which are not more immediately connected with the duties of some other department, but, nevertheless, the president, for the more easy and expeditious discharge of his executive duties, may direct some other department to make known the measures which he may think proper to take. They are equally his acts, whether they emanate from the department of state, or any other department. His immediate mandate to an inferior officer is in no case necessary. [2]

---

70 *From this modest beginning, the Executive Branch of the Government has grown to include 15 Departments (Cabinet level agencies) and 60 independent agencies (as of 2015).*

All commissions to officers issue from, and are signed by the president. When the president has nominated, the senate approved, and the commission is signed, the appointment is complete. If the officer be removable at the pleasure of the president, the commission may be arrested by him, if it is in the office of the secretary of state, but, if it is an office during good behavior, the appointment is not revocable, and, after it has received the approbation of the senate, cannot be annulled.

Delivery is not essential to the validity of a commission, nor is it affected by detention after it has been signed by the president, if the officer is not removable at pleasure. If in such case, the secretary of state being possessed of the commission, should refuse to deliver it, the judicial officer may nevertheless lawfully exercise his functions, and will be entitled to his legal compensations. [3]

Sickness, absence, or death, might delay the executing a commission, and the public interests in some cases, (as for instance the judge of a district court,) suffer great injury during the vacancy of the office. The commission is not the exclusive evidence of the appointment.

The appointments made, and commissions issued during the recess of the senate, are in force only till the end of the ensuing session when their advice and consent are given, it is to be considered not as a confirmation of the preceding appointment made during the recess, but strictly as a new one; a new official oath must be taken; and if it is an office in which security is required, a new security must be given.

It has been decided that persons who have become bound for the good conduct of the officer on the first appointment, are not responsible for his acts after the date of the second commission, which virtually suspends the first. [4]

CHAPTER NOTES
XIV

1. See Sergeant's *Constitutional Law*, p. 360.
2. 1 Peters' Rep. 471.
3. 1 Cranch, 137, *Marbury v. Madison*, and see particularly p. 167.
4. 9 Wheaton, 730. *United States v. Kirkpatrick.*

CHAPTER XV.

OF THE LIABILITY OF EXECUTIVE OFFICERS.

IT is a self-evident principle, that an illegal mandate or instructions from the president, can give no sanction to the conduct of a subordinate officer. On the contrary, the president would be liable to the action of a person injured in the same manner that a private individual would be. The law makes no distinction of persons, and the maxim that the king can do no wrong, so much admired in England, exists by no analogy in a republican government.

It may not be improper to consider why such a rule is admitted in monarchies, and why it cannot take place in a well constituted republic. In every monarchy, a quality termed prerogative, is attached to the monarch. It is defined by the learned commentator on the laws of England, "that "special preeminence which the king hath over and above all other persons, and out of the ordinary "course of law." [1] It cannot be shared with the people, for then it would cease to be prerogative: "it is that law in case of the king, which is law in no case of the subject." One of these prerogatives is, that no personal redress can be had from the king. He may actually, (it would seem,) commit any outrage on any of his subjects; he would be liable neither to a prosecution nor a civil action. "He is considered as a superior being, and entitled to that awful respect which may enable him "with greater ease to carry on the business of the government." [2] These doctrines, grating as they are to republicans, are palliated by the further remark, that prerogative is given for the "benefit of "the subject, in the confidence that it will only be exerted to the advantage of the realm — and that "to subject him to civil or criminal proceedings, would be to subvert the whole order of that species "of government." The theory is not unjust, and the remark of Locke, the great champion of a tempered system of popular rights, must be acknowledged to be cogent — "as to personal wrongs, "the harm which the sovereign can do, in his own person, not being likely to happen often, nor to "extend itself far; the inconvenience of some particular mischiefs, that may happen sometimes, "when a heady prince comes to the throne, are well recompensed by the peace of the public, and "the security of the government, in the person of the chief magistrate being thus sent out of the "reach of danger." But the principle which thus shields and protects the monarch; the sovereignty resident in himself, creates the distinction between him and the elected, though supreme, magistrate of a republic, where the sovereignty resides in the people.[71] All its officers, whether high or low, are but agents, to whom a temporary power is imparted, and on whom no immunity is conferred. An exemption from the power of the law, even in a small particular, except upon special occasions, would break in upon this important principle, and the freedom of the people, the great and sacred object of republican government, would be put in jeopardy. The exception adverted to, is that already noticed, of members of the legislature going to, attending at, or returning from a session of congress but even this exception is qualified; the commission of treason, felony, or the slightest breach of the peace, would convince the member, that his public function in nowise protected him from the administration of justice; but no other officer of government is entitled to the same immunity in any respect.

CHAPTER NOTES
XV

1. 1 Blackst. 239.
2. 1 Blackst. 240.

---

71 *The much-abused phrase of Jefferson in the Declaration of Independence that "all men are created equal" is explained here in its historical context. As Rawle states, under the system of monarchy the King is supreme to all citizens, and above the common law. The King is declared and denoted as the "Sovereign." Therefore, his will is law, whereas his subjects are bound by law. Under the republican system, the people of the sovereign community are sovereign; therefore, no one person is above the law, hence "all men are created equal." Nowhere in Jefferson's statement is there to be found the notion of absolute human equality. Jefferson believed in human inequality and in a society of degrees. Even still, Jefferson advanced the principle that the people of a political community were equal, and he promoted the idea of equality of opportunity. Jefferson Davis echoed this sentiment in his farewell address to the United States Senate when he stated, "... that men were created equal ... that there was no divine right to rule; no man inherited the right to govern."*

CHAPTER XVI.

ON COMMUNICATIONS TO BE MADE BY THE PRESIDENT TO CONGRESS.

IT is the duty of the president from time to time to give congress information of the state of the union; but although this alone is expressly mentioned in the Constitution, his communications naturally embrace a wider scope than internal affairs. Under the expression, he is to receive ambassadors, the president is charged with all transactions between the United States and foreign nations, and he is, therefore, the regular channel through which the legislature becomes informed of the political situation of the United States in its foreign, as well as its domestic relations; yet it has been always understood that he is not required to communicate more than, in his apprehension, may be consistent with the public interests. Either house may at any time apply to him for information; and, in the regular course of government, can apply only to him, where the matter inquired of, is principally under his superintendence and direction, although they frequently exercise the right to call upon the chief officers of executive departments, on matters peculiarly appertaining to them, and in like manner occasionally refer to the attorney general of the United States on subjects appropriate to Its office. The applications directly to the president, are generally accompanied with a qualification evincing a correct sense of the obligation on his part to avoid or suspend disclosures, by which the public interest, that both are bound to keep in view, might be affected.

Such disclosures the legislature in general expressly disclaims. In recurrence to our history, it must be obvious, that these official communications are chargeable with being rather more full and liberal than is common in other countries. In support of the practice it has been said, that in republics there ought to be few or no secrets; an illusory opinion, founded on ideal conceptions, and at variance with the useful practice of mankind. If all the transactions of a cabinet, whether in respect to internal or external business, were regularly exhibited to the public eye, its own operations would be impeded; the public mind be perplexed, and improper advantages would sometimes be taken. Foreign powers, pursuing as they invariably do, a different course themselves, would justly object to such proceeding.

The president is also required to recommend to their consideration such measures as he may deem expedient. This is an obligation not to be dispensed with. Exercising his office during the recess of the legislature, the members of which, when they return to the mass of citizens, are disengaged from the obligatory inspection of public affairs; supplied by his high functions with the best means of discovering the public exigencies, and promoting the public good, he would not be guiltless to his constituents if he failed to exhibit on the first opportunity, his own impressions of what it would be useful to do, with his information of what had been done. He will then have discharged his duty, and it will rest with the legislature to act according to their wisdom and discretion. These communications were formerly made in person at the opening of the session, and written messages were subsequently sent when necessary, but the whole is now done in writing. It was formerly the practice to return answers, which as a mere matter of ceremony is now disused. The course pursued at present is to refer the message to a committee, who commonly report an analysis of it, and the parts on which it appears necessary to act, are referred to other committees to prepare them for the deliberations of the whole.

CHAPTER XVII.

OF THE POWER TO GRANT PARDONS.

A POWER to grant reprieves and pardons is expressly given to the president.

That punishments should in all cases be strictly appropriate to the offence and certain in their execution, is indeed the perfection of criminal law, but the fallibility of human judgment would render an inflexible rule to this effect, too severe for human nature. An act may fall within the purview of the law and justly subject the party to conviction; yet there may be alleviating circumstances, which induce even those who deliver the verdict or pronounce the judgment, to feel repugnance at its being executed: but it would tend to overthrow the barriers of law, if the tribunal which is to decide on the guilt or innocence of the accused, were permitted to intermix other considerations. At first view, benevolent minds would not object to the admission of these principles in favor of the accused, on his trial, but the general interests of society have a stronger claim on the humanity of feelings justly regulated, than the particular case of the individual. The general interest requires that the administration of justice should not be diverted from its settled course, by an erroneous assumption of power and an irregular distribution of justice. If the law is plain, the duty of the tribunal is to conform to it, because the law is as compulsory on the tribunal as on the offender.

But the condition of society would be miserable if the severity of the law could in no form be mitigated, and if those considerations which ought not to operate on a jury or a judge could have no influence elsewhere.

Independently of other views, we may instance the case of treason against the state. Public policy may require that the offenders, though convicted, should be forgiven: severity may increase the opposition of that part of the community which was engaged in the combination; mercy may produce conciliation and submission; but if the guilt is proved, no such considerations can be admitted into the deliberations of the court. It is therefore expedient and wise, to deposit in some other part of the government, the power or granting pardons; a power, which notwithstanding the strange assertions of Blackstone and Montesquieu, is not inconsistent with the nature of a democratic government. [1] The most illustrious minds are sometimes seduced from plain and obvious truths by the illusions of theory, and when we are told that the power of pardon can never subsist in democracies, because nothing higher is acknowledged than the magistrate who administers the law, and because it would confound all ideas of right among the mass of the people, as they would find it difficult to tell whether a prisoner was discharged by his innocence, or obtained a pardon through favor, we must at once perceive that the position is fallacious, by being too general.

The inconvenience suggested in the latter member of it, corresponds indeed with what has been already observed, if confined to the judicial tribunal that originally acts on the case, but the first part of it indicates a want of acquaintance with the subdivisions of authority compatible with the purest democracy. It is the office of the judge to convict the guilty; the execution of the sentence is the duty of the executive authority, the time and place of execution are no part of the judgment of the court. [2] It is true, that during a vacancy in the office of president, which as has been seen, is carefully provided against, there would be no power to grant a pardon, but the moment the office is again filled, the power would be revived.

The power to grant pardons extends to all cases, except impeachments. Some considerations on the subject of impeachments will be presented hereafter; at present, it may not be improper to observe, that not only in the Constitution of the United States, but in those of almost every state in the Union, we find the English doctrine of impeachments introduced, but the difference in respect to granting pardons to the persons impeached is not preserved.

Impeachments are generally efforts of the people of that country through their representatives in the house of commons, to obtain redress before a distinct and independent tribunal, for the malpractices of the great officers of the crown. No pardon previously granted, can shelter the accused from a full inquiry, and thus his misconduct, if substantiated, is developed and exposed to the nation, but after the impeachment has been solemnly heard and determined, it is not understood that the royal grace is further restrained or abridged.

With us, no pardon can be granted either before or after the impeachment; and perhaps, if this mode of trial is retained at all, it is right that the sentence of a guarded and august tribunal, which, as we shall find, is exceedingly limited in the extent of its punishments, should be excepted from the general power of the president to defeat the effect of the condemnation.

In respect to another jurisdiction, it may be doubted whether he possesses the power to pardon.

It seems to result from the principle on which the power to punish contempt of either house of the legislature is founded, that the executive authority cannot interpose, in any shape, between them and the offender. The main object is to preserve the purity and independence of the legislature, for the benefit of the people. It acts, therefore, on its own power, without reference to, or dependence upon, any other. If the executive authority could, by granting a pardon, or, in any other mode, protect those who insidiously or violently interrupted or defeated their operations, the legislature, which is the superior body, would be so far dependent on the good will of the executive. And it would be only, as it were, by the permission of the latter, that it exercised a jurisdiction of so much importance to the people's rights. The Constitution is as silent in respect to the right of granting pardons in such cases, as it is in respect to the creation of the jurisdiction itself one arises by implication the other is excluded by implication.

In all other than these two cases, the power is general and unqualified. It may be exercised as well before as after a trial, and it extends alike to the highest and the smallest offences. The remission of fines, penalties, and forfeitures, under the revenue laws, is included in it, and in this shape it is frequently exercised: but although it may relieve the party from the necessity of paying money into the treasury, the president cannot, after the money has reached the treasury, compel the restitution of it no.

The Constitution where expressly describes any mode of punishment: it empowers congress in four enumerated cases to provide the punishment. They are treason, piracy, offences against the law of nations, and counterfeiting the securities and current coin of the United States. The power of congress to inflict punishment in other cases is derived from implication only, but it is necessary to carry the Constitution into effect, and is embraced in the general provision to pass all laws which may be necessary and proper. [3] The pardoning power is as extensive as the punishing power, and applies as well to punishments imposed by virtue of laws under this implied authority, as to those where it is expressed. The only exceptions are the two cases we have already mentioned, in one of which the power of pardoning is expressly withheld — and in the other it is incompatible with the peculiar nature of the jurisdiction.

In the exercise of the "benign prerogative of pardoning," as it has been justly termed, the president stands alone. The Constitution imposes no restraint upon him by requiring him to consult others. As the sense of responsibility is always strong in proportion as it is undivided, a single man will be most ready to attend to the force of those motives, which ought to plead for a mitigation of the rigor of the law, and less inclined to yield to considerations calculated to shelter proper subjects from its punishment. On the other hand; as men generally derive confidence from their number, they might often encourage each other in acts of obduracy [stubbornly inflexible], and be less sensible to apprehensions of censure for an injudicious or an affected clemency. [4]

In addition to this objection, there would be a great inconvenience in imposing on the president the necessity of consulting a body, which, whether already a permanent part of the government as the senate, or specially created for the purpose, it might be difficult to convene on occasions when perhaps an immediate decision would be highly expedient.

CHAPTER NOTES
XVII

1. 4 Blackstone, 397. Montesquieu, b. 6, c. 5.
2. 4 Blackstone, p. 404.
3. 6 Wheaton, 233.
4. Federalist, No. 74.

CHAPTER XVIII.

OF COMPENSATIONS TO PUBLIC OFFICERS.

THE principle of compensation to those who render services to the public, runs through the whole Constitution.

"The senators and representatives shall receive a compensation for their services, to be ascertained by law, and paid out of the treasury of the United States."

"The president shall at stated times, receive for his services a compensation, which shall neither be increased nor diminished during the period for which he shall have been elected, and he shall not receive within that period any other emolument from the United States, or any of them."

"The judges shall at stated times, receive for their services a compensation, which shall not be diminished during their continuance in office."

In the early stages of society, founded on a slender population, before any regular civil institutions took place, the tasks of government were probably performed without stated emoluments. In time, however, it was perceived that the public ought not to have their affairs administered without making compensation to those who postponed their private business for the general benefit. A compensation was therefore either exacted or voluntarily rendered. The former is always irregular and oppressive. We may refer as an illustration of it, to a practice which in early times prevailed in almost all the kingdoms of Europe. The monarch, for the supply of his court, his officers and attendants, was in the habit of seizing provisions and impressing horses and carriages, for which, an arbitrary and inadequate compensation was sometimes made, but any compensation whatever was frequently withheld. [1] The practice, though constantly complained of as a heavy grievance, equally inconsistent with the rights of the subject, and the real convenience of the crown, was not abolished in England till the restoration of Charles II. The government of a country is relieved from the necessity of exactions thus mutually injurious, by voluntary provisions on the part of the general society.

In respect to executive and judicial officers, no question has ever arisen: — It seems to be universally agreed, that compensations should be made for their services. The manner of making it is various, it is sometimes done by fixed salaries, and sometimes by fees and perquisites, which latter are exactly regulated as to the amount. Arguments are not wanting in favor of each of these plans. If a salary is granted which the officer is to receive, whether he does much or little of the business within his sphere, there is danger of remissness but to render him wholly dependent on the receipt of casual fees, would be inconsistent with the dignity that ought always to accompany a great executive or judicial office, and would tend to interrupt the dedication of his time to his high and important duties. In those cases, salaries are preferable. A legal remedy for neglect of duty may certainly be found, ill addition to the public reprobation, which must always attend upon it. But for inferior officers, not under the same control of public opinion, or at least not to the same extent, the payments by those whose business is transacted seems to form a proper fund.

In respect to the members of the legislature, our practice corresponds with that of some, though not of all the nations of Europe. In one, to which we are apt more frequently to look than any other, the ancient usage has melted away, and the members of parliament now receive no compensation for their attendance. The consequence is, that only men of fortune can take seats in the house of commons. This is inconsistent with the equality that ought to be found in a republic. Men of virtue and talent, though depressed by poverty, ought to have the avenues to public trust as open to them as to the most wealthy. We will venture to add that the compensation ought to be liberal: a generous people, if it is faithfully served, will never complain. But the compensation ought to bear as exact a proportion as possible to the time employed. An act of congress was passed a few years ago, [2] in which, a gross sum was allotted for an entire session. The dissatisfaction it occasioned, produced an early repeal.

The compensation of the president is not to be increased or diminished while he is in office; the legislature shall neither bribe nor terrify him in this mode. The compensations of judges shall not be diminished, but there is no restraint on their being increased, because their offices being in legal contemplation equivalent to offices for life; since the law benignly calculates that a judge will always behave well; the value of money may depreciate, and the salary become inadequate to the support intended to be allowed.

It may be observed, that the president and judicial officers are to receive their compensations at stated periods, the intention of which is, that services shall not be paid for, before they are performed; but no such restriction is imposed on the members of the legislature, because it is presumed that they will not violate a principle so just, and also, because from the uncertain duration of their sessions, no stated period can be fixed.

The military power is also in this respect to be distinguished from other executive offices; being liable to be employed in various places where it may be difficult or impossible to be regularly supplied with the means of discharging their pay, it would be impolitic to entitle them to demand it at certain periods. Their compensations cannot be diminished during the time for which they are engaged, because it would be a breach of the contract: they may be increased, because the public safety would not be endangered by it. Fortuitous additions, tending to stimulate their exertions are allowed: an army is entitled to share in some parts of what is taken from the enemy, which, according to the laws of war, become the property of the captors. A rule, however, which in modern practice is rather specious than profitable, for it is rarely enforced; but to the navy the same principle is often productive of great emolument; a discrimination having been long established between maritime captures and those on shore, on a foundation not perceptibly just. The property of peaceable and private individuals on the land is seldom considered in modern times, as a just subject of confiscation, although the owners are inhabitants of a hostile country;[72] but at sea, the merchant vessel, unarmed and unoffending, is the lawful prey of the commissioned cruiser [ship], and is condemned to his use, on being captured and brought into the ports of his country. The amount of these additional compensations is from time to time regulated by congress.

The appropriation for the support of the army and navy can be made only by congress, and in respect to the army, as has been already observed, for no longer time than two years. This may, at first view, appear inconsistent with the practice of enlisting soldiers for a longer time, but when we take a view of the whole political system and recollect that this limitation has been adopted as a suitable check upon the possible ill use of a regular army, we must allow a predominant operation to the greater principle. The military contracts must be construed, in all cases, as subject to the constitutional restriction,

---

72 *Lincoln and Republicans in Congress passed confiscation acts which "authorized" federal agents to size private property belonging to Southern citizens.*

which must be considered as a proviso introduced into every law that authorizes the president to raise an army.

To disband an army entirely, must be a legislative act. To dismiss any or all of the officers is, by the tenure of their commissions, within the power of the president. It is the practice in many countries when an army is reduced, to allow to the officers whose active services are no longer required, half the amount of their pay during life. Such compensations with us depend on the judgment of congress, and from that quarter also must proceed those charitable provisions which seem fairly due to the disabled and infirm soldier who has faithfully served his country.

A recent instance has proved that the charge of ingratitude cannot always be justly preferred against a republic.

Invited to revisit a country, to which in, early life he had rendered splendid and successful service; the heroism of General La Fayette has been rewarded, not merely by unbounded effusions of the public mind, but with a pecuniary compensation equally honorable to the donors and to the receiver.

CHAPTER NOTES
XVIII

1. See Barrington on Stat. 183, 237, 289. *Hume's History of Eng*. vol. v. 346. 519; and in 12 Coke, 19, it is considered as a prerogative inseparable from the person of the king, of which, even an act of parliament cannot deprive him.

2. March 19, 1816.

CHAPTER XIX.

OF INCOMPATIBLE OFFICES.

TWO offices may be so incompatible in their nature, that the same person shall not be admitted to hold them both. The Constitution in this respect is not altogether silent, and we shall endeavor to show the justness of the principles on which it proceeds. It is a rule of general law, that an officer who accepts another appointment inconsistent with the first, is held to have thereby resigned the first. [1] If the marshal of one of the districts were to be appointed judge of that district, it would virtually vacate his office as marshal. If a member of the house of representatives accepted an appointment as senator, he would cease to be a member of the house of representatives. But a man may hold two or more offices, if they are not incompatible in their nature, [2] and therefore there would seem no reason, other than general policy, for excluding some of the executive officers, below the president, from seats in either house, or, to prevent an individual from holding at the same time the office of secretary of state and of the treasury, or any similar offices. But although no reasons, merely of a legal nature, might be opposed to it, the impolicy of admitting such officers to compose a part of the legislature is exceedingly plain.

We must, once more recur to England, and examine the effects of their practice in this respect. The great officers of the crown, unless they are, members of the other house, are eligible as members of the house of commons. The whole administration partakes in one or the, other of the houses, of the legislative power. There is no doubt that some benefit is derived from it, in the facility of obtaining information in regard to public measures, and the inquiries of other members on such subjects, are usually answered with great courtesy; but this small advantage is counterbalanced by the influence they possess there, and by the total subversion of one of the chief pillars, on which the importance and value of the house of commons have always been asserted to rest.

Every panegyrist [one who praises] of the British Constitution delights to draw a perspective view of the house of commons as keeper of the purse of the nation; regulating its expenses and withholding supplies from the crown, except on such terms as the good of the people may require. But nothing is at present more remote from the fact. The whole scheme of taxation; the amount to be raised; the subjects to be taxed, and the objects to which the product is to be applied, are laid before them by the Ministers of the crown; not indeed in that capacity, but in the professed quality of members of the house, and perhaps since the restoration of Charles II. certainly not for many years back, the other members of the house, have never proposed other plans of finance, or undertaken to act on the old principle of representatives of the people, further than to object to and vote against the ministerial propositions. Thus the house of commons is rendered part of the machinery of the executive government, and whenever a minister becomes so unpopular as to lose his ascendancy in the house, either it must be dissolved, and the chance of one more pliant be taken by another election, or the minister resigns, and the crown employs new and more judicious or more dexterous servants. Great jealousy of the interference of the house of lords with money bills is retained, in which the ministerial part of the house of commons prudently unite; but no jealousy of the power of the ministry in their own house is collectively manifested. In short, the actual government of that country, as now administered, is purely the government of the crown, and the supposed representatives of the people, the house of commons, are merely what the first lord of the treasury, the chancellor of the exchequer, and similar great officers are avowedly; that is, the ministers of the executive government. It is true, that to keep up the appearance of its ancient character and independence certain interior officers of the excise and customs, &c. those who hold any office created since the year 1705 and persons holding pensions at the pleasure of the crown, or for a term of years, are ostentatiously excluded from seats in the house of commons; a sort of political flattery which can deceive only superficial observers; but the great managers of the whole machine remain in the heart of it, and direct all its internal springs and movements.

How is this open and undisguised process accomplished?

The answer is — by the almost entire destruction of their ancient principle of representation.

In very few parts of the kingdom is a seat obtained through the unbiassed and independent votes of the people. Boroughs, once populous and free, have become the actual property, in point of suffrage, of the crown, or of aristocratic families, and now are, in fact, mere subjects of sale or barter. The minister carefully avoiding to present himself as a candidate in those few places which are still actuated by the spirit of free suffrage, unless (as sometimes happens) the prevalent political opinions in such places should coincide with the party to which he belongs, procures a return in his favor without difficulty, and on the votes of some nominal electors, takes a place in the house, equal in legislative attributes to that conferred by the choice of thousands. All attempts at reformation in this respect are uniformly resisted by the ministers of the crown.

From such perversions of sound and regular principles, our Constitution effectually secures us. While decennial enumeration and apportionment continue, that is, while our Constitution lasts, no executive officer can insidiously creep into the number of our legislative representatives. The open and unfettered choice of the people only can place him there.

But would such a choice be consistent with sound policy, and the spirit of the Constitution?

The advantages derived to the people seem to be few — the objections many. The measures of the executive government, so far as they fall within the immediate department of a particular officer, might, it is true, be more directly and fully explained on the floor of the house; but we notice here also a striking difference between the two governments. In England, the measures of government are practically considered the measures of the ministers — it is not even allowed to introduce the king's name into a debate. [3] But the executive acts of the president, except in the two instances where the senate participates, are unshared with others, and the highest officer under him can constitutionally no more explain or account for them than any other individual. Besides, such modes of communication ought not to be encouraged, were they in use. The regular channels of communication from the president are pointed out in the Constitution, and if further information is desired, it is sought for in an open and public application, leaving it to the president to withhold what he may deem it injurious to disclose, and protecting him from the misapprehensions of others, by the necessity of reducing his communications to writing. Such a mode of obtaining information is infinitely superior to the sudden, and sometimes unguarded, answers returned to the verbal interrogations of the members of the house of commons in Great Britain.

But, among many other objections to the introduction of any of the great public officers into either house of congress, we must keep in view a great principle of all republican governments, that public offices are intended to be for the public service, and not for the benefit and emolument of the individuals who fill them. No more offices are created than the public needs require. If the duties are too few to occupy the time of the individual, the office is incorporated with another, unless the united weight of both should be too great. On the other hand, if the quantity of public business should so increase as to render it necessary to increase the number of persons who are to transact it, new offices are created. The whole system has a view only to the public benefit. We do not continue an office when its duties have expired. As Burke has justly observed, "when the reason of old establishments is gone, it is absurd to preserve nothing but the burden of them. This is superstitiously to embalm a carcass not worth the gums that are used to preserve it." [4]

The public officer being therefore considered with us as having actual living duties which he is bound to perform, and as having no more time than is necessary to perform them, the Constitution expressly excludes him from a seat. But a further caution is introduced into it. A member of either house may be appointed to an office existing previously to his being elected, if the emoluments of it have not been increased during the time for which he was elected. But if a new office has been created, or the emoluments of an old one increased during that time, the promise or the chance of receiving an appointment to it, may have an undue influence on his mind. Such an appointment is therefore forbidden by the Constitution during the time for which he was elected; and it is only to be regretted that it was not forbidden altogether. A dishonorable traffic in votes, should it ever become a characteristic of our country, would be more completely prevented, if to an office so created, or rendered more profitable, no one who had had an agency in either respect, could ever be appointed.

The Constitution contains no provision adverting to the exercise of offices under the United States and separate states at the same time, by the same persons. In some of the states it has been thought expedient to provide against it.

Those states appear to have acted under the apprehension of a possible collision between the two governments, and a jealousy lest the admission of the officers of the United States into places of trust and power in a state, might lead to a preference in the minds of those who hold offices under both to the prejudice of the state governments. [5] A counter apprehension did not exist in the people, when they formed the Constitution of the United States, although it has been the opinion of some enlightened men that there was more probability that if the balance ever should be disturbed, it would be by the preponderancy of the state governments. It has been observed, that the state governments are constituent and essential parts of the United States government, while the latter is in nowise essential to the organization or operations of the former. Without the intervention of the state legislatures, the president of the United States cannot be elected. The senate is elected immediately by the state legislatures. Even the house of representatives, though drawn immediately from the people, will be chosen very much under the influence of those whose own influence over the people obtains, for themselves an election into the state legislatures. On the other hand, the component parts of the state governments will in no instance be indebted for their appointments or their power to the direct agency of the general government.

The powers of the general government are few and defined, those which remain to the state government, numerous and indefinite.

The first and most natural attachment of the people will therefore be to their state governments, but in the general government they will see not a rival or an enemy to the state government, but the ultimate authority and common power, which they have themselves concurred to create, and therefore, as it will be their interest, it finally will be their endeavor to support and restrain both within their just constitutional bounds. [6]

It will not be foreign to this head to notice the oaths of office required by the Constitution.

The president is required by it to take an oath, (or affirmation,) that, "he will faithfully secure the duties of his office, and that he will preserve, protect, and defend the Constitution."[73] The senators, representatives, the members of the several state legislatures, and all executive and judicial officers, both of the United States and of the several states, shall be bound by oath or affirmation to support this

---

Note: The sworn duty of the President of the United States is to protect the Constitution — not the Union. The President's duty is to uphold the letter and spirit of the Constitution — a Constitution originally designed to limit the power of the Federal government while preserving the freedom, independence and sovereignty of the states that freely elected to accede to the union.

Constitution.

Although a promissory oath is not in point of law, ranked so high as a judicial oath; that is, it does not fall within the general provisions of the law in respect to perjury, yet it greatly increases the moral obligation of the party, and ought to make a deep impression on him. Every state officer, and every officer of the United States, on being elected or appointed, binds himself thereby,[74] not only to abstain from all opposition to the Constitution, but to give it his firm and active assistance.

It has been asked, why it was thought necessary that the state magistracy should be bound to support the Constitution of the United States, and unnecessary to impose an oath on the officers of the United States in favor of the state constitutions. The reason assigned, (as one of many,) by the authors of the Federalist, is, that the members of the general government will have no agency in carrying the state governments, into effect, but the members and officers of the state governments will have an essential agency in giving effect to the general government. [7]

This answer is a solid one. An official oath ought to be confined to the duties of the office. It is not so broad and comprehensive as a general oath of allegiance and fidelity which embraces all the duties of a citizen or subject. An officer appointed under the authority of the United States, is to perform only those duties which emanate from it; his obligation is limited by that authority, which, as repeatedly heretofore observed, is not controlled by the constitutions of the several states. An officer appointed under the authority of a state, is bound to support its constitution, but so far as the Constitution of the United States in any respect supersedes it, another rule of obligation arises, which he is equally bound to comply with; and, as it is essential to the true interests of all the states, that the powers granted to the general government should be fully effectuated, all their officers, legislative,

---

74 *It would be a false construction of logic to assert that, by this statement, elected officials must support every act of the Federal government. Only those acts which are PURSUANT to the Constitution should be considered as binding. Hamilton clearly indicates that a State may have to resist encroachments by the Federal agent: "… State governments will, in all possible contingencies, afford complete security against invasions of the public liberty by the national authority" (Federalist No. 28). Hamilton felt secure in "the disposition of the State legislatures to erect barriers against the encroachments of national authority." (Federalist No. 85). Real States' Rights enforces the Constitution.*

executive, and judicial, should expressly undertake to do so.[75]

The remarks on this subject may be concluded by drawing the attention of the reader to the liberal alternative of an oath or affirmation. No religious test, it is declared in the same sentence, shall ever be required as a qualification to any office or public trust under the United States. Not only a numerous and respectable sect, but many other persons not of the people called Quakers, feel an invincible repugnance to taking an oath in any form. If the term affirmation had been omitted, all such persons would have been excluded from public trusts on account of religious opinion. The abstract declaration of perfect equality in matters of religion is thus realized.

CHAPTER NOTES
XIX

1. 2 Rolle's Reports, 452. Brooke's ab. Commissions, 25. 3 Burr, 616. 2 Durn. & East, 85.
2. 4 Serg. & Rawle, 275.
3. "It is a constant rule," says Delolme, "never to mention him when they mean to blame the administration." And we may observe on all occasions when a majority adverse to the political measures of the day happens to prevail in the house of commons, that the language of resolutions and addresses is scrupulously pointed against the ministers who have advised the crown to adopt them — not against the monarch himself.
4. See his admirable speech on Economical Reform, in 1780.
5. Per Shippen, C. J. 3 Yeates's Reports, 315.
6. See the 45th and 46th numbers of the Federalist, in which this subject is fully discussed.
7. Federalist, No. 44.

---

75 *Here Rawle demonstrates how the States in forming the Federal government, did so in order to promote and to defend their own liberty and happiness. It is therefore in their own self-interest that they support the Constitution. This "safety and happiness" is what Madison in Federalist No. 43, states as the reasons for the formation of all governmental institutions. Force cannot maintain this safety and happiness; it must be maintained by the free will (consent) of the partners of the constitutional compact. If this safety and happiness no longer exists, then the institution of government no longer has a valid claim on the allegiance of the people of that society. Madison explained it "... the safety and happiness of society are the objects at which all political institutions aim, and to which* ***all such institutions must be sacrificed.*** *" [Emphasis added]. Madison, Federalist No. 43.*

CHAPTER XX.

OF SOME ARDUOUS PARTS OF THE PRESIDENT'S DUTIES.

ON a full view of the powers and duties of the president, the reader will probably perceive that they are of more importance in respect to foreign relations than to the internal administration of government.

At home his path, though dignified, is narrow. In the tranquility which we have hitherto in time of peace enjoyed, little more has been requisite, in either his legislative or executive functions, than regularly to pursue the plain mandates of laws, and the certain text of the Constitution.

In his legislative capacity, the power of objecting to acts of congress, has been fairly exercised and respectfully submitted to. In the executive department he has had indeed two insurrections to cope with, one of which was inconsiderable, and the other, though more extensive, disappeared before the mere display of the force collected to subdue it. The transaction itself afforded a valuable proof of the patriotism of the people, and their attachment to the Constitution. The regular militia of the three adjoining states, New Jersey, Maryland, and Virginia, cheerfully co-operated with that of Pennsylvania, in which the opposition existed, and the governor of Pennsylvania, as a military officer, obeyed the orders of the governor of Virginia, on whom the president conferred the chief command. A great proportion of this force consisted of volunteers; numbers of whom were men of considerable property and civil eminence, and the governors of the states we have mentioned, except that of Maryland, who was prevented by particular circumstances, voluntarily took the field in person.

If the pages of our history are soiled in any degree by transient resistance to the laws of the Union, the disgrace is redeemed by the proof of that wisdom, by which the general Constitution now appeared to have been framed, and of that determination to support it, by which the majority were actuated. And should instances of insurrection again occur, either against the laws of the Union, or the government of any particular state, it cannot be doubted that the same general and noble animation would be again displayed in support of the great political ark of our safety and happiness.

But it is in respect to external relations; to transactions with foreign nations, and the events arising from them, that the president has an arduous task. Here he must chiefly act on his own independent judgment. The Constitution authorizes him indeed to require the opinions of the principal officers in the executive departments; but however useful those opinions may be, they would afford no sanction for any errors he might commit. And although if required, they are to be given in writing, they would involve the officers in no responsibility.

In respect to treaties, it is only after they have received the approbation of the senate, that his responsibility is diminished by being divided. But he is not obliged to submit the inchoate [not yet completed or made effective] treaty to them. His instructions to the minister who negotiated it may have been misunderstood, or willfully disregarded; the national interests may have been plainly neglected, and it may be altogether such a compact as he would not ratify if he stood alone. Under such circumstances, it would be a timorous policy to endeavor to fortify his own disapprobation by obtaining the concurrence of the senate. And if he should continue to disapprove it, although it met their approbation, he would not be justified in giving it his further action. For by the express words of the Constitution, he in concurrence with the senate, and not the senate alone, is to make treaties. In case of an impeachment, it would be no valid defense, for him to allege that he submitted his own opinion to that of the senate. If indeed the case was at first of a doubtful nature, if he conscientiously desired the deliberate assistance of the senate, and if an honest conviction was produced in his own mind by the advice he received from them; his compliance with it would be personally honorable to him, and clearly consistent with the Constitution.

The power of receiving foreign ambassadors, carries with it among other things, the right of judging in the case of a revolution in a foreign country, whether the new rulers ought to be recognized. The legislature indeed possesses a superior power, and may declare its dissent from the executive recognition or refusal, but until that sense is declared, the act of the executive is binding. The judicial power can take no notice of a new government, till one or the other of those two departments has acted on it. [1] Circumstances may render the decision of great importance to the interests and peace of the country. A precipitate acknowledgment of the independence of part of a foreign nation, separating itself from its former, head, may provoke the resentment of the latter: a refusal to do so, may disgust the former, and prevent the attainment of amity and commerce with them, if they succeed. The principles on which the separation takes place must also be taken into consideration, and if they are conformable to those which led to our own independence, and appear likely to be preserved, a strong impulse will arise in favor of a recognition; because it may be for our national interest, which the president is bound pre-eminently to consult, to promote the dissemination and establishment, at least in our own neighborhood, of those principles which form the strongest foundations of good government.

But the most accurate and authentic information should be procured of the actual state and prospect of success of such newly erected states, for it would not be justifiable in the president to involve the country in difficulties, merely in support of an abstract principle, if there was not a reasonable prospect of perseverance and success on the part of those who have embarked in the enterprise. The caution of President Monroe in sending commissioners to South America, for the purpose of making inquiries on the spot, in preference to a reliance on vague rumors and partial representations, was highly commendable.

The power of congress on this subject cannot be controlled; they may, if they think proper, acknowledge a small and helpless community, though with a certainty of drawing a war upon our country; but greater circumspection is required from the president, who, not having the constitutional power to declare war, ought ever to abstain from a measure likely to produce it.

Among other incidents arising from foreign relations, it may be noticed that congress, which cannot conveniently be always in session, may devolve on the president, duties that at first view seem to belong only to themselves. It has been decided, that a power given to the president to revive an act relating to foreign intercourse, when certain measures, having a described effect should take place on the part of two foreign nations, was perfectly constitutional. The law thus rendered him the responsible judge of that effect. [2]

In case of war breaking out between two or more foreign nations, in which the United States are not bound by treaty to bear a part, it is the duty of the executive to take every precaution for the preservation of their neutrality; and it is a matter of justice, both to those nations and to our own citizens, to manifest such intention in the most public and solemn manner. The disquietude of the belligerent parties is thus obviated, our own citizens are warned of the course it becomes their duty to pursue, and the United States avoid all responsibility for acts committed by the citizens in contravention of the principles of neutrality. It is the office of the legislature to declare war; the duty of the executive, so long as it is practicable to preserve peace.

The proclamation issued in 1792, when the war broke out between England and France, was an example which, in similar cases, deserves to be followed.

The present state of this country in regard to the piratical depredations committed on its commerce, presents another striking feature of difficulty in, regard to executive duty.

The wretches who sally out from the ports of a Spanish island, seize the defenseless merchant vessel, and after removing or destroying the cargo, frequently glut their cruelty by the most barbarous destruction of human life, can be effectually suppressed by no exertion, however vigorous, of the marine force under the command of the president. It can only be effected by pursuing them on shore, by assuming, in some degree, the temporary command of a country, in which the local government is either too feeble or too corrupt to punish them. However strongly the voice of humanity and the interests of the country might urge the president to take such energetic but justifiable measures, it would involve him in great responsibility to do so — and yet it would be difficult for him wholly to restrain the zeal and indignation of the officers employed on the distant service, or on the other hand, by his own mere authority, to punish for an act committed from the best motives. If provided by congress with sufficient authority, these difficulties would be removed.

But notwithstanding all efforts to the contrary, we may be involved in war, by misconstructions of his acts, however justly intended and carefully regulated.

In such a case, whether immediate invasion ensues, or strong defensive measures become necessary, it is still the president who is to act on his own judgment, till congress can be convened. In every aspect directly or indirectly connected with foreign nations his duties are serious, and his responsibility great.

It was happy for this nation that at the time of adopting the Constitution, an individual was selected to preside, whose judgment never failed, and whose firmness never forsook him: whose conduct proved that the excellencies of the Constitution consisted not, merely in theory and contemplation, but could be realized in practice; that within its proper sphere no right was unprotected, and no evil unredressed. It ought to satisfy the people if the principles of George Washington's administration are faithfully followed by all his successors.

CHAPTER NOTES
XX

1. 3 Wheaton, 643. The same rule prevails in England.

2. 7 Cranch, 382.

SECTION V
CHAPTERS XXI-XXV

In the following section, Rawle discusses the need for and function of the judiciary system within a society. Rawle, being trained in the law, had a great respect for the American judicial system. Rawle points out that, in the United States, we have two judicial systems, one State and one Federal. The States had determined, by the adoption of the Constitution, that all laws and elected officials of both State and Federal governments would act according to and within the limits of the Constitution. The key point to be remembered, as stated by Hamilton in Federalist No. 33, is that all such laws or acts must be pursuant to or in keeping with the intent and meaning of the Constitution.

In this section, Rawle describes the foundation of our Republic, that is, the doctrine of the separation of powers among the Executive, Legislative, and Judicial Branches. Rawle has already demonstrated how our Republic is a Republic of Sovereign States[76] *where a coordinate system of government divides power between the State and the Federal governments. In Section V, he shows how power is further divided within the Federal government into three branches.*

This section also explains how the process of removing elected and judicial officials of the United States, and how a court martial proceeding, is accomplished.

Rawle views the United States Federal Courts from the perspective of 1829, and has a very high regard for the Court system of that time. The exercise of judicial powers in Rawle's time is in sharp contrast to the judicial activism of today. Currently, the Courts deem it necessary and proper to perform acts that in an earlier day were performed only by State or Federal legislation. Judging from Rawle's writings, we sense that he would not be pleased with the modern Courts' usurpation of the Legislative function.

---

76 *Rawle specifically referred to the Federal Union as an associations of people of republics and the great compound commonwealth. Hamilton in Federalist No. 69 used the term "Confederated America" and Madison in Federalist No. 51 used the term "compound republic of America."*

CHAPTER XXI.

OF THE JUDICIAL POWER.

NO form of government is complete unless it be accompanied with a judicial power.

To make laws and to execute them are the two great operations of government; but they cannot be fully and correctly executed unless there is somewhere resident a power to expound and apply them. This power is auxiliary to the executive authority, and in some degree partakes of its nature. But it is also required at times to control the executive, and what it decides to be unlawful, the executive cannot perform. It may also in some degree be said to participate in the legislative power. Its construction of the acts of the legislature is received as binding and conclusive, although it does not prevent the legislature from repairing its own defects, or clearing up its own ambiguities by subsequent laws, operating on subsequent cases. A high function also appertains to the judiciary in the exclusive right to expound the Constitution, and thereby to test the validity of all the acts of the legislature.

To the people at large, therefore, this institution is peculiarly valuable, and ought to be eminently cherished by them. On its firm and independent structure they repose with safety, while they perceive in it a faculty which is only set in motion when applied to, but which when thus brought into action, proceeds with competent power if required, to correct the error or subdue the oppression of both or either of the two other branches. A Constitution in which there was an omission to provide an adequate judiciary could not be successfully carried into effect; and if instead of being separate and independent, this power were either blended with the other two, or those who administer it were dependent on the will and pleasure of others, its luster would be tarnished and its utility destroyed.

The Constitution of the United States, therefore, required a judicial power, not as an adjunct, but as a necessary component part. The extraordinary complications of the authority of the United States with that of the several states, which seem at first view to throw so many difficulties in the way, fully prove its necessity. The state tribunals are no part of the government of the United States. To render the government of the United States dependent on them, would be a solecism almost as great as to leave out an executive power entirely, and to call on the states alone to enforce the laws of the Union. But it is not inconsistent with this principle that the United States may, whenever it is found expedient, elect to make use of a state tribunal to the same extent as any foreign power may, if it thinks proper to institute suits in the courts of other countries, which is in civil cases only.

The judicial power is general or limited, according to the scope and objects of the government. In a word, it must be fully and exactly commensurate with that of the legislature. It cannot by any terms of language, be made to exceed the legislative power, for such excess would be inconsistent with its nature. If by express words it should, on the other band, be restrained so as to embrace only a part of the subjects of legislation, it would impair the integrity of the whole system. The protection which it was intended to afford, in regard to the other branches of government, being confined to parts of their conduct, instead of embracing the whole, would produce the incongruous mixture of a theoretic, general power with partial debility and impotence. If general terms are used in describing it, there is no difficulty in defining its proper extent.

In the Constitution of the United States we perceive, not the express creation of a judicial power, but the recognition of it as a necessary part of the government, in which light it was justly considered and has been universally accepted. Its power extends to the great selected objects already noticed, and it is the duty of those who have to administer it, to carry it to that full extent, but never to exceed it. Experience has already shown that from a wise and temperate administration, the apprehension of inconvenience from serious collisions between the state judicatures and those of the United States was unfounded. It must be confessed that the merits of our Constitution have received ample support from the prudence and judgment with which it has been administered, and in no respect has a sounder discretion been exhibited than in the judicatory. If any objection could be sustained to the procedures of the judges of the supreme and circuit courts, it would be that of excessive caution, arising from a systematic anxiety not to exceed their jurisdiction. And it is a strong argument in favor of an elective government, that those men in whom the power of appointment is vested by the choice of the people, have, in regard to these judicial officers, exercised it with so much caution, judgment, and success.

But it is said that there is generally a propensity in public functionaries to extend their power beyond its proper limits, and that this may at some future time be the case with the courts of the United States.[77] The instances may be those in which the case is plain, and the encroachment upon state authority too obvious to be denied; as if a court of the United States should entertain a civil plea between two citizens of the same state in a case not authorized by the Constitution, or criminal proceedings on account of an offence merely against a state. In such an extreme, and therefore improbable case, as there would be no color of jurisdiction, the whole proceedings would be void. If, however, under the existing circumstances, it were doubtful and ambiguous, or if it were blended with matters in which they had jurisdiction, the rule commonly adopted among different courts, sitting precisely under the same authority, would probably be resorted to, and that which first obtained possession of the cause would be exclusively entitled to proceed.

Where the jurisdiction of the United States court and of a state court is concurrent, the sentence of either, whether of conviction or acquittal, may be pleaded in bar to a prosecution in the other, with the same effect as a judgment of a state court in a civil case may be pleaded in bar to an action for the same cause in a circuit court. [1]

A jurisdiction exclusive of the state courts, is not expressly given by the Constitution to any of the courts of the United States, but it is in several instances clearly implied. "Cases of admiralty and maritime jurisdiction and controversies between two or more states," must, by necessary construction, exclusively appertain to the courts of the United States: the first, because the whole system of maritime affairs with its connections and dependencies is withdrawn from the several states by their own consent, and vested in the general government; the second, because there can exist no other than the common tribunal, the supreme court of the United States, to entertain such suits. Indeed the jurisdiction itself is created by the Constitution, and vested in the supreme court of the United States alone, thus rendering the dignity of the tribunal correspondent to the dignity of the parties.

Cases affecting ambassadors, other public ministers and consuls, are also enumerated as falling within the jurisdiction of the courts of

---

77 *Rawle is anticipating the travesty which occurs with an activist Supreme Court that legislates from the bench and substitutes its will for objective interpretation of the Constitution or the laws of the several States — a "living constitution" that becomes a thing of clay to be molded by the will of unelected justices.*

the United States; reasons have been given for not considering this jurisdiction as entirely exclusive. It is true that an act of congress has declared that the jurisdiction is exclusive, and the practice is understood to have been in conformity to it, but the main question has never been brought to a judicial test. The same sentence extends the judicial power, "to all cases in law and equity arising under the Constitution, the laws of the United States, and treaties made, or which shall be made under their authority; to controversies to which the United States shall be a party; to controversies between a state and citizens of another state; between citizens of different states; between citizens of the same state claiming lands under grants of different states, and between a state or the citizens there of and foreign states, citizens or subjects." In some of these cases, it may be doubted whether it was intended, and whether it would be beneficial to the United States, that the jurisdiction should, be exclusive; it may conduce to its best interests at times to have recourse, not to the legislative or executive powers of a state, of which it should ever be independent, but to a state judicature, which if rightly constituted, can be influenced by no local partialities or political jealousies, and which can no more withhold justice from the United States than from the meanest individual.

Circumstances may render it expedient for the United States to institute civil suits for the recovery of debts, or damages for the breach of contracts due to themselves in the state courts. There is nothing in the Constitution to restrain them from so doing, nor to justify a refusal on the part of the state court to take cognizance of them. Such suits, indeed, are occasionally brought, and the United States, received as a plaintiff in the ordinary form, pursues them in the ordinary course to judgment and execution. But although the word "party" indicates a defendant as well as a plaintiff, it is not to be understood that suits can be brought in any court against the United States. Supreme head of the Union; center of the general power; it cannot be amenable to a judicial tribunal, unless by its own express consent, and the power to give this consent must appear in the Constitution itself to have been granted by the people. An ultimate and complete sovereignty for the practical purposes of a government, extending over all, protecting all, and binding all, is vested in them, by the confidence of the people, for the highest and most salutary purposes.

In some constitutions a power is given to the legislature to direct modes by which suits may be brought against the commonwealth. No power is given to congress to authorize suits against the United States in any case.

A citizen of one state is not precluded from suing a citizen of another state in the courts of the latter, nor a foreigner from a suit in the state court against a citizen of the United States, nor is there any thing to prevent one alien from suing another in a state court, or a citizen of one state from suing the citizen of another in the courts of a third state. A state may maintain a suit against an individual in its own courts or in those of another state. If two citizens of the same state claim land under grants of different states, the state courts are not precluded from jurisdiction in the first instance; nor are they precluded from holding cognizance of a right claimed under a treaty or statute of the United States, or an authority exercised under the United States, or a suit in which is drawn in question the construction of any clause of the Constitution. In all these cases a concurrent jurisdiction exists so far as relates to the language of the Constitution itself.

The Constitution containing a grant of powers in many instances similar to those already existing in the state governments, and some of these being of vital importance to state authority and state legislatures, a mere grant of such powers, in affirmative terms to congress, does not per se transfer an exclusive sovereignty on such subjects to the latter.

On the contrary, the powers so granted would not be exclusive of similar powers existing in the states, unless the Constitution had expressly given an exclusive power to congress, or the exercise of a like power were prohibited to the states, or there was a direct repugnancy or incompatibility in the exercise of it by the states.

In all other cases not falling within these classes the states retain concurrent authority.

There is this reserve, however, that in cases of concurrent authority where the laws of the states and of the United States are in direct and manifest collision on the same subject, those of the United States being the supreme law of the land are of paramount authority, and the state laws so far, and so far only, as such incompatibility exists must necessarily yield. [2] [78]

---

78 *In Marbury vs. Madison, 5 U.S. 137 (1803), the principle of judicial review was claimed by the court. This gave the Federal Court the sole right to decide if a State law was in conflict with a Constitutionally enacted Federal law, and if it were in conflict, the Federal law would be supreme. This has caused some to suggest that this principal means that the Federal government is superior to or has authority over States. Nothing*

The correct general position seems to be, that in civil cases the judicial power is, in some instances, unavoidably exclusive of state authority, and in many others it may be rendered so at the election of congress. [3]

In regard to criminal cases, there is more difficulty. The same act may amount to an offence both against the state and the United States. Resistance to the laws of the United States, may be accompanied with personal injuries to the officers. Robbing the mail, which by act of April 13th, 1810, is made highly penal, and in case of a second offence, punishable with death, might be cognizable as highway robbery under the state laws. Would the offender be amenable to both jurisdictions, or to only one, and which of them? One established rule may be resorted to as partly affording an answer. The greater crime includes and absorbs the less. [4] But this rule does not afford a complete solution of the difficulty. A prosecution may be commenced in the state court, before one is instituted in the United States court. If, for instance, the officer who was beaten, commenced and persisted in a prosecution for the battery, it would seem that the offender would not be acquitted, because it appeared in evidence that his general object was to resist the laws of the United States. If he were prosecuted at the same time for robbing the carrier of the mail, and for a common highway robbery, both of which are offences of the same grade, and the latter, according to the laws of the state in which it was committed, might be as, severely punished as the former; neither court would be bound to give way to the other, at least by the application of the rule before mentioned. A person convicted or acquitted in a court of competent jurisdiction, may plead such judgment in bar of a second indictment for the same offence, but he cannot plead an acquittal or a conviction of an inferior offence, in bar of an indictment for a higher offence, although each was part of the same act. [5] Where, however, the offences differ only in name, the acquittal may be pleaded, as a man indicted of murder and acquitted, is not liable on an

---

could be further from the truth. Rawle notes that the States, acting on their own free will, wrote and gave life to the Constitution. It is their creation, they empowered it with such powers as they deemed proper. They were acting in a manner to promote and protect their own interests, not creating an agent to be their Lord and Master. All laws passed "in pursuance" of the Constitution are "the supreme law of the land," but the operative words are "in pursuance." Unconstitutional acts of the Federal government are therefore null and void and can be so declared by a Sovereign State. See, Hamilton in Federalist 33.

indictment of petit treason for the same act, because both offences are in substance the same; [6] but when they are substantially different, though of equal degree, the acquittal in one does not constitute a bar to an indictment for the other.

It remains then to discover some other rule or principle to relieve us from this embarrassment. It has been laid down that the state courts retain their jurisdiction in all cases, which in their nature existed before the adoption of the Constitution, unless expressly excluded, or unless the exercise of it would be utterly incompatible with the authority granted to the Union. [7] In the case of offences which only arise by reason of the Union, as, for instance, treason against the United States, the state courts would have no jurisdiction. If in the state courts an indictment were preferred for murder or other capital crime, committed in the perpetration of treason, it must give way to the jurisdiction of the United States court, as well in respect to the superiority of jurisdiction, and the greater extent of public concernment, as the interior nature of the crime. But if the act committed, amounting at the same time to offences against both bodies, were still in regard to each of them, of the same degree, there seems no reason why each should not sustain its jurisdiction. It would not contravene the maxim that no one shall be twice punished for the same offence, for the offences are different in the eye of the law, although the result of the same act on the part of the culprit.

We must, indeed, avoid too broad a construction of this maxim, for a double punishment for the same act, is not wholly unknown to the law, if the forms of proceeding and the objects are different; thus, he who has committed an assault, battery, wounding, or mayhem, on the person of another, is liable both to an indictment, and to a civil action for damages. The satisfaction received by the public does not prevent the injured party from obtaining his peculiar redress. If the infliction of punishment by the state could impede the prosecution of the United States in such a case, a pardon granted by the state would have the same effect, yet it would be absurd to suppose that a pardon granted by the state for murder committed in the perpetration of treason, would bar the prosecution of the United States for such treason. On the whole, this difficult question may be fairly resolved on the principle, that immunity for one crime cannot be obtained by proving that in doing the act, the party committed another; and further, that each community is entitled, and its public officers are required, to prosecute offences committed against it. [8]

CHAPTER NOTES
XXI

1. *Houston v. Moore*, 5 Wheaton, 31. See also *Osborne v. Bank* of the United States, 9 Wheaton, 733.

2. *Houston v. Moore*, 5 Wheat. 48. Per Story, J.

3. 1 Wheaton, 337. But the author presumes to dissent from the opinion that it is competent for congress in all other cases to render it exclusive. Surely congress cannot exclude a state from holding plea of a suit by a citizen of another state against the citizen of a state in which the suit was brought, nor by or against an alien. Many other cases might be put in which the state courts could not be deprived of jurisdiction by any act of congress.

4. Opinion of Judge Chase, in Hall's *Journal of Jurisprudence*, 162.

5. Hawkins, b. 2. c. 39. § 5.

6. Ibid.

7. Federalist, No. 82. 4 Dallas, Appendix, xxx.

8. See the discrepant opinions of the judges of the Supreme Court of the United States in *Houston v. Moore*. The author of course adopts, and takes the liberty to say that in his own judgment he prefers, those of the majority.

CHAPTER XXII.

OF IMPEACHMENTS.

WE are next to consider what courts or judicial tribunals are created by the Constitution itself, and what have been created under the power to that effect given to congress. The language of the text is, that the judicial power of the United States shall be vested in, "one supreme court, and in such inferior courts as congress may from time to time ordain and establish."

But no mention is made in any part of this article, otherwise than by way of exception as to the mode of trial, of a very high tribunal, which seems rather to have been supposed to flow from the formation of the Constitution, than to be expressly created by it.

The first mention of it is contained in the following words, in a preceding article: "The house of representatives — shall have the sole power of impeachment."

In the third section of the same article, it is said, that the "senate shall have the sole power to try all impeachments. When sitting for that purpose, they shall be on oath or affirmation. When the president of the United States is tried, the chief justice shall preside, and no person shall be convicted without the concurrence of two-thirds of the members present."

Impeachments are thus introduced as a known definite term, and we must have recourse to the common law of England for the definition of them.

In England, the practice of impeachments by the house of commons before the house of lords, has existed from very ancient times. Its foundation is, that a subject entrusted with the administration of public affairs, may sometimes infringe the rights of the people, and be guilty of such crimes as the ordinary magistrates either dare not or cannot punish. Of these, the representatives of the people or house of commons cannot judge, because they and their constituents are the persons injured, and can therefore only accuse. But the ordinary tribunals would naturally be swayed by the authority of so powerful an accuser. That branch of the legislature which represents the people, therefore, brings the charge before the other branch, which consists of the nobility, who are said not to have the same interests, or the same passions as the popular assembly.

Such is the English theory, and it well suits a government in which there are three distinct and independent interests, and in which the crown, possessing the power of appointing the high officers, who are most frequently the subjects of impeachments, has also the sole power to carry on or withdraw prosecutions in the ordinary courts. For no misconduct, however flagrant, committed by such men, could the people obtain redress, if the monarch inclined to refuse it, unless a mode of proceeding had been invented which did not require his assent, and which he could not control, and therefore, as heretofore observed, he cannot defeat the inquiry by a previous pardon, although in the exercise of another branch of his prerogative, he may delay it by adjourning or proroguing [delay or postpone] the session of the parliament.

The difference between the two governments has no doubt already occurred to the reader. Our ordinary tribunals are not dependent on the pleasure of him who appoints the judges, nor are they to be influenced by the authority of the accuser in a case of this sort more than in any other, for with us the people are considered as the. accusers in all cases whatever. In England, the king is the accuser, (except in the instance now under consideration,) and all offences are charged to have been committed against his peace, his crown and dignity.

Still less are the weight and influence of any man, however exalted his station, or great his wealth, likely to deter our judges from an impartial administration of justice.

Yet although the reasons are not equally cogent, they will be found on examination sufficient to warrant the introduction of the system into our code.

We shall now proceed to consider —

1. The necessity or utility of impeachments.
2. The necessity or utility of erecting a separate tribunal for the trial of impeachments.
3. The propriety of rendering the senate such a tribunal.
4. The persons liable to be impeached.
5. The constitution of the court, its mode of proceeding, and the extent and effect of its judgments.

1. The delegation of important trusts, affecting the higher interests of society, is always from various causes liable to abuse. The fondness frequently felt for the inordinate extension of power, the influence of

party and of prejudice, the seductions of foreign states, or the baser appetite for illegitimate emolument, are sometimes productive of what are not unaptly termed political offences, [1] which it would be difficult to take cognizance of in the ordinary course of judicial proceedings.

2. The involutions and varieties of vice are too many, and too artful to be anticipated by positive law, and sometimes too subtle and mysterious to be fully detected in the limited period of ordinary investigation. As progress is made in the inquiry, new facts are discovered which may be properly connected with others already known, but would not form sufficient subjects of separate prosecution. On these accounts, a peculiar tribunal seems both useful and necessary. A tribunal of a liberal and comprehensive characters confined as little as possible to strict forms, enabled to continue its session as long as the nature of the case may require, qualified to view the charge in all its bearings and dependencies, and to appreciate on sound principles of public policy the defense of the accused; the propriety of such a separate tribunal seems to be plain, but not upon the assumed ground that the judges of the supreme court would not possess sufficient fortitude to perform the duty, or sufficient credit and authority to reconcile the people to their decisions. [2]

3. To compose this court of persons wholly distinct from the other branches of government — to form a permanent body for this single purpose — and to keep them always collected at the seat of government for the possible occurrence of an impeachment, would be as inconvenient as to appoint and collect such a body from time to time, when art impeachment is determined on.

On a review of all the departments of government provided by the Constitution, none will be found more suitable to exercise this peculiar jurisdiction than the senate.

Although like the accusers, they are representatives of the people, yet they are by a degree more removed, and hold their stations for a longer term. They are therefore more independent of the people, and being chosen with the knowledge that they may, while in office, be called upon to exercise this high function, they bring with them the confidence of their constituents that they will faithfully execute it, and the implied compact on their own parts that it shall be honestly discharged. Precluded from ever becoming accusers themselves, it is their duty not to lend themselves to the animosities of party or the prejudices against individuals which may sometimes unconsciously induce the house of representatives to the acts of accusation. Habituated to comprehensive views of the great political relations of the country, they are, naturally the best qualified to decide on those charges which may have any connection with, transactions abroad, or great political interests at home, and although we cannot say, that like the English house of lords they form a distinct body, wholly uninfluenced by the passions, and remote from the interests of the people, yet we can discover in no other division of the government a greater probability of impartiality and independence.

Nor does it form a solid objection in point of principle, that in this peculiar instance, a part of the legislative body should be admitted to exercise judicial power. In some degree all legislative bodies necessarily possess such a power. We have seen that for sufficient cause they may expel any of their own members — they may try and punish others for attempts to corrupt, bribe, or intimidate them, and they may punish for what are technically termed contempt committed in their presence, in all which they act judicially. But it is sufficient, to close the subject, that the people at large have concluded that this power would be best deposited in this body.

4. From the reasons already given, it is obvious, that the only persons liable to impeachment, are those who are or have been in public office. All executive and judicial officers, from the president downwards, from the judges of the supreme court to those of the most inferior tribunals, are included in this description. But in the year 1796, a construction was given to the Constitution, founded, it is believed, merely on its phraseology, by which a member of the senate was held not to be liable to impeachment. Their deliberations, after the arguments of counsel, being held in private, we can only infer from those arguments, that the term officers of the United States, as used in the Constitution, was held by a majority of the senate, not to include members of the senate, and on the same principle, members of the house of representatives would also be excluded from this jurisdiction.

An amendment to the Constitution in this respect would perhaps be useful. A breach of duty is as reprehensible in a legislator as in an executive or judicial officer, and if this peculiar jurisdiction possesses so much value in respect to the two latter, it is difficult to conceive why the public should not have the benefit of it in regard to the former.

No apprehensions of partiality in favor of one of their own body need to be carried so far as to require the substitution of another tribunal. In England, where there is not a greater portion of public virtue than here, peers are necessarily impeached before peers, and members of the house of commons have been frequently the subjects of impeachment. Judges are liable to trial for every offence before their brethren, and it is in no case to be presumed, that a fair and full administration of justice would be wanting. Of great public delinquencies the people do not long remain in ignorance. If the offences of a member of the house of representatives were culpably passed over by his brethren, the people by the recurrence of the periodical election would soon be enabled to substitute others to prefer the accusation, and, being sensible of this, the house would be slow to expose themselves to the reproach of their constituents, and the loss of public confidence, by omitting to do their duty.[79] The senate is obliged to receive and decide on the charge, and to the strongest moral obligations is added that of an oath or affirmation. It is not probable that the effect of these united impulses would be counteracted by other considerations, which would in themselves be criminal.

5. The legitimate causes of impeachment have been already briefly noticed. They can only have reference to public character and official duty. The words of the text are treason, bribery, and other high crimes, and misdemeanors. The treason contemplated must be against the United States. In general those offences which may be committed equally by a private person as a public officer, are not the subjects of impeachment. Murder, burglary, robbery, and indeed all offences not immediately connected with office, except the two expressly mentioned, are left to the ordinary course of judicial proceeding, and neither house can regularly inquire into them, except for the purpose of expelling the member. But the ordinary tribunals, as we shall see, are not precluded, either before or after an impeachment, from taking cognizance of the public and official delinquency.

We have hitherto had but three instances of impeachment, the

79 *When the modern reader of this ancient text reviews the activities of Congress, vis-à-vis the check-writing scam, the Congressional Post Office scandal (1992), and others that have been exposed subsequently, it is hard to feel as secure as Rawle does in the action of Congress or the voters. All these were severe breaches of public trust by Congress. In a 2013 public opinion poll confidence in Congress was down to 10 percent https://news.gallup.com/poll/163052/americans-confidence-congress-falls-lowest-record.aspx accessed 2/18/2020. In a 2018 opinion poll 62 percent had very little or no confidence in Congress; www.npr.org/2018/01/17/578422668/heres-just-how-little-confidence-americans-have-in-political-institutions*

first of which has already been noticed. As no decision was given on the merits, it is impossible to say whether the charges, which were chiefly founded on a conspiracy to invade the territories of the king of Spain, with whom the United States were at peace, and to excite the Creek and Cherokee Indians to concur in the outrage, would have been deemed by the senate sufficient, if proved, to support the impeachment. The second, on which a constitutional conviction took place, was against a judge of a district court, and purely for official misconduct. The third was against a judge of the supreme court, and was also a charge of official misconduct. It terminated in an acquittal, there not being a constitutional majority against him on any one article.

As articles of impeachment can only be exhibited by the house of representatives, if it should happen that the senate in the course of their executive functions or otherwise, became apprised of unlawful acts committed by a public officer, and in their opinions, meriting at least a public inquiry, it would be their duty to communicate the evidence they possessed, whether actual or presumptive, to the house of representatives, but the bare communication is all that would be consistent with their duty. They would cautiously avoid to recommend or suggest an impeachment, and the same would be the course pursued by the president.

Articles of impeachment need not to be drawn up with the precision and strictness of indictments. They must however be distinct and intelligible. No one is bound to answer to a charge so obscure and ambiguous that it cannot be understood. Additional articles may be exhibited, perhaps at any stage of the prosecution; certainly before the defendant has put in his answer or plea.

No precise number of senators is required to constitute the court, but no person can be convicted without the concurrence of two-thirds of the members, present. The vice president being the president of the senate, presides on the trial, except when the president of the United States is tried. As the vice president succeeds to the functions and emoluments of the president of the United States whenever a vacancy happens in the latter office, it would be inconsistent with the implied purity of a judge that a person under a probable bias of such a nature should participate in the trial and it would follow that he ought wholly to retire from the court. It is not stated in the Constitution whether the president of the senate is on the trial of an impeachment restricted, as in legislative cases, to the casting vote. As he is constituted one of the judges by being appointed to preside without any restriction, the fair inference would be, that he is entitled to vote like the other judges, but on the trial last mentioned of a judge of the Supreme Court, the vote of the vice president does not appear in the printed journal.

The defendant is entitled to the benefit of counsel but it is not necessary that he should be personally present; the trial may proceed in his absence if he has had due notice to appear.

The consultations of the senate, as well upon incidental points as on the main questions, are conducted in private, but the judgment is rendered in public.

The judgment is of a limited and peculiar nature — it extends no further than to removal from office, and disqualification to hold and enjoy any office of honor, trust, or profit, under the United States.

Herein we may perceive the importance and utility of this system under our regulations. In England impeachments may be prosecuted for capital crimes and the court may award capital punishment, of which many instances occur in the history of that kingdom. Lord Strafford in the reign of Charles I. and Lord Stafford in the reign of Charles II. were beheaded on the sentences of the court which decided without the aid of a jury, and both of them have been considered rather as victims to the spirit of the times, than as merited oblations to justice. But with us, although the party accused may be found guilty of the highest crime, his life is not in danger before this tribunal, and in no cases are his liberty and property affected: indictment, trial, judgment, and punishment, still await him according to the usual course of law.

Why then, it may be asked, has this system been introduced, and why, if the firmness and integrity of the ordinary tribunals cannot be overpowered by any supposed influence of character, wealth, or office, have we deemed it expedient to copy from a foreign nation an institution for which there is not the same necessity, and which we do not allow altogether to produce the same effects? One answer is, that the sentence which this court is authorized to impose cannot regularly be pronounced by the courts of law. They can neither remove nor disqualify the person convicted, and therefore the obnoxious officer might be continued in power, and the injury sustained by the nation be renewed or increased, if the executive authority were perverse, tyrannical, or corrupt: but by the sentence which may be given by the senate, not only the appointment made by the executive is superseded and rendered void, but the same individual may be rendered incapable of again abusing an office to the injury of the public. It is therefore right and proper that the president should be disabled from granting a pardon, and restoring the offender to his former competency; but there is no restraint on his pardoning when a conviction in the common course ensues, for such pardon extends only to the punishment which is then pronounced, and does not affect the sentence of the senate.

We may perceive in this scheme one useful mode of removing from office him who is unworthy to fill it, in cases where the people, and sometimes the president himself would be unable to accomplish that object. A commission granted during good behavior can only be revoked by this mode of proceeding. But the express words of the Constitution also extend to the president and vice president, who partake of the legislative capacity, and are chosen by the people. When this corrective jurisdiction is thus applied; when it reaches all judicial officers, all civil officers appointed by the president during pleasure, and involves in its grasp the vice president and the president himself, it is difficult to conceive that it was intended to exempt men whose treachery to their country might be productive of the most serious disasters, because they do not come precisely within a verbal description supposed to be exclusively applicable to those who, except in the two instances of specific enumeration, receive commissions from the president. A member of either house of the legislature betraying his trust and guilty of the most culpable acts of an official nature is, under the decision of the senate, liable, indeed, to expulsion, but not to impeachment; liable to the ordinary course of legal proceedings, but not to disqualification. Yet as from the judgment of this high tribunal there is no appeal; as the decision which has been given in the case adverted to is a judicial one, and probably will be held binding on themselves on all future occasions, we must now receive it as the settled construction of the Constitution.

Whether an amendment of the Constitution in this respect will ever be made, is not for the author to anticipate.

CHAPTER NOTES

XXII

1. Federalist, No. 65.

2. This is one of the few points in which the author is compelled to differ from that excellent work the Federalist.

CHAPTER XXIII.

OF ANOTHER SPECIAL JURISDICTION.

THERE is another species of courts having a special jurisdiction, from which trial by jury is also excluded, yet whose power extends to pecuniary mulcts [to punish by imposing a monetary fine], deprivation of office, imprisonment, personal chastisement, and even loss of life. It will be at once perceived that we allude to courts martial.

Although not expressly mentioned in the Constitution, the power to institute them is unquestionably given by the authority vested in congress to make rules for the government and regulation of the land and naval forces, and the amendment heretofore noticed, which before a person shall be held to answer for a capital or otherwise infamous crime, requires a presentment or indictment by a grand jury, excepts the land and naval forces, and the militia when in actual service in time of war or public danger, thereby indirectly recognizing the establishment and the efficient powers of courts martial.

Congress has reasonably and moderately executed this power, but the details are inconsistent with the plan of this work. The subjects of a court martial are only those who fall within the above descriptions. Martial employment creates martial law, and requires martial courts. On the civil class of the community, it can never operate, except perhaps in one instance, which on our part, could not well apply to one of our own citizens or inhabitants. It is a settled principle of the laws of war that a spy may be put to death. One detected in his obnoxious employment within our lines in time of war, although not himself a soldier, is a legitimate subject of this severity; and upon the same principle we should be bound to admit the right of the enemy to execute any of our citizens or soldiers, apprehended by them in the performance of the same act.

We have heretofore adverted to the procedure of president Madison in the case of a citizen of the United States who had joined the enemy during the late war, and was apprehended as a spy within our lines on the frontiers: the course pursued by his directions, was both humane and consistent with the true principles of law. It gave to the individual the fairer prospect of acquittal on a trial by jury accompanied with all the guards and precautions allotted to charges of treason; while it more extensively enforced a principle of which all should be apprized, that it is lawful for no one to desert his country in the hour of her danger, and lift a parricide arm against her.

CHAPTER XXIV.

OF GENERAL TRIBUNALS, AND FIRST OF THE SUPREME COURT.

A VIEW of the general system will now be taken.

The only tribunal expressly noticed in the Constitution is the Supreme Court, whose power is co-extensive with all the exigencies of the government, and pervades every part of the United States, and the territories belonging to them. In many particulars, however, it possesses only an appellate jurisdiction; in a few, its jurisdiction is original.

In the latter are embraced all, "cases affecting ambassadors, other public ministers and consuls, and those in which a state shall be a party."

Cases of the first description may be either civil or criminal. The protection afforded by the laws of nations to diplomatic functionaries, extends, however, so far that it is not easy to conceive any case in which a person invested with that high character can be subjected either to criminal or civil proceedings. But he may be entitled to prosecute others — he may have received outrages or insults affecting his national character, for which redress may be justly due. The United States, who are responsible to foreign nations for their Ministers receiving all due respect, and an almost unlimited freedom in the exercise of their functions, supply the proper means for these purposes, by taking on themselves and vesting in their highest tribunal, the cognizance of such cases. When the proceedings are against one of these officers, we must consider the jurisdiction of the United States as being from its own nature exclusive of the state courts.

It may not be equally clear, if he should be the complainant, and seek redress in either a criminal or civil case in the forum of a state, that the latter could not take cognizance of it. The unity of the system would perhaps be better promoted, if the state courts were authorized to decline the cognizance of all such cases. The United States are responsible to foreign nations for the due administration of justice in their own tribunals only, and it might involve them in some difficulties, if state courts, whose judges they do not appoint, and whom on account of misconduct they could not impeach, were to intermeddle even on the application of the minister himself in cases of this nature. But if the state courts are not prohibited by their own constitutions, it does not appear that they could justly refuse their assistance to a foreign minister who thought it expedient to apply to them, although perhaps some political inconvenience may occur to the mind reflecting on the possibility of widely different views being entertained on the same subject by a state court and a court of the United States.

Congress [1] has declared the jurisdiction of the Supreme Court to be exclusive in all such suits or proceedings against ambassadors or other public ministers, their domestics, &c. as a court of law can have or exercise consistently with the law of nations, but they have gone no further.

Such cases certainly come within the terms used in the Constitution affecting ambassadors, &c., and such jurisdiction must have been intended to be exclusive.

The power given to congress to define and to punish offences against the law of nations, has been partly executed by congress, [2] — offering violence to the person of an ambassador or other public minister, and suing out process against him or his domestics, are declared to be offences subjecting the parties to fine and imprisonment. Having been defined by congress, they may properly be said to arise under the Constitution and to be cognizable under the authority of the United States. But other violations of the law of nations than those expressly enumerated, may be committed, and if it is a sound doctrine, (which is intended to be hereafter examined,) that the criminal jurisdiction of the courts of the United States is confined to cases expressly provided for by statute, either such offences, however flagrant, must go unpunished, and the United States incur a national disgrace, or the state courts must be resorted to.

In respect to civil suits, when a foreign minister may sue an alien, the jurisdiction is confessedly concurrent, [3] but it would seem that if a foreign nation brought a civil suit in a court of the United States, it ought to be in the supreme court, although here also it is apprehended that the state courts might sustain it.

The reason for placing consuls on the same footing, deserves inquiry. Consuls are not diplomatic functionaries, or political representatives of a foreign nation. Their general character is that of commercial agents. They may be citizens or subjects of the foreign power, or they may be citizens and permanent inhabitants of the United

States. The president may, at his discretion, acknowledge their capacity or refuse to do so. When he deems it expedient, he may revoke the admission of them, [4] by which act they would be at once stripped of their privileges and immunities, and reduced to the level of private persons.

It may sometimes happen, that a consul in the absence of the proper minister of his country, may be charged with higher national duties, but in this case, the greater character absorbs the smaller.

In respect to the citizens or subjects of their own nations, they are sometimes admitted by the nation which receives them to exercise functions partaking of a judicial nature, but they cannot be carried so far as to affect others, nor be exercised at all without the permission of the government. And their procedures must be distinguished from a court, or an establishment in the nature of a court, affecting the interests of any others than the nation to which the consul belongs. In the year 1793, the French consuls attempted to exercise prize jurisdictions in the United States over captures made from the British, with whom France was at war; but the supreme court at once decided, that no foreign power can of right institute or erect any court or judicature of any kind within the United States, unless warranted by and in pursuance of treaties. [5]

But whether such functions are permitted and exercised or not, the other trusts and duties of consuls require that they should be treated with much respect. The sovereign who receives them, tacitly engages to afford them all the freedom and protection necessary to enable them to execute their functions, without which the admission would be illusory and vain. [6]

What may be done in some other countries by the mere grant of the executive magistrate, must with us be effected by constitutional or legislative provisions; and therefore, although a total exemption from civil and criminal process is not required by the nature of the office, yet a limitation of the general judicial power operating to a certain degree as a national protection, was deemed expedient, and cannot be disapproved.

The legislative provisions that have been made in respect to them, may be considered as founded on the same article in the Constitution. If the law of nations considers them as entitled to protection, offences against them fall within the class of offences against the law of nations.

Cases in which a state shall be a party, originally signified those in which a state was either plaintiff or defendant, as well suits brought by a state against individuals as those by individuals against a state, and also those in which the controversy was between two states; but the Constitution having since been altered, [7] and a state being no longer liable to a private action, this provision must be confined to the other two cases.[80]

General expressions must always be construed according to the subject. It has been justly decided that the words cases in law or equity, apply as well to criminal as to civil matters, [8] but it cannot be conceived that a state was intended by the Constitution to be able to prosecute in the Supreme Court of the United States one of its own citizens for an offence committed against itself, although it might have the power to institute in that court a suit on a civil contract either between itself and its own citizens, or citizens of another state, or foreigners.

In all other cases, the Supreme Court possesses jurisdiction only by appeal or writ of error; that is, it may revise and correct the proceedings in a cause instituted in an inferior tribunal, but cannot originate a cause; and the power thus withheld from it by the Constitution cannot be given to it by the legislature. When an instrument organizing a judicial system; divides it into one supreme and so many inferior courts as the legislature may ordain and establish; then enumerates its powers, and proceeds so far to distribute them as to define the jurisdiction of the Supreme Court, by declaring the cases in which it shall have original jurisdiction, and those in which it shall have appellate jurisdiction, it follows, that in one class its jurisdiction is original and not appellate, and that in the other it is appellate and not original. [9]

It has already been observed, that it does not rest with congress to give a binding construction to the Constitution. It can neither diminish nor enlarge the powers of the Supreme Court.

By the act of the 24th of September, 1789, congress undertook to

---

80 *In Chisholm v. Georgia, 2 U.S. 419 (1793), the State of Georgia was ordered before the Federal Supreme Court. Georgia refused to submit to this Federal order on the grounds that a sovereign State could not be compelled to act against its will. So incensed were the States, by the action of the Federal Judicial System, that the States passed the Eleventh Amendment to the Constitution. This Amendment prohibits a State from being sued in Federal Courts by an individual. The Eleventh Amendment is a strong endorsement of the idea of State sovereignty and States' Rights. It was ratified by both Northern and Southern States. The American principle of States' Rights belongs all Americans.*

vest in the Supreme Court, the power to issue writs of mandamus [a judicial command], in cases warranted by the usages and principles of law, to any courts appointed by, or persons holding office under, the authority of the United States. In a case which did not come within the description of original jurisdiction, contained in the Constitution, a mandamus was moved for in the supreme court, to be directed to a person holding an office under the authority of the United States, and therefore the case was within the letter and spirit of the act of congress; but the act was, in this respect, clearly held to be unconstitutional and void, and the mandamus was refused. [10] The same act provides, that the supreme court shall have power to issue writs of habeas corpus, where persons are in custody, under or by color of the authority of the United States, or are committed for trial before some court of the same. A writ of habeas corpus was moved for, in a case where the prisoner was committed by the circuit court of the District of Columbia, on a charge of treason against the United States. The writ was granted because it amounted only to a revision of the decision of an inferior court of the United States, [11] and therefore was of an appellate nature.

CHAPTER NOTES
XXIV

1. By the act of 24th Sept. 1789.
2. Act of April 30, 1790.
3. Act of Sept. 24, 1789.
4. Case of Du Plaine, consul at Boston, in 1793.
5. 3 Dallas, 6.
6. Vattel, I. 2. § 34.
7. The eleventh amendment is in these words: "The judicial power of the United States shall not be construed to extend to any suit in law or equity commenced or prosecuted against one of the United States by citizens of another state, or by citizens or subjects of any foreign state."
8. 6 Wheaton, p. 399.
9. 1 Cranch, 175, *Marbury v. Madison.*
10. Ibid.
11. *Ex parte* Bollman, 4 Cranch, 75.

CHAPTER XXV.

OF TRIBUNALS INFERIOR TO THE SUPREME COURT.

IN respect to all the other subjects of the judicial power, the original jurisdiction is vested in the inferior tribunals ordained and established by congress, which consist of circuit courts, district courts, and territorial courts. These are all courts of the United States — the judges are appointed by the president — their power is limited to the power which is possessed under the Constitution of the United States — and the decisions of them all may be ultimately reviewed, reversed, or affirmed in the supreme court. But congress has undertaken, in some instances, to vest in state courts a power of proceeding for offences committed against the United States, which has produced a question of considerable magnitude, not yet definitively settled. Some of the state courts have refused to exercise this jurisdiction, and there seems much weight in their objections.

The principle on which the judicial power of the Constitution is founded, has already been observed to be, its forming an integral part of the system of government. It was deemed as necessary to keep the judicial powers of the states and the United States separate and distinct, as the legislative and executive powers.

To admit the state courts to a share of the judicial powers of the United States in criminal cases, would tend, it was supposed, not only to break down those barriers which were deemed important to the self-preservation of the United States, but would produce perplexity and confusion, dangerous to the harmony of both.

The office of congress is to appoint those courts which are to receive the powers vested in the United States, not to grant those powers to the courts. Congress are not the donors, but the mere agents of distribution. Impressions sometimes arise, and consequences often flow from the latter capacity, which do not regularly attend the former. The gratification of making donations cannot be enjoyed by those who are only the agents to distribute, and when not only that which is to be distributed is precisely defined and limited, but those who are exclusively to receive it are exactly described, there seems so little latitude in the power as to excite some surprise that it should have been carried so far. But the motives for it were of the best kind. It was deemed a convenience to individuals to give them a forum as near to their residence as possible: it was also perhaps considered indicative of a confidence in the state governments, and if the Constitution had been accommodated to these principles, this donation of power might have been justifiable, but unless the vesting jurisdiction in a tribunal already ordained and established by a state, can be considered as ordaining and establishing a court by congress, the objections to this well meant measure seem insurmountable.

This is not, however, to be confounded with the legal principles that arise when an act amounts to an offence both against the state and the United States. As congress cannot in one case confer jurisdiction, they cannot in the other abridge it; hence those acts of congress providing for the punishment of counterfeiting the current coin of the United States, [1] and forgery of the notes of the bank of the United States, [2] which declared that nothing therein contained should be construed to deprive the state courts of jurisdiction under the laws of the several states of offences made cognizable therein, were strictly constitutional and proper.

In no case can the circuit or district courts exercise jurisdiction, unless it be so provided by congress. The judicial part of the Constitution, except so far as relates to the supreme court, must be set in motion by congress. It is, therefore, proper to show to what extent the power has been exercised by congress, observing at the same time that nothing prevents them from extending the jurisdiction of those or other courts which they may hereafter ordain and establish, provided they do not exceed the limits of the Constitution.

The original jurisdiction of the circuit court now extends to suits in which the United States are plaintiff; or petitioners, to suits between citizens of different states and those in which an alien is a party, to suits relative to patents granted under the authority of the United States, and to suits brought by or against the Bank of the United States.

In criminal cases the circuit court has original jurisdiction of all crimes and offences cognizable under the authority of the United States, except, as we have seen, proceedings against ambassadors and other public ministers or their domestics, which, whenever a court of law can exercise a jurisdiction consistently with the law of nations, are reserved for the supreme court.

The original jurisdiction of the district court in civil cases includes all causes of admiralty and maritime jurisdiction; seizures under laws of impost, navigation or trade of the United States, made on waters navigable from the sea by vessels of ten or more tons burthen, within their respective districts or on the high seas; seizures on land, or other waters than aforesaid; penalties and forfeitures; suits brought by an alien for a tort only in violation of the laws of nations, or a treaty of the United States; suits at common law where the United States sue, and the matter in dispute amounts, exclusive of costs, to one hundred dollars; suits against consuls or vice consuls.

In criminal cases, cognizance is given to the district courts of all crimes and offences cognizable under the authority of the United States, committed within their respective districts, or on the high seas, when whipping not exceeding thirty stripes, a fine not exceeding one hundred dollars, or a term of imprisonment not exceeding six months is to be inflicted, [3] and with this qualification it may sustain prosecutions against consuls or vice consuls.

In respect to the latter, it deserves notice, that this legislative provision subjecting them in certain supposed cases to the jurisdiction of the lowest court in the Union, is somewhat at variance with the high rank that they are placed in by the Constitution. It cannot, however, be said to be inconsistent with the Constitution itself, which in respect to all the jurisdiction of the supreme court contains nothing exclusive of the inferior courts of the United States, yet the entire omission of this clause, which, qualified as it is, is really inoperative, would have better harmonized with the principles manifestly kept in view by the Constitution.

CHAPTER NOTES
XXV

1. Act of April 21, 1806.

2. Acts of February 24, 1807, and April 10, 1816.

3. This part of the criminal jurisdiction of the district court is as yet a dead letter. There is no crime or offence against the United States, for which a punishment within the limits above mentioned is prescribed. It cannot be understood that prosecutions for offences punishable by

the acts of congress in a more severe manner, can be sustained with a view to the judgment of the court being reduced within these limits.

SECTION VI
CHAPTER XXVI-XXIX

In the following Section, Rawle discusses under what conditions a defendant can have his case removed from a State Court to a Federal Court.

Rawle explains how the Federal Courts have both appellate jurisdiction (the right to hear an appeal from a lower Federal court) as well as original jurisdiction (court where a case is originally filed). Under the legal theory of "diversity of citizenship" citizens of two different states may have their "state" case moved to Federal court. As Rawle points out, the Federal Courts have original jurisdiction only in those areas specified in the Constitution. Rawle also notes that the Federal Courts (at the time in which he was writing) gave deference to the acts of State Supreme Courts.

CHAPTER XXVI.

REMOVAL FROM STATE COURTS.

OTHER parts of the judicial power are by acts of congress provided for as follows: —

If a suit be commenced in a state court against an alien, or by a citizen of the state in which a suit is brought against a citizen of another state; the defendant may have the benefit of the unbiased judicatures of the United States, by removing the suit into the circuit court of the same district, provided it be done immediately, for the complainant ought not to suffer by the hesitation or delay of his opponent — but if the alien or citizen of another state has commenced the suit, he cannot afterwards remove it, for he is bound by his own election, nor can the defendant remove it, for he is not to be apprehensive of the injustice of the courts of his own state.

If there is a controversy in a state court respecting the title to land between two citizens of the same state, and either party shall make it appear to the court, that he claims and shall rely upon a right under a grant from a state other than that in which the suit is pending, and the other party claims under a grant from the last mentioned state, the party claiming under the grant first mentioned, whether plaintiff or defendant, may remove the suit to the circuit court for the same district, but neither party so removing the cause, shall be allowed to plead or give evidence on the trial in the circuit court of any other title than that by him so stated as the ground of his claim. This is perfectly consistent with the principle, that in all controversies the most impartial tribunal that can be formed, shall be selected, and the propriety of adopting this somewhat circuitous mode, instead of enabling the claimant under the grant of another state to bring his action at once in the United States court, arises from the juridical rule that the defendant, unless some express provision is made to compel him, shall not at law be obliged to show on what title he relies, before the commencement of the trial. A citizen of another state or an alien, (in those cases where an alien may hold land,) is not obliged nor indeed allowed to adopt this course, because he may commence a suit in the United States courts or remove it there, as noticed before, immediately on its, being commenced against him, and it is his own folly not to avail himself of this benefit in the first instance.

No other court of the United States than the supreme court can entertain a suit brought by a state, either against another state or against individuals. In this respect, congress has no further legislated than to declare that the jurisdiction of the supreme court shall be exclusive, except between a state and its citizens. This inference would indeed flow from the words of the Constitution, which could never be so construed as to prevent a state from suing its own citizens, or those of other states or aliens, in its own courts. In regard to suits against states, they were unknown before the Constitution, and since the amendment already adverted to, the only remaining class is above the jurisdiction of the circuit courts.

Jurisdiction by way of appeal or writ of error, according to the nature of the case, is given to the circuit from the district court, and to the supreme from the circuit court. But a pecuniary qualification is annexed both to the original and appellate jurisdiction in most cases. The district court has cognizance of all civil suits brought by the United States where the matter in dispute, exclusive of costs, amounts to one hundred dollars. The original jurisdiction of the circuit court is described as applying to cases where the matter in dispute, exclusive of costs, exceeds five hundred dollars. Yet it would seem, that if any sum exceeding three hundred dollars was found due, the court could sustain the jurisdiction, although the plaintiff would be liable to costs. To sustain the jurisdiction on a suit for the violation of a patent right, any sum, however small, that may be recovered, is sufficient.

To sustain the jurisdiction of the Supreme Court on writs of error, the matter in dispute, exclusive of costs, must exceed two thousand dollars. There is perhaps too much disproportion in these sums, and there seems little reason for excluding a stranger or a citizen of another state from the benefit of a revision of the judgment, for any sum below five hundred dollars. No pecuniary limit is adverted to in the Constitution, and although there is weight in the suggestion that the dignity of a court is impaired by giving an ear to trifling controversies, yet the humblest suitor is entitled in some shape to relief; and the principle on which the classification of the subjects of judicial cognizance is founded, ought not to be impaired by a standard of value, which to a poor man may amount to a denial of justice.

In this chapter, there is (as occasionally elsewhere) a deviation from the original plan of confining ourselves to an exposition of the Constitution. The legislative development of principles, briefly expressed in the great text, when it correctly explains and applies those principles, is highly useful.

CHAPTER XXVII.

OF THE PLACES IN WHICH JURISDICTION IS TO BE EXERCISED.

HAVING thus shown the subjects to which this jurisdiction extends, and the courts among which it is distributed, we shall proceed to consider the places in which it is to be exercised, and the rules and principles by which it is to be administered.

The geographical limits of the United States and those of the territories, are subject to the jurisdiction of all the courts of the United States, in all matters within the scope of their authority.

For the better administration of justice, the United States are divided into districts, in forming which, the convenience of suitors is chiefly consulted. It has ever been a principle with us, to bring justice as much as possible home to the doors of the people. These districts may be altered at the pleasure of congress. The jurisdiction of the particular courts is of course confided to them. But some courts possessing only a special jurisdiction as to the subject, are without restriction as to the place. Such is the senate in respect to impeachments, both houses when acting judicially in respect to contempt and breach of privileges, and courts martial.

The extent of the admiralty jurisdiction at sea, has already been noticed.

In these the subjects are limited, but a general jurisdiction appertains to the United States over ceded territories or districts.

If the land, at the time of cession, is uninhabited, except by the Indians, of whose polity we take no account, it is in the power of congress to make such regulations for its government as they may think proper. Whoever subsequently becomes an inhabitant, is of course bound to conform to the system which may be thus established; if there be a number of civilized inhabitants previously settled there, enjoying the advantages of a particular code of laws, they have a just right to claim a continuance of those laws. Thus in the first cession of this kind, which was from the states of Massachusetts, Connecticut, New York, and Virginia, and formed what was termed the territory North-west of the Ohio, there was a saving to the French and Canadian inhabitants, and other settlers of the Kaskaskias, St. Vincents, and the neighboring villages, who had theretofore professed themselves citizens of Virginia, of the laws and customs then in force among them relative to the descent and conveyance of property, and in the treaty by which Louisiana was ceded to the United States in 1803, it was expressly stipulated that the inhabitants should retain their ancient laws and usages.

With these restrictions, congress has always been considered as entitled not only to regulate the form of government, but also to reserve to themselves the approbation or rejection of such laws, as may be passed by the legislative power which they may establish. In regulating the government of the territory northwest of the Ohio, which was the act of congress under the confederation, and which has been the model of most of the subsequent regulations of the same nature, it is declared that the governor and judges who, until the population amounted to five thousand male inhabitants, were to compose their legislature, should adopt such laws of the original states as might be necessary and suitable to their circumstances, which, unless disapproved by congress, should be in force until the organization of a general assembly, which was to take place when the population reached the number before mentioned. These laws may therefore be considered as emanating from the United States, and the judicial authority is to be regarded as the judicial authority of the United States.

In respect to those portions of land which become the property of the United States for the purposes of arsenals, dockyards, &c. it may be observed, that exclusive legislation generally implies exclusive jurisdiction. Yet the peculiar nature of this possession may require some qualification, and, therefore, a reservation by a state of the power to serve its civil and criminal process therein by its own officers, is not objectionable. It prevents the particular spot from becoming a sanctuary for criminals or debtors, and from the assent of the United States it results, that the state officers, in executing such process, act under the authority of the United States. [1] Indeed, a general provision to this effect has been made by an act of congress, [2] although no reservation be made by the state.

The power of exercising exclusive legislation over such districts as should become the seat of government, like all others which are specified, is conferred on congress, not as a mere local legislature, but as the legislature of the Union, and cannot be exercised in any other character. A law passed in pursuance of it is the supreme law of the land; is binding as such on the states, and a law of a state to defeat it would be void. The power to pass such a law, carries with it all those incidental powers which are necessary to its complete and effectual execution; and such law may, it seems, be extended in its collateral operation throughout the United States, if congress think it necessary to do so. But if it be intended to give it a binding efficacy beyond the district, language showing this intention ought to be used, especially if it is to extend into the particular states, and to limit and control their penal laws. [3]

So also the power vested in congress to legislate exclusively within any other place ceded by a state, carries with it a right to make that power effectual. They may therefore provide by law for apprehending a person who escapes from a fort, &c. after committing a felony, and for conveying him to or from any other place for trial or execution. So they may punish those for misprision of felony [the offense of concealing knowledge of a felony or treason by one not engaged to the act], who, out of a fort conceal a felony committed within it. [4]

Where a fortress within the acknowledged limits of a state, was surrendered under the treaty of 1794 with Great Britain, and was afterwards constantly possessed and garrisoned by the United States, but was never purchased from the state by the United States, or ceded to the latter by the former, the United States do not possess the right of exclusive legislation or exclusive jurisdiction over such fortress, but crimes committed therein may be punished under the laws and by the courts of the state. To give the United States exclusive legislation and jurisdiction over a place, there must be a free cession of the same, for one of the purposes specified in the Constitution. They cannot acquire it tortuously or by disseisin [unlawful depriving of property or rights] of the state, or by occupancy with merely the tacit consent of the state, when such occupancy is as a military post, though obtained after a treaty by which foreign garrisons were withdrawn from our posts. And the rule is the same, although the title to such place be vested in the United States, by purchases from individuals, and it has been occupied by them as a military post; for if there has been no cession by the legislature of the state to the United States, the right of legislation and jurisdiction over such place, remains exclusively in the state where it is situated. [5]

CHAPTER NOTES
XXVII

1. Commonwealth v. Clary, 8 Mass. 72.
2. Act of March 2, 1795.
3. *Cohens v. Virginia*, 6 Wheaton, 264. See *United States v. Moore*, 3 Cranch, 159.
4. 6 Wheaton, 264.
5. Hall's *Journal of Jurisprudence*, p. 47.

CHAPTER XXVIII.

OF THE APPELLATE JURISDICTION.

THE general expressions of the Constitution are, that the supreme court shall have, "appellate jurisdiction in all cases of law and equity, both as to law and fact, with such exceptions and under such regulations as congress shall make, of all controversies to which the United States shall be a party; controversies between two or more states; between a state and citizens of another state; between citizens of deferent states; between citizens of the same state claiming lands under grants of different states, and between a state or the citizens thereof and foreign states, citizens or subjects."

The power given to except and to regulate does not — *ex vi termini*—[from the very meaning of the expression used] carry with it a power to enlarge the jurisdiction; so far therefore as it relates to the subjects of jurisdiction, we must consider it as confined by the enumeration of them.

But on another question the Constitution is not equally explicit. It is not said whether the revision of the sentences of other courts extends to state courts, or is limited to the courts of the United States. Some discussions took place on this subject in the state conventions, and the question was not perhaps entirely at rest till the year 1821, when it again arose in the supreme court, received its close attention, and it is presumed, its final decision.

The clear and convincing elucidations of the chief justice [Federalist, John Marshall] would suffer by abridgement, and could not be improved by the substitution of other language.

He observes that the United States for many and most important purposes form a single nation.

"In making peace, we are one people. In all commercial regulations, we are one and the same people. In many other respects, the American people are one, and the government which is alone capable of controlling and managing their interest in all these respects, is the government of the Union, and in that character the people have no other. America has chosen to be in many respects and to many purposes a nation; and for all these purposes, her government is competent and complete. The people have declared, that in the exercise of all powers given for these objects, it is supreme. It can, then, in affecting these objects, legitimately control all individuals or governments within the American territory. The constitution and laws of a state, so far as they are repugnant to the Constitution and the constitutional laws of the United States, are absolutely void. These states are constituent parts of the United States. They are members of one great empire — for some purposes sovereign; for some purposes subordinate.

"In a government so constituted, is it unreasonable that the judicial power should be competent to give efficacy to the constitutional laws of the legislature? That department can decide on the validity of the constitution or law of a state if it be repugnant to the Constitution or to a law of the United States. Is it unreasonable that it should also be empowered to decide on the judgment of a state tribunal enforcing such unconstitutional law? Is it so very unreasonable as to furnish a justification for controlling the words of a constitution?

"When a government is confessedly supreme, in respect to objects of vital interest to the nation, there is nothing inconsistent with sound reason, or incompatible with the nature of government, in making all its departments supreme, so far as respects those objects, and so far as is necessary in their attainment. The exercise of the appellate power over those judgments of the state tribunals which may contravene the Constitution or laws of the United States, is essential to the attainment of those objects.

"The propriety of entrusting the construction of the Constitution, and laws made in pursuance thereof, to the judiciary of the Union, has not, as yet, been drawn into question. It seems to be a corollary from this political axiom, that the federal courts should either possess exclusive jurisdiction in such cases, or a power to revise the judgment rendered in them by the state tribunals. If the federal and state courts have concurrent jurisdiction in all cases arising under the constitution, laws, and treaties of the United States; and if a case of this description, brought in a state court, cannot be removed before judgment, nor revised after judgment, then the construction of the constitution, laws, and treaties of the United States, is not confided particularly to their judicial department, but is confided equally to that department, and to the state courts, however they may be constituted. 'Thirteen independent courts,' says a very celebrated statesman, (and we have now more than twenty such courts,) 'of final jurisdiction over the same causes, arising upon the same laws, is a hydra in government, from which nothing but contradiction and confusion can proceed.'

"Dismissing the unpleasant suggestion, that any motives which may not be fairly avowed, or which ought not to exist, can ever influence a state or its courts; the necessity of uniformity, as well as correctness in expounding the Constitution and laws of the United States, would itself suggest the propriety of vesting in some single tribunal, the power of deciding in the last resort, all cases in which they are involved.

"We are not restrained, then, by the political relations between the general and state governments, from construing the words of the Constitution, defining the judicial power, in their true sense. We are not bound to construe them more restrictively than they naturally import.

"They give to the Supreme Court appellate jurisdiction, in all cases arising under the Constitution, laws, and treaties of the United States. The words are broad enough to comprehend all cases of this description, in whatever court they may be decided. In expounding them, we may be permitted to take into view, those considerations to which courts have always allowed great weight in the exposition of laws.

"The framers of the Constitution would naturally examine the state of things existing at the time; and their work sufficiently attests that they did so. All acknowledge that they were convened for the purpose of strengthening the confederation by enlarging the powers of the government, and by giving efficacy to those which it before possessed, but could not exercise. They inform us themselves, in the instrument they presented to the American public, that one of its objects was to form a more perfect union. Under such circumstances, we certainly should not expect to find, in that instrument, a diminution of the powers of the actual government.

"Previous to the adoption of the confederation, congress established courts which received appeals in prize causes decided in the courts of the respective states. This power of the government, to establish tribunals for these appeals, was thought consistent with, and was founded on, its political relations with the states. These courts exercised appellate jurisdiction over those cases decided in the state courts, to which the judicial power of the federal government extended.

"The confederation gave to congress the power of 'establishing courts for receiving and determining finally appeals in all cases of captures.'

"This power was uniformly construed to authorize those courts to receive appeals from the sentences of state courts, and to affirm or reverse them. State tribunals are not mentioned; but this clause in the confederation necessarily comprises them. Yet the relation between the general and state governments was much weaker and much more lax, under the confederation than under the present Constitution; and the states being much more completely sovereign, their institutions were much more independent.

"The convention which framed the Constitution, on turning their attention to the judicial power, found it limited to a few objects, but with respect to some of those objects extending in its appellate form to the judgments of the state courts. They extended it, among other objects, to all cases arising under the Constitution, laws, and treaties of the United States; and in a subsequent clause declare, that, in such cases, the supreme court shall exercise appellate jurisdiction. Nothing seems to be given which would justify the withdrawal of a judgment rendered in a state court on the Constitution, laws, or treaties of the United States from this appellate jurisdiction.

"Great weight has always been attached to contemporaneous exposition. No question, it is believed, has arisen to which this principle applies more unequivocally than to that now under consideration.

"In discussing the extent of the judicial power, the Federalist says, 'Here another question occurs: what relation would subsist between the national and state courts in these instances of concurrent jurisdiction? I answer, that an appeal would certainly be from the latter to the supreme court of the United States. The Constitution in direct terms gives an appellate jurisdiction to the supreme court in all the enumerated cases of federal cognizance in which it is not to have an original one, without a single expression to confine its operation to the inferior federal courts. The objects of appeal, not the tribunals from which it is to be made, are alone contemplated. From this circumstance, and from the reason of the thing, it ought to be construed to extend to the state tribunals. Either this must be the case, or the local courts must be excluded from a concurrent jurisdiction in matters of national concern, else the judicial authority of the Union may be eluded at the pleasure of every plaintiff or prosecutor. Neither of these consequences ought, without evident necessity, to be involved; the latter would be entirely inadmissible, as it would defeat some of the most important and avowed purposes of the proposed government, and would essentially embarrass its measures. Nor do I perceive any foundation for such a supposition. Agreeably to the remark already made, the national and state systems are to be regarded as one whole. The courts of the latter will of course be natural auxiliaries to the execution of the laws of the Union, and an appeal from them will as naturally be to that tribunal which is destined to unite and assimilate the principles of natural justice, and the rules of national decision. The evident aim of the plan of the national convention is, that all the causes of the specified classes shall, for weighty public reasons, receive their original or final determination in the courts of the Union. To confine, therefore, the general expressions which give appellate jurisdiction to the supreme court, to appeals from the subordinate federal courts, instead of allowing their extension to the state courts, would be to abridge the latitude of the terms in subversion of the intent, contrary to every sound rule of interpretation.'

"A contemporaneous exposition of the Constitution, certainly of not less authority than that which has been just cited, is the judiciary act itself. We know that in the congress which passed that act, were many eminent members of the convention which formed the Constitution. Not a single individual so far as is known, supposed that part of the act which gives the supreme court appellate jurisdiction over the judgments of the state courts in the cases therein specified, to be unauthorized by the Constitution.

"While on this part of the argument, it may be also material to observe, that the uniform decisions of this court on the point now under consideration, have been assented to, with a single exception, [1] by the courts of every state in the Union, whose judgments have been revised. It has been the unwelcome duty of this tribunal to reverse the judgments of many state courts in cases in which the strongest state feelings were engaged. Judges, whose talents and character would grace any bench; to whom a disposition to submit to jurisdiction that is usurped, or to surrender their legitimate powers, will certainly not be imputed, have yielded without hesitation to the authority by which their judgments were reversed, while they perhaps disapproved the judgment of reversal.

"This concurrence of statesmen, of legislators, and of judges, in the same construction of the Constitution, may justly inspire some confidence in that constructions." [2]

In this case, as may have been perceived from the course of reasoning, the appellate jurisdiction was exercised over a state court. In 1824, the consideration of the same question was again thrown on the supreme court, on an appeal from the circuit court of the United States for the district of Ohio, in an equity case.

In the extract we shall also give of the decision pronounced by the chief justice in this case, we shall perceive some further important principles laid down which will be found serviceable in a future view of the powers of the United States courts that will be presented to the reader; at the same time we must not be understood to have a design to apply arguments, evidently intended only for cases of a civil nature, further than fair reasoning will justify.

"In support of the clause, in the act incorporating the subscribers to the Bank of the United States, it is said that the legislative, executive, and judicial powers, of every well constructed government, are co-extensive with each other. That is, they are potentially co-extensive. The executive department may constitutionally execute every law which the legislature may constitutionally make, and the judicial department may receive from the legislature the power of construing every such law. All governments which are not extremely defective in their organization, must possess within themselves the means of expounding as well as enforcing their own laws. If we examine the Constitution of the United States, we find that its framers kept this political principle in view. The second article vests the whole executive power in the president, and the third declares, that 'the judicial power shall extend to all cases in law and equity arising under this Constitution, the laws of the United States, and treaties made, or which shall be made under their authority.'

"This clause enables the judicial department to receive jurisdiction to the full extent of the Constitution, laws, and treaties of the United States, when any question respecting them shall assume such a form that the judicial power is capable of acting on it. That power is capable of acting only when the subject is submitted to it by a party who asserts his rights in the form prescribed by law. It then becomes 'a case,' and the Constitution declares that the judicial power shall extend to 'all cases arising under the Constitution, laws, and treaties of the United States.'

"The suit of the Bank of the United States v. Osborne and others, is 'a case,' and the question is, whether it arises under a law of the United States?

"The appellants contend that it does not, because several questions may arise in it, which depend on the general principles of the law, not on any act of congress.

"If this were sufficient to withdraw a case from the jurisdiction of the federal courts, almost every case, although involving the construction of a law, would be withdrawn; and a clause in the Constitution relating to a subject of vital importance to the government, and expressed in the most comprehensive terms, would be construed to mean almost nothing. There is scarcely any case, every part of which depends on the Constitution, laws, or treaties of the United States. The questions whether the fact alleged as the foundation of the action be real or fictitious; whether the conduct of the plaintiff has been such as to entitle him to maintain his action; whether his right is barred; whether he has received satisfaction, or has in any manner released his claims — are questions, some or all of which may occur in almost every case; and if their existence be sufficient to arrest the jurisdiction of the court, words which seem intended to be as extensive as the Constitution, laws, and treaties of the Union — which seem designed to give the courts of the government, the construction of all its acts, so far as they affect the rights of individuals, would be reduced to almost nothing.

"In those cases in which original jurisdiction is given to the Supreme Court, the judicial power of the United States cannot be exercised in its appellate form. In every other case, the power is to be exercised in its original or appellate form, or both, as the wisdom of congress may direct. With the exception of those cases, in which original jurisdiction is given to this court, there is none to which the judicial power extends, from which the original jurisdiction of the interior courts is excluded by the Constitution. Original jurisdiction, so far as the Constitution gives a rule, is co-extensive with the judicial power. We find in the Constitution, no prohibition to its exercise, in every case in which the judicial power can be exercised. It would be a very bold construction to say that this power could be applied in its appellate form only, to the most important class of cases to which it is applicable.

"The Constitution establishes the Supreme Court, and defines its jurisdiction. It enumerates cases in which its jurisdiction is original and exclusive; and then defines that which is appellate, but does not insinuate that in any such case the power cannot be exercised in its original form by courts of original jurisdiction. It is not insinuated that the judicial power, in cases depending on the character of the cause, cannot be exercised in the first instance, in the courts of the Union, but must first be exercised in the tribunals of the state; tribunals over which the government of the Union has no adequate control, and which may be closed to any claim asserted under a law of the United States.

"We perceive, then, no ground on which the proposition can be maintained, that congress is incapable of giving the circuit courts original jurisdiction in any case to which the appellate jurisdiction extends.

"We ask, then, if it can be sufficient to exclude this jurisdiction, that the case involves questions depending on general principles? A cause may depend on several questions of fact and law. Some of them may depend on the construction of a law of the United States; others on principles unconnected with that law. If it be a sufficient foundation for jurisdiction, that the title or right set up by the party, may be defeated by one construction of the Constitution or law of the United States, and sustained by the opposite construction, provided the facts necessary to support the action be made out; then all the other questions must be decided as incidental to this, which gives that jurisdiction. Those other questions cannot arrest the proceedings. Under this construction, the judicial power of the Union extends effectively and beneficially to that most important class of cases, which depend on the character of the cause. On the opposite construction, the judicial power never can be extended to a whole case, as expressed by the Constitution, but to those parts of cases only which present the particular question involving the construction of the Constitution or the law. We say, it never can be extended to the whole case, because, if the circumstance that other points are involved in it, shall disable congress from authorizing the courts of the Union to take jurisdiction of the original cause, it equally disables congress from authorizing those courts to take jurisdiction of the whole cause on an appeal; and thus, words which in their plain sense apply to a whole cause, will be restricted to a single question in that cause; and words obviously intended to secure to those who claim rights under the Constitution, laws or treaties of the United States, a trial in the federal courts, will be restricted to the insecure remedy of an appeal upon an insulated point, after it has received that shape which may be given to it by another tribunal into which he is forced against his will.

"We think, then, that when a question, to which the judicial power of the Union is extended by the Constitution, forms an ingredient of the original cause, it is in the power of congress to give the circuit courts jurisdiction of that cause, although other questions of fact or of law may be involved in it." [3]

From these two decisions we collect, among other matters, that the appellate jurisdiction does not depend on the court where the decision was given, but on the subject to which it relates; that it is not necessary that the subject should be purely and abstractedly of a single nature within the view of the Constitution, but may be connected with other matter, and the entire subject so formed, falls within the appellate jurisdiction; that this jurisdiction is essential to the well-being of the nation, and that the Supreme Court have not the power to decline its exercise. A tribunal so high, fully submitting to its constitutional obligations, when motives may easily be conceived of a personal nature, to tempt it to relax or evade their performance, affords an example for the imitation of all. [4]

CHAPTER NOTES
XXVIII

1. Supposed to be the case of *Hunter's lessee v. Martin*, of which the particulars may be seen in 7 Cranch, 604, and 1 Wheaton, 304. The ultimate acquiescence of the state tribunal restored the harmony of the general system. We are all fellow citizens, and all have but one interest.

2. 6 Wheaton, 413. *Cohens v. Virginia.*

3. 9 Wheaton, 733. *Osborne v. Bank of the United States.*

4. In these quotations the author has retained, without approving of, the expression *federal*, frequently applied to the courts of the United States. The government not being strictly a federal government, its tribunals are not properly federal tribunals. He refers to his antecedent remarks, to show how little of the pure federative quality, was intended to be retained in it, nor on the other hand, is it liable to the objection sometimes raised, that its warm advocates aim at rendering it a consolidated government, destructive of state sovereignty. The minority, who at first opposed its adoption, were, no doubt, sincere in the alarm they professed in this respect: **but time has proved that it is utterly groundless, and the state sovereignties are, in all respects not**

voluntarily ceded to the United States, as vigorous as ever *[emphasis added]. [What was true in 1829, was put to death in 1865 and regretfully has not been resurrected as of yet.]*

CHAPTER XXIX.

OF THE RULES OF DECISION.

THE rules and principles by which the judicial power is to be administered, form the next subject of consideration, and here we have, in the Constitution, the benefit of a text which in some respects is explicit, and in all others, supplies a foundation on which it is apprehended we may securely rest.

The laws of the United States and treaties made under their authority, form the explicit principle of the judiciary power, and in respect to their high obligation no question can arise: but another part of the same sentence leads us into a wider field of inquiry.

The Constitution itself is the supreme law of the land, and all cases arising under it are declared to be within the judicial power. To every part of this well-digested work we are bound to give an efficient construction. No words are there used in vain: as a literary composition, the union of precision with brevity constitutes one of its chief ornaments and recommendations. When we find a distinction between cases arising under the Constitution and under laws and treaties, we are not at liberty to suppose that the former description was introduced without a definite meaning. The other designations are not more plain than this. We understand what is meant by cases arising under laws and under treaties, but something more is evidently meant. We may recollect that in another article of the Constitution, laws made in pursuance thereof, and treaties made under the authority of the United States, are declared to be the supreme law of the land. The subordination of all legislative acts to the Constitution is thereby provided for, and it is inconsistent with the whole frame of its composition to consider any part of it as an useless repetition of words. We are therefore bound to say, that cases may arise under the Constitution which do not arise under the laws, and if this point is conceded or established, we are next to inquire what are those cases.

Of a civil nature nothing can properly be said to arise under the Constitution, except contracts to which the United States are parties. Jurisdiction is given to them over controversies in which states and individuals of certain descriptions are concerned, but those cases would exist although the Constitution did not exist. The courts of the United States are, in these respects, merely the organs of justice, and by the first act of congress relative to the judicial establishment [1] it is expressly declared that the laws of the several states, except where the Constitution, treaties, or statutes of the United States shall otherwise require or provide, shall be regarded as rules of decision in trials at common law, in courts of the United States, in cases where they apply.

The term, laws of the several states embracing as well their common as their statute laws, there is no difficulty on this subject. It is admitted, that every state in the Union has its peculiar system and rules of decision in cases for which no positive statutes are provided, and of these general rules the United States have the benefit in all cases of contract which may occasion suits on their behalf, either in their own courts or in those of the several states.[81] To their own courts a similar power could not be given by congress unless warranted by the Constitution, but if the Constitution does warrant it, congress may give it. No one has doubted that although no express adoption of this general principle is apparent, it is necessarily contained in the Constitution, in relation to all civil matters.

Contracts obligatory on the party, though merely implied by reason of principles not found in the text of any statute, but originating in universal law, may as well be made by the United States acting through the agency of their executive officers, as by private individuals. No one has doubted that they may be enforced. But it cannot be supposed that in such cases the United States would be obliged to have recourse to the state courts to obtain redress.

In respect to foreigners and citizens of different states, it would be illusory and disgraceful, to hold up to their view a jurisdiction destitute of the necessary means of expounding and deciding their controversies, and therefore inferior in its efficacy to those state tribunals from whose supposed partialities or imperfections, it tendered an asylum.

We cannot therefore otherwise understand the constitutional extension of jurisdiction in the cases described, than as a declaration that whatever relief would be afforded by other judicial tribunals in similar cases, shall be afforded by the courts of the United States,

---

81 *Rawle recurs here to his theme of State sovereignty. The fundamental rule of States' Rights as provided for in the 9th & 10th Amendments to the Constitution acknowledges the individual States as autonomous in their Court decisions and rule-making.*

or a strange anomaly would be presented. We may consider it as an inherent and a vital principle in the judicial system, that in all civil cases those rules of decision founded on reason and justice which form the basis of general law, are within the reach and compose parts of the power of our tribunals. And it is apprehended that although the legislature on the creation of inferior tribunals unquestionably possesses the right to distribute the judicial authority among them, it cannot control the constitutional qualities appertaining to such portions of the judicial power as it may vest in any one of those tribunals. Thus it may create a court for the trial of suits to which an alien is a party, or it may wholly omit to institute any such court. By such omission, what may be termed the national promise to provide impartial tribunals, would in this respect remain unexecuted, but whenever it was intended to be redeemed by the erection of a court, the national promise would only be fulfilled by the tribunal being possessed of all the powers necessary to render it efficient.

The act of September 24th, 1789, essentially depends for its validity on the Constitution. Unless the legislature is authorized by the Constitution to declare that the laws of the several states shall be the rules of decision; it is certain that a declaration to that effect would be vain. But the subject may be further pursued.

Legislative expositions of the Constitution, although not binding, are entitled to the greatest respect — and when such laws apply immediately to the action of the judicial power, and are fully adopted and uniformly acted upon by the latter, a joint sanction is thus conferred on the construction thereby given to the Constitution. Now the memorable language of this act is, that in trials at common law, the laws of the several states shall govern the courts of the United States. But whence do we derive the first position? By what authority do the courts of the United States try causes at common law? Unless the Constitution confers this power they do not possess it — nor does congress profess to give it to them, but considers it as already given. The law serves only to modify it, and render it more convenient and practicable.

In another respect, the view here taken, appears to receive some support both from the silence of the act, and from judicial practice.

We find a distinction taken between common law and equity, not only in the section before mentioned, but in that which describes the jurisdiction of the circuit court. "The circuit courts shall have original cognizance concurrent with the courts of the several states, of all suits of a civil nature at common law or in equity, when the United States are plaintiffs or petitioned or an alien is a party, or the suit is between a citizen of the state where the suit is brought and a citizen of another state." In other parts of the same act the distinction is between law, without the prefix "common," and equity. The provision in regard to the laws of the several states is therefore not in words extended to suits in equity. And the course pursued has been to make use of those forms and modes of proceeding adopted in that country from which "we derive our knowledge of the "principles of common law and equity." It is observed that in some states no court of chancery exists, and courts of law recognize and enforce in suits at law, all the equitable claims and fights which a court of equity would recognize and enforce; in others such relief is denied, and equitable claims and rights are considered as mere nullifies at law. A construction that would adopt the state practice in all its extent would extinguish in some states the exercise of equitable jurisdiction altogether. [2]

Where, for want of a court of equity, rights of an equitable character are enforced in a state court of law, the United States courts will afford relief in the same manner. [3]

But although the forms of proceeding are regulated in this manner under an act of congress, [4] the principles of decision are in nowise modified or regulated by congress. They are therefore to be drawn directly from the Constitution, and the construction given by the supreme court in this respect must be received as decisive, that the word equity there introduced means equity as understood in England, and not as it is expounded and practiced on in different states. Yet, perhaps in every state having courts of equity, there are variations and peculiarities in the system. Equity is not to be viewed as a pure system of ethics, formed only on the moral sense. Every lawyer knows that it is now a definite science, as closely bound by precedents as the law itself, and its local character would seem to require as much regard from the courts of the United States as the common law of a particular state. It does not appear that this point has yet been directly decided.

We have therefore before us, in all cases at law, a rule so convenient and appropriate, that it would probably have been adopted by the courts, if no act of congress had been passed on the subject, and which would be so justly applicable to cases in equity, that we may consider it likely to be adopted, whenever the necessity shall arise, and in each respect, and however the latter may be settled, we find that in civil cases the judicial power is not confined to positive statutes.

We now proceed (*minibus certe tremulis,*) to the application of the same principles to of a criminal nature. [5] In a matter so important, and on which there has been such a variety of opinions, it seems incumbent distinctly to state the process of reasoning, by which a conclusion apparently differing from that which has influenced so many wise and virtuous members of our community has been attained.

The four following propositions form the basis of this conclusion.

1. On the formation of society, prior to positive laws, certain rules of moral action necessarily arise, the foundation of which is the observance of justice among the members of the society.
2. On the formation of the Constitution of the United States, such rules arose without being expressed: the breach of them constitutes offences against the United States.
3. If no judiciary power had been introduced into the Constitution of the United States, the state courts could have punished those breaches.

The creation of such judiciary power was intended to confer jurisdiction over such and other offences, not to negative or destroy it.

1. It was intended by Divine Providence that men should live in a state of society. Reason and reflection were given to him to be used and improved. Social affections were created, as natural impulses to promote their use and improvement, by leading and keeping mankind together. When societies commence, certain rules of action are necessary. Men are not equally honest and virtuous; without some restraint, injustice and violence would soon throw the association, however small, into disorder and confusion. Hence arises at once a law of tacit convention, founded on a few plain principles. It requires no positive law to have it understood, that one shall not, without cause, deprive another of his property, or do injury to his person. When the period arrives for the formation of positive laws, which is after the formation of the original compact, the legislature is employed, not in the discovery that these acts are unlawful, but in the application of punishments to prevent them. In every code we find a distinction between things *mala* in *se*, things in themselves unlawful; and *mala prohibita*, things which become unlawful from being prohibited by the legislature. But circumstances may delay the formation or the action of a legislative body, or its provisions may be inadequate

to the redress of experienced or expected evils. In this interval can no rights to property be acquired or preserved — can no binding contracts be made — are theft, robbery, murder, no crimes? Opinions so monstrous can be entertained by none. On the contrary, the human heart, the universal sense and practice of mankind, the internal consciousness of the Divine will, all concur in pointing out the rules and obligations by which we are bound.[82]

Emphatically termed the law of nature, it is implanted in us by nature itself; it is felt, not learned; it is never misunderstood, and though not always observed, never is forgotten. Cicero in his *Treatise de Legibus*, remarks that law, (and he explains that he speaks of general, not positive law,) is the perfection of reason, seated in nature, commanding what is right, and prohibiting what is wrong. Its beginning is to be traced to times before any law was written, or any express form of government adopted.

This proposition is indeed too plain to be contradicted; and we therefore pass on to the second, which may require a closer examination.

2. We have seen that the Constitution of the United States was the work of the people. It was the formation of a new and peculiar association, having for its objects the attainment or security of many important political rights, which could not otherwise be fully attained or secured; but not embracing in its sphere of action all the political rights to which its members were individually entitled. So far as related to those other rights, the people were satisfied with other associations, in each of which the law of nature, under the usual appellation of the common law, prevailed. So far as related to the new rights and duties, springing from the new political association, the same tacit compact which is acknowledged to exist in all society, necessarily accompanied this. Nothing short of express negation could exclude it. Every member of society has a direct interest in the prevention or punishment of every act contrary to the well being of that society. Before the Constitution was adopted, every act of such a tendency, having relation to the state association, was punishable by the common law of such state, but when it was adopted, certain actions, whether

82 *Rawle explains here the inalienable rights in criminal law described as procedural due process. Due process includes such things as adequate notice of alleged crimes, a fair hearing, and subsequent fair trial conducted according to established rules regulating judicial proceedings — typically by a jury of one's peers. These rights originate in equity or what our society views as fair play.*

considered in reference to persons, to particular places, or to the subject itself, were either expressly or by implication withdrawn from the immediate cognizance of the states. The people of the United States did not, however, mean that if those actions amounted to offences they should go unpunished. The right of prosecution and of punishment was not meant to be surrendered. In this instance, the converge of the well known proposition, that whatever is not delegated to the United States is reserved to the people, is the true construction. The people possessed at the moment the full right to the punishment of offences against the law of nature, though they might not be the subject of positive law. They did not surrender this right by adopting the Constitution. An offence against them in a state capacity, became in certain cases an offence against them in relation to the United States. In fact, there is no offence against the United States which is not an offence against the people of the United States. They did not, perhaps we may even say, that without being in some degree guilty of political suicide, they could not cede or relinquish the right to punish such acts. If they had so done, the system itself would soon dissolve. They gave no power to congress to pass any penal laws whatever, except on this basis. Every act, declaring a crime and imposing a penalty, rests upon it. It follows that this source of the power of congress must be admitted. It may be attenuated by positive law, but it never can be exhausted, unless we can suppose that positive laws may meet and provide for all the incalculable varieties of human depravity. But in no country has this been found practicable.

In the very terms made use of in the Constitution, it is manifest that a new and distinct class of duties were to arise which would tend to produce a new and distinct class of offences. The words are, as we have already seen — that the judicial power shall extend to all cases in law and equity arising under this Constitution, the laws of the United States and treaties. No jurisdiction over crimes is given, except as they are included in the antecedent words, cases in law; but it is declared that they shall be tried only by jury. We have thus three divisions of judicial subjects.

I. Cases including crimes arising under the Constitution.

II. Cases including crimes arising under acts of congress.

III. Those arising under treaties.

There may then be crimes arising under the Constitution, on which no act of congress has been passed; but if such an act has been passed, as in all countries positive laws control the, common law, the act is punishable under such positive law.

If only the infraction of treaties and acts of congress had been considered as criminal acts, there would have been a manifest impropriety in the introduction of those words "arising under the Constitution." But they were certainly used with. the intention that they should have the same effect in criminal as in civil cases. The construction we venture to affix, appears to us to render the whole system harmonious, efficient, and complete.

3. Our next position is, that if the Constitution of the United States had been wholly unfurnished with a judicial power, offences of this description could be punished through the medium of the state courts.

In the year 1779, one Cornelius Sweers, a deputy commissary of the United States, was indicted in a court of oyer and terminer [to hear and determine] then held by the judges of the Supreme Court of Pennsylvania, for forging and altering two receipts given to him by persons of whom he had purchased, goods for the use of the United States. The indictment, in compliance with judicial forms, was laid to be against the peace and dignity of the commonwealth of Pennsylvania, with intent to defraud the United States. McKean, C. J. after hearing the arguments of counsel, supported the indictment. [6] It is a memorable instance of the power of the common law to accommodate itself to the attainment of substantial justice. Even the articles of confederation did not then exist, but the court recognized the United States as a corporation. It was an offence against the United States, in which the state of Pennsylvania had no other interest than as one of thirteen states. But the prosecution was technically supported as an offence against the state of Pennsylvania. Another important consideration arises from this case. There existed at that time no act of assembly in Pennsylvania which rendered such an action a crime. By the English common law it was not forgery. The court must have proceeded therefore on higher ground. The principles laid down in our second position support their judgment. The soundness of this decision, as well as, that in the case of De Long Champs, [7] has never been questioned. We may therefore safely infer, that the state judicatures would, if it were necessary, afford an easy and a certain remedy in all cases of a criminal nature, arising tinder the Constitution of the United States.

4. It only remains to inquire, whether the addition of a judiciary system to the Constitution of the United States diminishes the power

of punishing offences arising under it. It is well understood that the motives for annexing a judiciary power were to give force and energy to the government. It was apprehended that less interest in the concerns of the Union, and less uniformity of decision might be found in the state courts; and it was thought expedient that a suitable number of tribunals under the authority of the United States should be dispersed through the country, subject to the revision of superior courts, and finally centering in a common head, the Supreme Court. To these tribunals was imparted the power which the state courts would, it is presumed, have otherwise continued to exercise, of expounding and enforcing whatever was properly cognizable as an offence against the United States. But it cannot be conceived, that a system intended to strengthen and invigorate the government of the Union, can impair and enfeeble it. It cannot be supposed, that the effect of providing weapons for its defense, is to strip it of its armor. Neither can it be supposed that it was intended to establish a system so incongruous as to confine the United States courts to the trial of offences against positive law, and to rely upon the state courts for relief against acts of another description injurious to the United States; nor yet that the United States, having so strong an interest in being protected against such acts, meant to relinquish and abandon the remedies against them altogether.

In addition to these general grounds, we ought not to omit the peculiar jurisdiction given by the Constitution over districts ceded by states for certain purposes, and also over the territories acquired from the states or from foreign powers. A construction which implies that in such places any offence not expressly prohibited by an act of congress may be committed with impunity, cannot be a sound one.

Let us also consider persons of a certain description. The Constitution, as we have already seen, gives to the courts of the United States jurisdiction in all cases affecting consuls. Congress, in creating the interior courts, assigned to them an exclusive jurisdiction in criminal cases over consuls. In 1816, a foreign consul was charged with the commission of an atrocious crime within the state of Pennsylvania, for which an indictment was found against him. He denied the jurisdiction of the state court, and was discharged. He still goes untried, laboring under an unmerited imputation if innocent, and if guilty, unpunished, which, if the doctrine here opposed is correct, is an unavoidable consequence.

Still, however, although these positions may be considered as sound, some serious objections remain for discussion.

1. In the inquiry, whether the courts of the United States possess jurisdiction of a criminal nature in any case not provided for by an act of congress, it has always been supposed that the common law of England was alone to be considered. Chase, J. says, "If the United States can for a moment be supposed to have a common law, it must, I presume, be that of England." [8]

Thus the attention has been confined to a part only of the general question; and if it is understood by courts, that they are only to decide whether the common law of England is in such cases to be the sole rule of decision, it is easy to account for some of the opinions that have been given. Both Chase, J. and Johnson, J. justly observe, that the common law of England has been gradually varied in the different states, and that there exists no uniform rule by which the United States could be governed in respect to it. The latter, with great truth and effect remarks, that if the power implied on the formation of any political body, to preserve its own existence and promote the end and object of its own creation, is applicable to the peculiar character of our Constitution, (which he declines to examine,) it is a principle by no means peculiar to the common law [of England.] "It is coeval probably with the first formation of a limited government, belongs to a system of universal law, and may as well support the assumption of many other powers, as those peculiarly acknowledged by the common law of England." [9]

We may account for most of the opposition in various parts of the Union from the question having been misunderstood. That the common law of England was kept in view, to a certain extent by the framers of the Constitution, even in criminal cases, and as such adopted by the people, cannot be doubted. The instances are numerous. Impeachment, treason, felony, breach of the peace, habeas corpus, the trial by jury, and many other phrases and appellations, derived from the common law of England, appear both in the original text and the amendments. But this, as justly observed by a learned jurist, [10] was not intended as a source of jurisdiction, but as a rule or mean for its exercise. In this sense alone we are to accept those technical terms, and by no means as evidence that if any common law was intended by the Constitution to be adopted as a rule of action, it was the common law of England.[83]

---

83 *The bulk of the United States Civil and Criminal laws originate from the English*

2. It is plausibly urged, that a system of law which defines crime, without appropriating punishment, possesses no efficacy and does not merit adoption, and it is inquired in what manner are offences against the law of nature to be punished.

The question is not without its intrinsic difficulty, and an answer cannot be attempted without some diffidence, but it is hoped that the following view will be satisfactory.

1. We may lay it down as an axiom, that in every system of law, whether express or implied, crime is held to be liable to punishment of some sort.

The mere sense of guilt, however unhappy it may render the offender, yields no compensation, and affords to security to society.

2. Punishment ought always to bear a just relation to the nature and degree of the offence. Positive law is sometimes arbitrary and unreasonably severe; but the united sense of the community, some of whom may commit, and all of whom may suffer from the commission of crimes, is generally apposite [appropriate] and reasonable. If there is any deviation from the strict measure of punishment, it is generally on the side of humanity.

3. Recurring, as far as we have materials, to the history of ancient law in Europe, for we cannot take Asia or Africa as our guides, we find that although the injured individual, or his nearest friends, were sometimes held to be entitled to take redress into their own hands, and pursue the offender by their own power; a practice so dangerous was gradually overruled, and punishment, rendered the act of the whole, afforded through the medium of the whole, satisfaction proportioned to the offence. [11]

4. In remote times, and in most countries, this satisfaction consisted in the forfeiture of something of value; we have to this affect the authority of Homer, Iliad, b. 9, v. 743. The price of blood discharged, the murderer lives." Of Tacitus, in respect to the ancient Germans, *"Luitur etiam homicidium certo armentorum ac pecorum numero,"* &c. homicide is also punished by the forfeiture of a certain number of cattle or sheep; and he adds, that those convicted of other crimes were fined in proportion, a part of which was paid to the prince, and part to him who was wronged, or to his relations. Imprisonment was added either to coerce payment, or as a further punishment.

Common Law. However, as Rawle points out, this may give English Common Law persuasive authority in American courts, the English Common Law does not have mandatory authority in American courts.

There was a time, says Beccaria, when all punishments were pecuniary. [12] Lord Kaimes lays down the same position, and it is a settled principle in the ancient law of England, that where an offence has been committed to which no specific punishment is affixed by statute, it is punishable by fine and imprisonments. [13]. Here then we have materials which laborious inquiry would probably increase, for ascertaining the nature of those punishments that by common consent preceded positive law. Their mildness ought not to lead us to reject them. It would be a sorry argument to say, that because a severe punishment cannot be inflicted, the offender shall not be punished at all. Judge Story truly remarks, [14] that it is a settled principle, that when an offence exists to which no specific punishment is affixed by statute, it is punishable by fine and imprisonment, but when he adds, that if treason had been left without punishment by an act of Congress, the punishment by fine and imprisonment must have attached to it; we must recollect that the power to declare the punishment being expressly given to congress, it seems to be taken out of the general principle that would otherwise be applicable.

On the whole, we arrive at the conclusion, that crimes committed against society have been at all times the subject of punishment of some sort; that independent of positive law, the forfeiture of property, or personal liberty, has been the general, though not perhaps the universal character of punishment; for a difference of manners will always have a strong influence on the extent of punishment, as the people are mild and peaceable or rugged and ferocious; and that the tribunals of justice in every case within their jurisdiction, are thus provided with a guide, which if found inadequate to the safety of society, may at any time be rendered more effectual by the legislative power.

It has been said, that to give it effect, the common law ought to have been expressly enacted as part of the Constitution. But how could this have been done? Should it have been described as the common law of England? It was not contemplated. The common law of any particular state in the Union? This would have been equally inadmissible. It could have been introduced in no other than some phrases as the following:

"The law of nature, or the just and rational obligations of men in a state of political society, "shall be the rule or decision in all cases not otherwise provided for." And surely it would have been deemed a most unnecessary declaration. It has been well observed that the attempt to enumerate the powers necessary and proper to call the general power into effect, would have involved a complete digest of laws on every subject to which the Constitution relates — accommodated not only to the existing state of things, but to all possible changes; for in every new application of a general power, the particular powers, which are the means of attaining the object, must often necessarily vary, although the object remains the same. [15]

In delivering the opinion of the Supreme Court in the United States v. Hudson and Goodwin, Judge Johnson observes, that it "is not necessary to inquire whether the general "government possesses the power of conferring on its courts a jurisdiction, in cases similar to the "present, it is enough that such jurisdiction has not been conferred by any legislative act, if it does "not result to these courts as a consequence of their creation." With great deference to an authority so respectable, it is submitted that if the preceding observations are correct, that jurisdiction has been expressly given by the act of September 24, 1789, which although repealed by the act of February 13, 1801, was revived by the act of March 8, 1802, and is now in full force. By this act the circuit courts are expressly invested with the cognizance, (the exclusive cognizance says the law,) of all crimes and offences cognizable under the authority of the United States, except where the laws of the United States shall otherwise direct. If the offences of which we have been speaking, arise under the Constitution, they must be cognizable under the authority of the United States, and are thus rendered cognizable in the circuit courts.

The same learned judge in a subsequent case, when he also delivered the opinion of the Supreme Court, most correctly drew from the Constitution itself, certain principles necessary to support the asserted jurisdiction of a legislative body to punish contempt against itself, which he justly observes involves the interest of the people.

"The interests and dignity of those who created the public functionaries, require the "exertion of the powers indispensable to the attainment of the ends of their creations." [16]

The question before the court was only on the jurisdiction of the house. The precise nature of the offence committed, did not appear on the face of the pleadings. It was observed by him, "that we are not to decide that this jurisdiction does not exist, because it is not expressly given. It "is true, that such a power, if it exists, must be derived from implication, and the genius and spirit "of our institutions are hostile to the exercise of implied powers. Had the faculties of man been "competent to the framing of a system in which nothing would have been left to implication, the "effort would undoubtedly have been made. But in the whole of our admirable Constitution, there "is not a grant of powers, which does not draw after it others not expressed, but vital to their "exercise, not substantive and independent, but auxiliary and subordinate."

Now we may be permitted to remark, that the jurisdiction thus raised and supported by necessary implication, could in this case, have operated only on those acts, which, by an implication equally necessary, were to be considered as offences. No act of congress has declared what shall constitute those offences. They must therefore essentially be, what are termed contempt, or breaches of privilege at common law. It was competent for the Supreme Court, (was it not incumbent on them?) to notice that the non-existence of any legislative provisions on the subject, rendered it impossible to justify an imprisonment by virtue of the speaker's warrant for a non-existing offence. But the observation is, that "the power to institute a prosecution must be "dependent on the power to punish. If the house of representatives possessed no power to punish "for contempt, the initiatory process issued in the operation of that authority, must have been "illegal; there was a want of jurisdiction to justify it." And the omission to take this ground, seems to support the argument excluding the necessity of a statutory provision.

On the same ground we may advert to the exercise of the power of impeachment. In neither of the cases already mentioned, were the acts charged on the parties accused, statutory offences. Yet the doctrine opposed in this work would render the power of impeachment a nullity, in all cases except the two expressly mentioned in the Constitution, treason and bribery; until congress pass laws, declaring what shall constitute the other "high crimes and misdemeanors."

And thus the question seems to be at rest in the contemplation of both these courts, for such they must be termed, when acting in those capacities, and both of them are courts from whose decision there is no appeal.

CHAPTER NOTES
XXIX

1. Act of September 24, 1789.

2. 3 Wheaton, 222. *Robertson v. Campbell.* 4 Wheaton, 414. *United States v. Howland.*

3. 3 Wheaton, *ubi supra*, and 3 Dallas, 425. Sims's lessee v. Irvine.

4. May 8, 1792. The language of the act is general. It speaks of the principles, rules, and usages "which belong to courts of equity as contra-distinguished from courts of common law."

5. It does not appear that this interesting question, though often discussed, has yet been definitively settled by the supreme court of the United States. It was first raised in the case of the *United States v. Warrell*, 2 Dall. 297, when Judge Peters dissented from Judge Chase. The clear and manly, though brief exposition of the opinion of the former, merits great attention. In the following year, 1799, in the case of the *United States v. Williams*, Chief Justice Ellsworth held that the common law of this country remained the same as it was before the revolution. Other decisions, not reported, are believed to have taken place. In the *United States v. M'Gill*, Judge Washington is represented to have said, that he had often so decided it, 4 Dall. 429. The case of the *United States v. Hudson and Goodwin*, came into the supreme court in 1812, it was not argued. In 1816 another case was brought up. The judge of the circuit court for the district of Massachusetts, maintaining a common law jurisdiction in opposition to the district judge, the case of the *United States v. Coolidge*, was removed according to the provisions of the judiciary bill into the supreme court. Unfortunately the attorney-general again declined the argument. Three of the seven judges observed that they did not consider the question as settled, but the court declared that although they would have been willing to hear the question discussed in solemn argument, yet, under the circumstances, they would not review their former decision or draw it into doubt. See 1 Wheaton, 415, and for the original case, 1 Gallison, 488. Two cases, earlier than any of these, *United States v. Ravara*, in 1792, and *United States v. Henfield*, in 1793, are passed over, because the question was not distinctly raised in either. And for the same reason no reliance is placed on the *United States v. Pickering*, on an impeachment before the senate in 1804, all the charges in which were purely at common law.

6. 1 Dallas, 41.

7. The case of De Long Champs in 1783, though not equally strong, was of the same nature. This was after the articles of confederation in which the intercourse with foreign powers was exclusively reserved to the United States. The defendant had assaulted the secretary of the legation from France. The indictment here was remarkable. It described the person assaulted as secretary of the legation of France — consul general to the United States, and consul to the State of Pennsylvania, and it concluded — "In violation of the law of nations, against the peace and dignity of the United "States, and of the commonwealth of Pennsylvania." It was learnedly argued; but the court without difficulty decided that they had jurisdiction, and that it was punishable as an offence against the law of nations. — 1 Dallas, 111. Some parts of the opinion of Chief Justice Kent in Lynch's case, 11 Johnson, 549, coincide with these remarks.

8. 2 Dallas, 384.

9. 7 Cranch, 32. *United States v. Hudson.* As this case was not argued by counsel, it does not distinctly appear why it was deemed by the court to depend on the common law of England, and why it should not have been taken up on the general principle alluded to by Judge Johnson. This spontaneous assumption of the ground of decision in the court below, confines the judgment of the supreme court to the question on the common law of England.
In the *United States v. Burr*, Chief Justice Marshall also refers to that "generally recognized and long established law, which forms the substratum of the laws of every state." (See Robertson's Report of the Trial of Aaron Burr.)
The Chief Justice of Pennsylvania, in a case in 5 Binney, 558, truly observes, that "every nation has its common law." And are not the United States a nation?

10. Mr. Duponceau in his late work on the jurisdiction of the courts of the United States.

11. See the elegant elucidation of this subject by Lord Kaimes in his historical law tracts.

12. C. 17, § 46.

13. See also Grotius, b. 1, c. 2. Puff. b. viii. c. 3, § II, to the same effect.

14. *United States v. Coolidge*, 1 Gallison, 488.

15. Federalist, No. 44.

16. 6 Wheaton, 204. Anderson v. Dunn.

SECTION VII
CHAPTERS XXX-XXXI

In the following section, Rawle explains why a judicial system is necessary at the State and Federal level in America. Rawle demonstrates why the written constitutions (State and Federal) are superior to the unwritten constitutions as in the British system.

Two points Rawle makes clear: one, the rights protected by a written constitution cannot be usurped (legally) at the will of a legislature, whereas, in the unwritten constitution of the British the rights of the people are at risk from acts of the legislature. The second point Rawle notes is that the State Constitutions preceded the Federal Constitution.

Rawle points out that even under the best of circumstances, errors can and will occur because the institutions in question are the making of imperfect men. He points out that all institutions of government are subject to abuse. Any form of government from a dictatorship to mass democracy (including republican systems) may lead to the misuse of power. As Rawle states, "Create a government of any kind, and invest its officers with powers so extensive and uncontrollable, and there will be the same abuses." Thus the need for an educated and aware citizenship to be stewards of the nation as they elect only people of quality to high office, thereby preventing the perversion of liberty into tyranny.

CHAPTER XXX.

OF CHECKS AND RESTRAINTS ON THE JUDICAL BRANCH.

FROM these general views of the judicial power, we collect that it is in the nature of a principle incorporated for useful purposes into the Constitution, vested in various agents, some of whom derive their authority from the United States, and some from the states, and holding their offices, as will appear by reference to those constitutions, on various tenures, but all possessing the right of deciding on the validity of a law.

If this power is in itself inordinate, if it is not consistent with the true interests of the people, it might have been excluded from, or carefully qualified in, the Constitution; but it has been established by the people on full deliberation; and a few additional reflections on its nature and utility may be admitted.

In the first place, we may observe, that a judicial power with such extensive attributes, is probably peculiar to this country. Where there is not a fixed and settled constitution, whether written or unwritten, which cannot be altered by the legislature, the judiciary has no power to declare a law unconstitutional. In such countries, the people are at the mercy of the legislature. The appeals which they may make to their constitutions are disregarded if they cannot be enforced, and the constitution possesses merely a nominal value. It tends indeed to excite discontents, by exhibiting rights that cannot be enjoyed, and promising restraints on government that may be broken with impunity.

The Constitution of the United States was not framed, in this respect, on ground new to us. The principle had been previously inserted in all the state constitutions then formed. It has been preserved in all those since established, and none of the alterations which we have heretofore noticed, have been extended to this point.

We may then inquire, in what mode or form of language it could have been excluded from the Constitution, and what would have been the effect of such exclusion. Being in itself a necessary incident to a regular and complete government, its existence is implied from the mere fact of creating such a government; it is intended that it should not be commensurate with all the powers and obligations of the government, or that it should not form any part of it whatever, express terms of qualification or exclusion would certainly be required.

Now it would be difficult to reconcile the minds of freemen, to whom was submitted the consideration of a scheme of government, professing to contain those principles by which a future legislature and executive were to be regulated, to any declarations that a subversion or abandonment of those principles, by either branch, and particularly by the legislature, should be liable to no resistance or control. The judicial power potentially existed before any laws were passed; it could not be without an object; that object, is at first the Constitution. As the legislature proceeds to act, the judicial power follows their proceedings. It is a corrective imposed by the Constitution on their acts. The legislature are not deceived or misled. Nothing indicates that they alone are to decide on the constitutionality of their own acts, or that the people who may be injured by such acts, are unprovided with any other defense than open resistance to them. But without an adequate power in the judiciary to the effect required, the people would either be driven to such resistance; obliged to wait till they could obtain redress through the exercise of their elective powers; or be compelled to patient submission.

The rights of the people are better secured by the general undefined judicial power, necessarily inferred from the general language of the Constitution itself, pre-existing in their own state constitutions, and never surrendered to the United States. In the last mentioned aspect, it would appear surprising that those who were most apprehensive of the self-increasing power of the general government, did not perceive the bulwark of their safety. The courts and the judges of every state possess, as before observed, the right to decide on the constitutionality of a law of their own state and of the United States. The principle itself, and not the mere tribunal, constitutes the public security. That such decisions are subject to the appellate jurisdiction heretofore spoken of, forms no objection to their usefulness. The object of this jurisdiction is to produce uniformity. Instead of reducing, it enhances the value, while it proves the universal bearing of the principle itself.

In the organization of this power thus salutary, thus necessary, is found the only difficulty. To render it wholly independent of the people, is objected to by many: to affect its necessary independence by the modes of creating and appointing its ministers, is liable to equal objections. In the first case, arbitrary and despotic proceedings are apprehended. It is supposed to be the natural disposition of man, when placed above control, to abuse his power, or, if no corrupt motives produce this consequence, there sometimes are found a laxity, a carelessness, a want of sufficient exertion and deliberate judgment in the exercise of it. On the other hand, if instead of availing himself of his own knowledge and capacity, the judge submits to be governed by the opinions of others; if he allows the desire to retain his office, the fear of giving offence, or the love of popularity, to form any part of the ingredients of his judgment, an equal violation of his trust is apparent. It is therefore not without anxiety that the patriotic mind endeavors so to regulate the organization of this all essential power, that it shall be safely steered between the two extremes.

In all governments retaining a semblance of the preservation of popular rights, it is believed that the structure of the judicial power ought to be founded on its independence. The tenure of office is therefore generally during good behavior. But in some of our state governments, judges are appointed for a term of years. In some, the appointments are made by the executive, in some by the legislative power. The mode of appointment is of little consequence as to the principle, if, when it has been made, the magistrate is independent of the further favor of the appointing power. The more important question is the condition and duration of the appointment. The condition of good behavior necessarily accompanies all judicial appointments, for whatever term they may be granted. There are none during pleasure in this country, although the case is otherwise as to some high judicial stations in England. [1] Cases of misbehavior are therefore to be provided against. Honest errors in judgment do not amount to misbehavior. The court of the last resort is to correct all those which take place in the previous tribunals. If this court shall itself be deemed to have committed an error, there can be no redress, because from the nature of things, there must be some point at which to stop: and it is better that an individual should sustain an injury, than that the whole system should be thrown into disorder.

This last resort may be differently constituted, but there must be some final mode of deciding.

On some occasions of dissatisfaction with the decisions of the supreme court, different modes of revising even their decisions have been suggested. The last of these known to the author has been to convert the senate into the final court of error and appeal.

Of their competency in a practical view, no doubt can be entertained, but of the benefit which the public would derive by their unavoidable suspension of legislative business, with other high functions devolved on them, while their time was occupied in the trial of causes, there would be much room for doubt.

But, however this ultimate tribunal may be constituted, it is still to be the last resort; and, since human infallibility can no where be found, it may also pronounce erroneous judgments for which there would be no redress.

In all these institutions we must therefore recognize the imperfection of man, and content ourselves with the intention to act rightly, although the decision, in the apprehension of many, may be wrong.

In some states, a power is, given to the executive authority on the application of a certain proportion of the legislature to remove a judge from office. Reasons will occur both for and against such a provision. If a judge should be incapacitated by infirmity. or age, or be otherwise, without any fault of his own, prevented from performing his duties, he would not be a proper subject for removal by impeachment; yet, where duties cannot be performed, the officer should not be continued. The incapacity should, however, be established in the specific case, and to lay down a general rule, that on the attainment of a certain age, the judge shall no longer be admitted to act, may withdraw from the service of the public a person capable of being highly useful to them. In New York the commission expires at the age of sixty years; in Connecticut at seventy years; and thus their constitutions seem to intend to impose laws on nature itself, or to drive from their own service men in whom may still reside the most useful faculties, improved by time and experience. The Constitution of the United States abstains from this error.

But the power of removal intended, in those states where it is found, to be exercised in cases of actual and not implied incapacity, may in practice be carried further, and if the representatives of the people hold the opinion that the proceedings of a judge are contrary to the public interests, an application for his removal may be made to the governor. If, for instance, he has decided that one of their laws is unconstitutional, and they retain a different opinion, or if his constructions of, and proceedings under a law not objectionable in itself, differ from their own views of the same subject, dissatisfaction with his conduct which may be very honestly felt, may occasion an address for his removal, not as a mode of avoiding or reversing his decisions, for that could not be the effect, but as an example to others, and perhaps in some degree, it might be calculated for a punishment to himself.

Now, laying aside all party considerations which sometimes may operate, perhaps unconsciously, with the best men, we must inquire into the principle on which such removal would be founded, and we shall find it to be that of setting up the judgment of the people through their representatives to correct the judgment of the judicial power.

If the Constitution of the particular state fairly admits of this construction, it is the will of the people, and must be obeyed. It is a control reserved to themselves over the general character of the judicial power, and to that extent impairs its absolute independence. In the absence of corrupt motives, which might justify an impeachment, it is the only mode of rectifying a course of erroneous judgments tending to produce public injury. But it is liable to the objection that those who thus undertake to decide, are seldom so well qualified for the task as those whose peculiar studies and occupation may be considered as having enabled them to judge. Another objection is, that removal in this manner being in every sense an evil, a fear of displeasing the legislature may always hover over the mind of the judge, and prevent his being the impartial 'and inflexible mediator between the legislature and the people, which the people intended he should be.

The advantages and disadvantages of the whole subject must have been duly considered by the framers of our Constitution, and the people at large have confirmed the result of their judgment.

There is, however, one power vested in the legislature, of which they cannot be deprived. They are authorized "from time to time" to ordain and establish tribunals inferior to the supreme court, and such courts they may at any time abolish. Thus, as before noticed, the act of 1801, establishing certain circuit courts was repealed in 1802, and the commissions granted to the judges were consequently avoided.

To this instance we may be permitted to refer, for the purpose of showing the high independence of all party considerations, that appertains to the character of a judge. The supreme court, which affirmed a decision by which the validity of the repealing act was established, [2] was at that time composed entirely of men politically adverse to that which, by a sudden revolution, had become the predominant party in the legislature. Yet the decision was unanimously given, one of the judges only being absent on account of ill-health. And such are the true nature and spirit of a judicial institution, that there can be no doubt that the same principle; the same entire repudiation of party spirit, would govern men of all political impressions, when required to act on similar occasions by the Constitution and their country. Party spirit seldom contaminates judicial functions.

On the whole, it seems that with the right to new model all the inferior tribunals, and thereby to vacate, the commissions of their judges, and with the power to impeach all judges whatever, a sufficient control is retained over the judiciary power for every useful purpose; that it is a branch of government which the people have the strongest motives to cherish and support, and that if they value and wish to preserve their Constitution, they ought never to surrender the independence of their judges.

CHAPTER NOTES
XXX

1. The lord chancellor, the judges of the courts of admiralty, vice-admiralty, &c.

2. *Stuart v. Laird*, 1 Cranch, 308.

CHAPTER XXXI.

OF CHECKS AND CONTROLS ON OTHER BRANCHES OF THE GOVERNMENT.

IS there any foundation for the position, that in a republic the people are naturally betrayed by those in whom they trust?

Is it true that personal, power and independence in the magistrate, being the immediate consequence of the favor of the people, they are under an unavoidable necessity of being betrayed? [1]

Were this objection well founded, we should shrink with horror from the formation of a republic. Let us examine how it is attempted to be supported.

The first postulate is, that those who are in possession of power, generally strive to enlarge it for their own advantage in preference to the public good. In those governments where no restraint on the conduct of public officers is provided, we see to what an extent this propensity has been sometimes carried. Rome is the favorite example adduced to support the proposition.

It was found impossible for the people of that state, ever, to have faithful defenders. Neither those whom they expressly chose, nor those whom some personal advantages enabled to govern the assemblies, were united to them by any common feeling of the same concern. The tribunes pursued with zeal and perseverance, no greater object than to procure admission to all the different dignities in the republic. To admit the plebeians to participate in offices previously confined to patricians, was considers a it great victory over the latter. The use they made of the power of the people was to increase prerogatives, which they falsely called the prerogatives of all, but which the tribunes and their friends alone were likely to enjoy. But it does not appear that they ever set bounds to the terrible power of the magistrates, or repressed that class of citizens who knew how to make their crimes pass unpunished, or to regulate and strengthen the judicial power; precautions without which men might struggle to the end of time, and never attain true liberty.

Such are the views taken of this great, but internally imperfect republic, and a general proposition is illogically deduced from a particular instance.

If a Constitution is so framed that official power becomes at once absolute and independent of law; if the magistrates who are to administer the law are authorized like the prætors [*a Roman magistrate ranking below a consul and having chiefly judicial duties*], to make it from time to time as they think proper, and if a competition is admitted among the public officers, as to who shall exercise the most authority, and he who succeeds the best, cannot be compelled by the people either to surrender or reduce it; the very appointment, in such case, tends to stimulate all the evil propensities, and create a dereliction of all the moral obligations of man. But it is an error to suppose, (if it is supposed,) that this is confined to republican forms. The distinction would only be in name. Create a government of any kind, and invest its officers with powers so extensive and uncontrollable, and there will be the same abuses. The only difference will be that in one case we shall say the people are oppressed; in the other that they are betrayed.

A knowledge of human nature, too perspicacious not to perceive the danger, and too cautious not to provide against it, dictated in the composition of our Constitution, those checks and balances on which its purity and continuance were calculated to depend. While all necessary power was granted, every sound precaution was adopted to prevent its abuse.

We have already considered the express restrictions on the legislature, and have seen that on some points they cannot legislate at all, and on many others they can act only to a limited extent; but a wider view may be now taken, and an examination of the entire context will fully exhibit a pervading principle, which, while it secures the due performance of public duty, prevents its abuse.

The legislature is in the first place restrained by a fixed and absolute Constitution, over which it has no sort of power. In wine countries, and in one of our own states, [2] the legislature laying their hands on the Constitution, may so mold it from time to time, as to give a sanction to measures not within its original contemplation. But the Constitution of the United States, the work of the people, alterable only by the people, possesses a sacred and intangible character in respect to the legislature. This is, therefore, the great restraint. When the legislature feels that it has no power unless the Constitution has given it, the mere shame of being defeated in any step which cannot be supported, compels it to look to the Constitution for its authority, and if it cannot find it there, to desist from the measure.[84]

Secondly, as this may not always be a sufficient restraint, the judicial power presents an effectual barrier against its excesses, the observations on which head need not be, repeated. But, as observed, the judicial power possesses no spontaneous motion — it must be called into action by the application of others either individuals, or constituted authorities, — and in the mean time, the obnoxious law may not only take its place in the statute book, but be injuriously acted upon. The third corrective therefore, is the hands of the people, who do not, as disingenuously remarked, [3] make no other use of their power than to give it away. The biennial election of the house of representatives, of which the people can by no artifice be deprived, secures to them the power of removing every member of that house who has shown, either an inability to comprehend, or an unwillingness to conform to the transcendent obligations of the Constitution, which he has sworn to support. Here, then, we have the protection and safety unknown to those countries where, either the legislature elect themselves, or enjoy an hereditary right, or where, although the representative principle may be nominally kept up, its exercise may be suspended or postponed at the pleasure of another part of the government.

It is true, that this mode of reforming the abuse, is not at first full and complete. The senate, which must have concurred in the unconstitutional law, is not renewed at the same period, but the Constitution, which for reasons heretofore assigned, conferred on this body a longer duration of office, has regulated the continuance of each senator, so that at the end of every two years one-third of the whole must be chosen anew. The sense of the people, indicated by a full change in the house of representatives, and by the change of one-third of the senate, could not be without effect, and in two years more it would be imperious and irresistible.

A further restraint, though less definite, yet not without considerable weight, may be conceived in the influence arising from the portion of sovereignty remaining in the states.

Although, to the full extent established by the Constitution, the

84 *At one time, acts of Congress were held up to the Constitution to ascertain if Congress had a right to legislate on that subject. But today, any act, law, rule, or regulation deemed necessary by the ruling elite in Washington, D.C. is automatically considered to be within the purview of Congress. But as Rawle explains, this has not always been the case nor was it the intent of the founding fathers.*

power of the legislature of the United States is superior to that of the states, yet in the smallest particular in which they pass beyond the true line, the power of the states is in full effect. The states will always maintain a reasonable jealousy on this subject.

In all matters not transferred to the general government, the rights and interests of the people are confided to the care of the state governments, and an anxiety to secure and defend them has been uniformly apparent in all the states. The desire of preserving harmony and order, nay, the very love of power, always more valuable where it is least resisted, will operate with great effect on the national legislature to prevent its falling into unnecessary collisions with the states. This consideration will have the greatest influence with the members of the senate, who, although they do not in any sense sit and act as states in a federative quality, and are not bound by instructions — yet cannot but look with much respect to, and feel a close connection with the legislature of the state that appoints them.

2dly. The fears of those theoretical writers, who have gratified themselves by lamenting the internal dangers of our republic, have been chiefly directed against the tendency of the executive authority to overpower the freedom of the people.

It is supposed that much is to be apprehended from the influence of an officer who has the power of appointing so many other officers, and who is entrusted with the management of the military force. It is true, they admit that as he has not exclusively the appointment to office, this influence is thereby somewhat diminished, but the recommendations proceeding from him alone, and the power of dismission being exclusively with him, the hope of the one, and the fear of the other, must confer on him an excessive and alarming influence. All these considerations may have weight, yet the evil consequences predicted are not likely to ensue.

The military force, as we have seen, is well regulated not only by the constitutional prohibition to provide for its support for a longer term than two years, but also by the power that congress have to shorten even that period, and by the great improbability that an American army would consent to substitute for regular subsistence and the approbation of their countrymen, the tumultuary and precarious exactions of internal warfare, and convulsions, personal dangers which must be certain, and eventual ruin from which they cannot be exempted. The influence supposed to arise in respect to the appointments to, or dismissions from office, can operate only in a narrow circle, and however far it might be carried, would not tend to the subversion of the government, or even to any material alteration of it, since the value of the offices would always depend on the preservation of the Constitution and the laws, and their emoluments could not be carried beyond their legal limits.

No person is eligible to the office of president before he attains the age of thirty-five years, nor unless he has been a resident within the United States for fourteen years.

The object of the latter provision is, that his habits and opinions shall be as much as possible purely American, but temporary absence on public business, and particularly on an embassy to a foreign nation, would not be an interruption of residence in the sense here affixed to it.

The senator must have attained the age of thirty years, and the members of the house of representatives the age of twenty-five years.

In some of the states, the chief executive magistrate is not again eligible, until an interval has elapsed, after having served a certain time. The Constitution of the United States, on the contrary, admits the same individual to be continued in office by re-election during his life.

The propriety of a rotation in office, has had some warm advocates. The chief arguments in its favor seem to be,

1. That it renders the people more secure in their rights against an artful and ambitious man. If it were impossible that the chief magistrate should be re-elected after serving for a given time, it would be in vain for him to concert plans and create an insidious influence for the promotion of his own continuance in power.

2. On an opposite principle, it is supposed that he would be more independent in the exercise of his office: when, knowing that he could not be re-elected to it, he would not be under the necessity of courting the popular favor.

And 3dly. It has occurred to the imaginations of some, that there would be no small danger that the great powers of Europe, being interested in having a friend in the president of the United States, would interpose in his election, and the dangers and misfortunes of Poland be renewed in America. [4]

In answer to these objections, it has been said with great truth and force:

1st. That one ill effect of the exclusion would be a diminution of the inducements to good behavior. Less zeal would be felt in the discharge of a duty, when the advantage of the station must be relinquished at a determinate period. The desire of reward is one of the strongest incentives of human conduct, and the best security for fidelity, is to make interest coincide with duty. Even the love of fame, the ruling passion of noble minds, prompting a man to plan and undertake arduous enterprises for the public benefit, which might require time to perfect them, would deter him from the undertaking, if he foresaw that he must quit the scene before he could accomplish the work, and commit it, together with his own reputation, to bands that might be unequal or unfriendly to the task.

2dly. Experience is the parent of wisdom, and highly desirable in the first magistrate of a nation. It would be injurious and absurd to declare, that as soon as it is acquired, its possessor shall be compelled to abandon the station in which he acquired it, and to which it is adapted.

3dly. A third ill effect of the exclusion would be, the banishing men from stations in which their presence might be of the greatest moment to the public interest on particular emergencies. An ordinance which prevents a nation from making use of its own citizens, in the manner best suited to peculiar exigencies and circumstances, must be unwise. Suppose, for instance, a war to exist, and the president then in place, peculiarly fitted by his military talents and experience to conduct it to advantage: to be obliged to exclude him from office, perhaps to substitute inexperience for experience, and thereby unhinge and set afloat the settled train of administration, might be of the greatest, detriment. [5]

The apprehension of the interference of foreign nations in regard to the office of president, unless he was at first elected for life, seems to be without foundation. While he is elected only for four years at a time, it is evident that it would be of no use to foreign powers to corrupt him, unless they can intimidate or corrupt those who elect him; but by the guarded provisions of the Constitution, it is impossible to know for a long time beforehand, who those electors will be. As, however, this mode of election has now become the act of the people, and the electors are merely nominal, the whole body of the people, or at least a majority of them, must be corrupted or intimidated, before such a scheme can succeed; a measure not very practicable by any foreign power. It is well known that in Poland, the king was elected, not by the people at large, but by an aristocratic class, small in number, and therefore accessible to foreign intrigues.

If it were desired by such powers to obtain an undue ascendancy in our government, the attempts would be made, not on the president, but on the members of the legislature, and particularly of the senate, but in no government is it recollected that a necessary rotation in office was ever imposed on the members of the legislature.

Down to the present moment, nothing in point of fact has occurred among us to excite a regret at the continued eligibility of the same individual. No undue influence has been practiced, and the voice of the people, sovereign in fact, as well as in theory, has been independently exercised, both in the continuance and in the removal of their public agents. The predominant feature of the American character, seems, in truth, to be that sort of good sense, which invariably leads to just distinctions between partial and general benefit. It is not pretended, that party ebullitions do not sometimes overpower the calm reflection of the community, but the illusions are temporary, and the sound judgment which never wholly departs from the entire body, ultimately recovers its ascendancy.

That universal phrenzy of the nation, of which Europe, both in ancient and modern times has exhibited instances, never found place with us. Temperate and self-collected in the most trying seasons, America always pursued a regular course, terminating in that security and peace, which violent agitations and tumultuous passions could not have procured. Their good sense displays itself in the utter rejection of personal influence, when the pursuits of the party are hostile to the general sentiment. What is believed to be for the public good, is never sacrificed to the views of any individual, however distinguished.

But there are certain legitimate restraints on the office of president, which remove from the people every cause of uneasiness in respect to it.

These restraints consist, in part, of those already mentioned in regard to the legislative bodies. In the first place, he is equally bound by the Constitution, and must feel the same interest in conforming to it, that is felt by those bodies. He has even less to do in respect to alterations of the Constitution than the two houses have. He cannot recommend to the people an amendment of it, and if the two houses resolve to submit one to them, his concurrence in their so doing is not required, [6] and perhaps would not be allowed.

Self-interest, (as just before observed,) is one of the strongest permanent influences of human action, and wherever it can be coupled with public duty, it affords great reason for believing that they will act in concert.

Now, if we consider that the president, being a single officer, without those combinations which may be formed by the members of the two houses; not at any time during his official existence, returning to and mixing with the mass of the people, and thereby to some extent enabled to deceive and mislead them; but whatever may personally be his social habits and republican simplicity, still separated from extensive practical intercourse by the very nature of his office; we shall at once perceive that all eyes being constantly fixed on him, his motions will always be scrupulously watched, and so much of the regular execution of his power as may be considered to depend on popular acquiescence, will be diminished, in proportion as he evinces a design to extend it beyond its constitutional bounds.

Nor would the supposed influence of the other executive officers support him in such cases. Compared with the mass of the people, their numbers are small, and their very dependence on him would render them suspected. But the interests of those officers would operate in another direction: as a willful infringement of the Constitution will naturally terminate in some way, in a destitution of the president's power, their interest would not be promoted by contributing to an event injurious to themselves, since his successor would of course manifest a deference to public opinion by removing all the promoters and participators of the preceding delinquency.

The Constitution may therefore be considered as having a still stronger hold on the president, than on the legislative body.

2dly. If, from its nature, any political or casual motives could have an effect on the judicial interposition when regularly called forth, it would seem that it would be exercised with more alacrity against a single officer, already become the subject of general suspicion or disapprobation, than against those acts which must be considered as the measures of the entire government.

But this is altogether an illegitimate view of the character of the judicial power and mode of action. On the contrary, the president, while laboring under public reprobation, would look forward to the judiciary, with a certain confidence that prejudice and error would find no room in the judgments by which the legality of his conduct would be decided.

This check upon him would therefore be the more complete by being unbiassed and certain.

3dly. But, as before observed in regard to the legislature, the opportunity for this judicial intervention in its common form, may be remote, and one transgression not resisted, may lead to another, till the accumulation becomes too heavy to be borne.

Then, the power of the people arises in its majesty, and through their appropriate organs, the house of representatives, the judicial power is appealed to in another, a most imposing and conclusive form.

The dignified tribunal which the Constitution has provided for the trial of impeachments, has now the eyes of the public immovably fixed on it. Guilt or innocence, not prejudice or party motives, form the ground of decision, and although the senate does not directly vacate or annul the illegal acts that have taken place, which are still left to the redress of the ordinary tribunals; it prevents the possibility of their being again committed by the same individual, and the probability of their being copied by another.

4thly. And so effectual are the disqualifications which the senate may pronounce, that if the people, subsequently imposed on and misled by the discarded president or his partisans, were inclined again to confide a public trust to him, it would not be in their power to do so. The sentence of the senate is immutable.

No similar caution, no analogous defense of the people against their own dangerous clemency or forgetfulness, are to be found elsewhere. The ostracism of Athens, the interdictions from fire and water of Rome, the disqualifications in sentences on impeachments in England, might all be repealed, and the party, however politically dangerous, be restored to his former rank.

It may be inquired, why the power of pardoning should be absolutely excluded in such a case as this? The answer has already been given. The safety of the people is the supreme law: their liberties properly regulated and secured are the cardinal objects of republican constitutions. Those who have evinced the capacity to abuse a public trust ought not to have a second opportunity to do so. If it were possible to remove the disqualification thus solemnly imposed, the state might be thrown into disorder; factions in favor of the delinquent be formed; contrary pretensions be warmly, perhaps forcibly asserted — and the bloody, civic contests of ancient Rome might be renewed on the polluted arena of a modern and a temperate republic. It is infinitely preferable that one man should be meritedly [justly] deprived of part of the rights and privileges of citizenship, than that the peace and happiness of the whole community should be endangered.

The sentence itself is at the utmost a mild one; but the object of it is still liable to the ordinary process of justice. If his crime should be of that high class which subjects him to the forfeiture of life, the president for the time being still possesses the power to prevent its infliction. The individual with the accumulated weight of two convictions, might safely be pardoned in respect to the second. He never could again become an object of public confidence.

To these views of the checks upon this office, we may add the power of the people, when the quadrennial period of election returns, to remove him, whose conduct, although it may not have amounted to actual delinquency, has excited even their suspicion.

Referring, without repeating it, to the last chapter, we may thus recognize in every part of the Constitution those cautious provisions, forming, adequate checks on every power it confers, restraining all from doing wrong, yet not productive of an inconvenient interference with each other when all do right; contributing to preserve a necessary purity and vigor, and rendering the mere distribution of power the means of correcting its abuse.

CHAPTER NOTES
XXXI

1. See this bold assertion and its feeble illustration, in Delolme, book 2, ch. ix.

2. The state of Maryland. The legislature of that state may alter or abolish any part of the Constitution or the bill of rights, provided the bill for that purpose is passed three months before a new election, and is confirmed by the general assembly at the first session after such election, the object of which proviso undoubtedly is to afford the people an opportunity to testify by the removal of the members a disapprobation of their measures.

3. By Delolme, in the chapter already referred to.

4. See debates in Virginia convention, vol. iii. p. 67.

5. Federalist, No. 72.

6. *Hollingsworth v. Virginia*, 3 Dallas, 378.

SECTION VIII-Appendix
CHAPTER XXXII

Chapter XXXII, dealing with the means by which a Sovereign State may secede from the Union, will no doubt, in today's world, be the most controversial chapter of Rawle's book. Controversial by today's standards but in Mr. Rawle's day and in the day of the framers of the Constitution, the right of secession was not viewed as an extreme or evil idea.

In the year 1825 when Rawle's first edition was published, it was reviewed by the North American Review, a politically orthodox publication in Boston, Massachusetts. In this review, Rawle's view on the constitutional right of a State to secede from the Union was not criticized. Why should it be? After all, the statesmen of New England had, at the Hartford Convention only a few years earlier, proclaimed the very right of secession which Rawle advocates in Chapter XXXII.

The early history of the United States was at the time of Rawle's book still fresh enough in the minds of Americans that it would have been difficult for a politically astute person to regard the right of secession as anything other than correct. The secession of the American Colonies from the Union with Great Britain, the secession of each State from the Articles of Confederation, and the accession of each State into the Union were actions providing proof enough of the correctness of the secession of one political society from another.

In its approximately 2,000-word review of Rawle's book, this Boston journal never issued a single word of protest about Rawle's view of the constitutional right of a State to secede from the Union. Rawle, a Pennsylvanian and a friend of both George Washington and Benjamin Franklin, was blessed by this Northern journal for his book, A View of the Constitution of the United States of America. It should be apparent to any open-minded person that the right of secession, being a constitutional right, is anything but treason. In the last chapter of his book, Rawle explains the correctness of this view.

For a more complete history of Rawle's book, and its use as a textbook at West Point Military Academy, the reader is directed to the Introduction to the annotation of this edition.

The last portion of Chapter XXXII is devoted to the text of President Washington's address. There are no fewer than six points that are clearly made in this famous address:

1. The name "American" is a shared name which belongs to all citizens in the national capacity. Acting for all the States, the Federal government is the sole representative for the States on the international stage. Although slight differences exist among the people of the States and of various regions, the defense of our common liberty and safety is the sole reason that American's exist in a national capacity.
2. The reasons why the Union should be guarded and preserved are listed by regions. Washington explains how each section would benefit from a common national government. No one region is given dominion over the others, but the protection of the safety and happiness of each would impel all to maintain the "indissoluble community of interest." The common interests of each region are the justification for the Union.
3. By a joint effort of all States, their mutual defense from "foreign attack and intrigues" is secured. At that time in American History, many European nations were still hoping to acquire territory in North America by subverting the United States and causing a breakup of the whole into smaller antagonistic parts. The joint effort of all the States in a common defense and a mutually agreeable Union was a guarantee against foreign intrigues or attack.
4. An overgrowth of the military establishment is warned against. Washington, with appropriate knowledge of history, feared for the liberty of the common people if a large military were available to suppress the people's right to free government. In Washington's day, the militia of each State was an integral part of the nation's defense. This militia was not part of the national government's regular army but was composed of civilian members of a State and, if necessary, called up for Federal service. (In no way can the National Guard be said to be a militia. The National Guard is part of the United States Army.) This citizen army was not to be feared, but a large "professional" army was considered to pose a potential danger to republican institutions.
5. The Union is viewed as the main prop of liberty; therefore, the love of liberty "ought to endure you to the preservation of the other [Union]." As John C. Calhoun said, "The Union! Next to our liberties, most dear." The Union was established to provide a bulwark and defense for our hard-won liberties. As James Madison stated in The Federalist No. 43, the reason for the formation of any govern-

mental institution is the "safety and happiness of a society." As Madison states, when this "safety and happiness" no longer exist, the sole reason for the existence of any institution is removed. The Union must, as Washington points out, be viewed as the stabilizing force for the maintenance of our liberty. If the Union becomes destructive to those ends, it forfeits its claim to legitimacy.

6. *Washington's final point expresses distrust of the patriotism of those who would weaken the bonds of a union calculated for the preservation of liberty.*

CHAPTER XXXII.

OF THE PERMANENCE OF THE UNION.

Quassata respublica multa perderet et ornamenta dignitatis et præsidia stabilitatis suæ. Oratio pro Marcello. [A shattered republic with many trappings might destroy the defenses of ones dignity and stability. Spoken on behalf of Marcellus.]

HAVING thus endeavoured to delineate the general features of this peculiar and invaluable form of government, we shall conclude with adverting to the principles of its cohesion, and to the provisions it contains for its own duration and extension.

The subject cannot perhaps be better introduced than by presenting in its own words an emphatical clause in the Constitution.

"The United States shall guarantee to every state in the Union a republican form of government, shall protect each of them against invasion, and on application of the legislature, or of the executive when the legislature cannot be convened, against domestic violence."

The Union is an association of the people of republics;[85] its preservation is calculated to depend on the preservation of those republics. The people of each pledge themselves to preserve that form of government in all. Thus each becomes responsible to the rest, that no other form of government shall prevail in it, and all are bound to preserve it in every one.

But the mere compact, without the power to enforce it, would be of little value. Now this power can be no where so properly lodged, as in the Union itself. Hence, the term guarantee, indicates that the United States are authorized to oppose, and if possible, prevent every state in the Union from relinquishing the republican form of government, and as auxiliary means, they are expressly authorized and required to employ their force on the application of the constituted authorities of each state, "to repress domestic violence." If a faction

85 *Note: Rawle refers to the Union as "an association of the people of republics." In other places, page 107, "the great compound commonwealth." He never refers to the Union as a singular entity. The United States was created as a Republic of Sovereign States, not a single, supreme, nation ruled over by elites in Washington, DC.*

should attempt to subvert the government of a state for the purpose of destroying its republican form, the paternal power of the Union could thus be called forth to subdue it.

Yet it is not to be understood, that its interposition would be justifiable, if the people of a state should determine to retire from the Union, whether they adopted another or retained the same form of government, or if they should, with the, express intention of seceding, expunge the representative system from their code, and thereby incapacitate themselves from concurring according to the mode now prescribed, in the choice of certain public officers of the United States.

The principle of representation, although certainly the wisest and best, is not essential to the being of a republic, but to continue a member of the Union, it must be preserved, and therefore the guarantee must be so construed. It depends on the state itself to retain or abolish the principle of representation, because it depends on itself whether it will continue a member of the Union. To deny this right would be inconsistent with the principle on which all our political systems are founded, which is, that the people have in all cases, a right to determine how they will be governed.

This right must be considered as an ingredient in the original composition of the general government, which, though not expressed, was mutually understood, and the doctrine heretofore presented to the reader in regard to the indefeasible nature of personal allegiance, is so far qualified in respect to allegiance to the United States. It was observed, that it was competent for a state to make a compact with its citizens, that the reciprocal obligations of protection and allegiance might cease on certain events; and it was further observed, that allegiance would necessarily cease on the dissolution of the society to which it was due.

The states, then, may wholly withdraw from the Union, but while they continue, they must retain the character of representative republics. Governments of dissimilar forms and principles cannot long maintain a binding coalition. "Greece," says Montesquieu, "was undone as soon as the king of Macedon obtained a seat in the amphictyonic council." [1] It is probable, however, that the disproportionate force as well as the monarchical form of the new confederate had its share of influence in the event. But whether the historical fact supports the theory or not, the principle in respect to ourselves is unquestionable.

We have associated as republics. Possessing the power to form monarchies, republics were preferred and instituted. The history of the ancient, and the state of the present world, are before us. Of modern republics, Venice, Florence, the United Provinces, Genoa, all but Switzerland have disappeared. They have sunk beneath the power of monarchy, impatient at beholding the existence, of any other form than its own. An injured province of Turkey, recalling to its mind the illustrious deeds of its ancestors, has ventured to resist its oppressors, and with a revival of the name of Greece, a hope is entertained of the permanent institution of another republic. But monarchy stands by with a jealous aspect, and fearful lest its own power should be endangered by the revival of the maxim, that sovereignty can ever reside in the people, affects a cold neutrality, with the probable anticipation that it will induce to barbarian success. Yet that gallant country, it is trusted, will persevere. An enlightened people, disciplined through necessity, and emboldened even by the gloom of its prospects, may accomplish what it would not dare to hope. [2]

This abstract principle, this aversion to the extension of republican freedom, is now invigorated and enforced by an alliance avowedly for the purpose of overpowering all efforts to relieve mankind from their shackles. It is essentially and professedly the exaltation of monarchies over republics, and even over every alteration in the forms of monarchy, tending to acknowledge or secure the rights of the people. The existence of such a combination warrants and requires that in some part of the civilized world, the republican system should be able to defend itself. But this would be imperfectly done, by the erection of separate, independent, though contiguous governments. They must be collected into a body, strong in proportion to the firmness of its union; respected and feared in proportion to its strength. The principle on which alone the Union is rendered valuable, and which alone can continue it, is the preservation of the republican form.

In what manner this guaranty shall be effectuated is not explained, and it presents a question of considerable nicety and importance.

Not a word in the Constitution is intended to be inoperative, and one so significant as the present was not lightly inserted. The United States are therefore bound to carry it into effect whenever the occasion arises, and finding as we do, in the same clause, the engagement to protect each state against domestic violence, which can only be by the arms of the Union, we are assisted in a due construction of the means of enforcing the guaranty. If the majority of the people of a state deliberately and peaceably resolve to relinquish the republican form of government, they cease to be members of the Union. If a faction, an inferior number, make such an effort, and endeavor to enforce it by violence, the case provided for will have arisen, and the Union is bound to employ its power to prevent it.

The power and duty of the United States to interfere with the particular concerns of a state are not, however, limited to the violent efforts of a party to alter its constitution. If from any other motives, or under any other pretexts, the internal peace and order of the state are disturbed, and its own powers are insufficient to suppress the commotion, it becomes the duty of its proper government to apply to the Union for protection. This is founded on the sound principle that those in whom the force of the Union is vested, in diminution of the power formerly possessed by the state, are bound to exercise it for the good of the whole, and upon the obvious and direct interest that the whole possesses in the peace and tranquility of every part. At the same time it is properly provided, in order that such interference may not wantonly or arbitrarily take place; that it shall only be, on the request of the state authorities: otherwise the self-government of the state might be encroached upon at the pleasure of the Union, and a small state might fear or feel the effects of a combination of larger states against it under color of constitutional authority; but it is manifest, that in every part of this excellent system, there has been the utmost care to avoid encroachments on the internal powers of the different states, whenever the general good did not imperiously require it.

No form of application for this assistance is pointed out, nor has been provided by any act of congress, but the natural course would be to apply to the president, or officer for the time being, exercising his functions. No occasional act of the legislature of the United States seems to be necessary, where the duty of the president is pointed out by the Constitution, and great injury might be sustained, if the power was not promptly exercised.

In the instance of foreign invasion, the duty of immediate and unsolicited protection is obvious, but the generic term invasion, which is used without any qualification, may require a broader construction.

If among the improbable events of future times, we shall see a state forgetful of its obligation to refer its controversies with another state to the judicial power of the Union, endeavor by force to redress its real or imaginary wrongs, and actually invade the other state, we shall perceive a case in which the supreme power of the Union may justly interfere; perhaps we may say is bound to do so.

The invaded state, instead of relying merely on its own strength for defense, and instead of gratifying its revenge by retaliation, may prudently call for and gratefully receive the strong arm of the Union to repel the invasion, and reduce the combatants to the equal level of suitors in the high tribunal provided for them. In this course, the political estimation of neither state could receive any degradation. The decision of the controversy would only be regulated by the purest principles of justice, and the party really injured, would be certain of having the decree in its favor carried into effect.

It rests with the Union, and not with the states separately or individually, to increase the number of its members. [3] The admission of another state can only take place on its own application. We have already seen, that in the formation of colonies under the denomination of territories, the habit has been, to assure to them their formation into states when the population should become sufficiently large. On that event, the inhabitants acquire a right to assemble and form a constitution for themselves, and the United States are considered as bound to admit the new state into the Union, provided its form of government be that of a representative republic. This is the only check or control possessed by the United States in this respect.

If a measure so improbable should occur in the colony, as the adoption of a monarchical government, it could not be received into the Union, although it assumed the appellation of a state, but the guaranty of which we have spoken, would not literally apply — the guaranty is intended to secure republican institutions to states, and does not in terms extend to colonies. As soon, however, as a state is formed out of a colony, and admitted into the Union, it becomes the common concern to enforce the continuance of the republican form. There can be no doubt, however, that the new state may decline to apply for admission into the Union but it does not seem equally clear, that if its form of government coincided with the rules already mentioned, its admission could be refused. The inhabitants emigrate from the United States, and foreigners are permitted to settle, under the express or implied compact, that when the proper time arrives, they shall become members of the great national community, without being left to an exposed and unassisted independence, or compelled to throw themselves into the arms of a foreign power. It would seem, however, that the constitution adopted, ought to be submitted to the consideration of congress, but it would not be necessary that this measure should take place at the time of its formation, and it would be sufficient if it were presented and approved at the time of its admission. The practice of congress has not, however, corresponded with these positions, no previous approbation of the constitution has been deemed necessary.

It must also be conceded, that the people of the new state retain the same power to alter their constitution, that is enjoyed by the people of the older states, and provided such alterations are not carried so far as to extinguish the republican principle, their admission is not affected.

The secession of a state from the Union depends on the will of the people of such state.[86] The people alone as we have already seen, bold the power to alter their constitution. The Constitution of the United States is to a certain extent, incorporated into the constitutions or the several states by the act of the people. The state legislatures have only to perform certain organic operations in respect to it. To withdraw from the Union comes not within the general scope of their delegated authority. There must be an express provision to that effect inserted in the state constitutions. This is not at present the case with any of them, and it would perhaps be impolitic to confide it to them. A matter so momentous, ought not to be entrusted to those who would have it in their power to exercise it lightly and precipitately upon sudden dissatisfaction, or causeless jealousy, perhaps against the interests and the wishes of a majority of their constituents.

But in any manner by which a secession is to take place, nothing is more certain than that the act should be deliberate, clear, and unequivocal. The perspicuity and solemnity of the original obligation require correspondent qualities in its dissolution. The powers of the general government cannot be defeated or impaired by an ambiguous or implied secession on the part of the state, although a secession may perhaps be conditional. The people of the state may have some

86 *Rawle teaches that the decision of a sovereign state to withdraw from the Union is dependent upon the will of the people "of such state." The will of those who hold the reins-of-power in the Federal government is not a legitimate part of a State's decision to secede from the Union. Consent to accede to the Union was freely given by the people of the state and the decision to withdraw their consent, the decision to secede, can only be legitimately made by the people "of such state." As Jefferson Davis noted, "The alternative to secession is coercion." Davis, Jefferson,* Rise and Fall of the Confederate Government, *Vol. 1, (1881, William Mayes Coats, Nashville, TN: circa 1980), 177.*

reasons to complain in respect to acts of the general government, they may in such cases invest some of their own officers with the power of negotiation, and may declare an absolute secession in case of their failure. Still, however, the secession must in such case be distinctly and peremptorily declared to take place on that event, and in such case — as in the case of an unconditional secession, — the previous ligament with the Union, would be legitimately and fairly destroyed. But in either case the people is the only moving power.

A suggestion relative to this part of the subject has appeared in print, which the author conceives to require notice.

It has been laid down that if all the states, or a majority of them, refuse to elect senators, the legislative powers of the Union will be suspended. [4]

Of the first of these supposed cases there can be no doubt. If one of the necessary branches of legislation is wholly withdrawn, there can be no further legislation, but if a part, although the greater part of either branch should be withdrawn it would not affect the power of those who remained.

In no part of the Constitution is a specific number of states required for a legislative act. Under the articles of confederation the concurrence of nine states was requisite for many purposes. If five states had withdrawn from that Union, it would have been dissolved. In the present Constitution there is no specification of numbers after the first formation. It was foreseen that there would be a natural tendency to increase the number of states with the increase of population then anticipated and now so fully verified. It was also known, though it was not avowed, that a state might withdraw itself. The number would therefore be variable.

In no part of the Constitution is there a reference to any proportion of the states, except in the two subjects of amendments, and of the choice of president and vice-president.

In the first case, two-thirds or three-fourths of the several states is the language used, and it signifies those proportions of the several states that shall then form the Union.

In the second, there is a remarkable distinction between the choice of president and vice president, in case of an equality of votes for either.

The house of representatives, voting by states, is to select one of the three persons having the highest number, for president, a quorum for this purpose shall consist of a member or members from two-thirds of the states, and a majority of all the states shall be necessary for the choice.

The senate not voting by states, but by their members individually, as in all other cases, selects the vice president from the two persons having the highest number on the list. A quorum for this purpose shall consist of two-thirds of the whole number of senators, and a majority is sufficient for the choice.

Now, if by the omission of the legislators of more than one third of the states, there were no senators from such states, the question would arise whether the quorum is predicated of the states represented, or of all the states, whether represented or not.

The former opinion is most consistent with the general rule, that we should always prefer a construction that will support, to one that has a tendency to destroy an instrument or a system. Other causes than design on the part of a state legislature, may be imagined to occasion some states to be unrepresented in the senate at the moment.

It seems to be the safest, and is possibly the soundest construction, to consider the quorum as intended to be composed of two-thirds of the then existing senators.

But we may pursue the subject somewhat further.

To withdraw from the Union is a solemn, serious act. Whenever it may appear expedient to the people of a state, it must be manifested in a direct and unequivocal manner. If it is ever done indirectly, the people must refuse to elect representatives, as well as to suffer their legislature to re-appoint senators. The senator whose time had not yet expired, must be forbidden to continue in the exercise of his functions.

But without plain, decisive measures of this nature, proceeding from the only legitimate source, the people, the United States cannot consider their legislative powers over such states suspended, nor their executive or judicial powers any way impaired, and they would not be obliged to desist from the collection of revenue within such state.

As to the remaining states among themselves, there is no opening for a doubt.

Secessions may reduce the number to the smallest integer admitting combination. They would remain united under the same principles and regulations among themselves that now apply to the whole. For a state cannot be compelled by other states to withdraw from the Union, and therefore, if two or more determine to remain united, although all the others desert them, nothing can be discovered in the

Constitution to prevent it.

The consequences of an absolute secession cannot be mistaken, and they would be serious and afflicting.

The seceding state, whatever might be its relative magnitude, would speedily and distinctly feel the loss of the aid and countenance of the Union. The Union losing a proportion of the national revenue, would be entitled to demand from it a proportion of the national debt. It would be entitled to treat the inhabitants and the commerce of the separated state, as appertaining to a foreign country. In public treaties already made, whether commercial or political, it could claim no participation, while foreign powers would unwillingly calculate, and slowly transfer to it, any portion of the respect and confidence borne towards the United States.

Evils more alarming may readily be perceived. The destruction of the common hand would be unavoidably attended with more serious consequences than the mere disunion of the parts.

Separation would produce jealousies and discord, which in time would ripen into mutual hostilities, and while our country would be weakened by internal war, foreign enemies would be encouraged to invade with the flattering prospect of subduing in detail, those whom, collectively, they would dread to encounter.

Such in ancient times was the fate of Greece, broken into numerous independent republics. Rome, which pursued a contrary policy, and absorbed all her territorial acquisitions in one great body, attained irresistible power.

But it may be objected, that Rome also has fallen. It is true; and such is the history of man. Natural life and political existence alike give way at the appointed measure of time, and the birth, decay, and extinction of empires only serve to prove the tenuity and illusion of the deepest schemes of the statesman, and the most elaborate theories of the philosopher. Yet it is always our duty to inquire into, and establish those plans and forms of civil association most conducive to present happiness and long duration: the rest we must leave to Divine Providence, which hitherto has so graciously smiled on the United States of America.

We may contemplate a dissolution of the Union in another light, more disinterested but not less dignified, and consider whether we are not only bound to ourselves but to the world in general, anxiously and faithfully to preserve it.

The first example which has been exhibited of a perfect self-government, successful beyond the warmest hopes of its, authors, ought never to be withdrawn while the means of preserving it remain.

If in other countries, and particularly in Europe, a systematic subversion of the political rights of man shall gradually overpower all rational freedom, and endanger all political happiness, the failure of our example should not be held up as a discouragement to the legitimate opposition of the sufferers; if, on the other hand, an emancipated people should seek a model on which to frame their own structure; our Constitution, as permanent in its duration as it is sound and splendid in its principles, should remain to be their guide.

In every aspect therefore which this great subject presents, we feel the deepest impression of a sacred obligation to preserve the union of our country; we feel our glory, our safety, and our happiness, involved in it; we unite the interests of those who coldly calculate advantages with those who glow with what is little short of filial affection; and we must resist the attempt of its own citizens to destroy it, with the same feelings that we should avert the dagger of the parricide.

This work cannot perhaps be better concluded than with a quotation from the valedictory address of one whose character stamps inestimable value on all that lie has uttered, and whose exhortations on this subject, springing from the purest patriotism and the soundest wisdom, ought never to be forgotten or neglected. [5]

In this address Washington expressed himself as follows: [87]

"The name of American, which belongs to you in your national capacity, must always exalt "the just pride of patriotism, more than any appellation derived from local discriminations. With "slight shades of difference, you have the same religion, manners, habits, and political principles "— you have in a common cause fought and triumphed together; the independence and liberty you "possess, are the work of joint counsels, and joint efforts, of common dangers, sufferings, and "successes.

"But these considerations, however powerfully they address themselves to your sensibility, "are greatly outweighed by those which apply more immediately to your interest. Here every "portion of our

87 *As President Washington leaves office, he gives his fellow countrymen sound advice regarding the Union. He notes that North, South, East, and West are bound together by the mutual benefits arising from their Union. It is the mutuality of benefits that held the original and legitimate Union together. Such a Union was a free, happy and prosperous Union — all sharing both benefits and burdens equally. Lincoln's Union was pinned together by bloody bayonets.*

country finds the most commanding motives for carefully guarding and preserving "the union of the whole.

"The North in an unrestrained intercourse with the South, protected by the equal laws of a "common government, finds in the productions of the latter, great additional resources of maritime "and commercial enterprise, and precious materials of manufacturing industry.

"The South, in the same intercourse, benefiting by the same agency of the North, sees its "agriculture grow and its commerce expand. Turning partly into its own channels the seamen of "the North, it finds its particular navigation invigorated, and while it contributes in different ways "to nourish and increase the general mass of the national navigation, it looks forward to the "protection of a maritime strength, to which itself is unequally adapted. The East in a like "intercourse with the West, already finds, and in the progressive improvement of interior "communications by land and water, will more and more find, a valuable vent for the commodities "which it brings from abroad or manufactures at home. The West derives from the East supplies "requisite to its growth and comfort, and what is perhaps of still greater consequence, it must of "necessity owe the secure enjoyment of indispensable outlets for its own productions, to the "weight, influence, and the future maritime strength of the Atlantic side of the Union, directed by "an indissoluble community of interest as one nation. Any other tenure by which the West can hold "this essential advantage, whether derived from its own separate strength, or from an apostate and "unnatural connection with any foreign power, must be intrinsically precarious.

"While, then, every part of our country thus feels an immediate and particular interest in "union, all the parts combined cannot fail to find in the united mass of means and efforts, greater "strength, greater resource, proportionably greater security from external danger, a less frequent "interruption of their peace by foreign nations, and what is of inestimable value, they must derive "from union an exemption from those broils and wars between themselves which so frequently "afflict neighboring countries, not tied together by the same government, which their own "rivalships alone would be sufficient to produce, but which opposite foreign alliances, attachments, "and intrigues, would stimulate and embitter. Hence, likewise, they will avoid the necessity of "those overgrown military establishments, which, under any form of government are inauspicious "to liberty, and which are to be regarded as particularly hostile to republican liberty. In this sense, "it is that your union ought to be considered as a main prop of your liberty, and that the love of the "one ought to endear to you the preservation of the other.

"These considerations speak a persuasive language to every reflecting and virtuous mind, "and exhibit the continuance of the Union as a primary object of patriotic desire. Is there a doubt "whether a common government can embrace so large a sphere? Let experience solve it. To listen "to mere speculation in such a case were criminal. We are authorized to hope that a proper "organization of the whole, with the auxiliary agency of governments for the respective "subdivisions, will afford a happy issue to the experiment. With such powerful and obvious "motives to union, affecting all parts of our country, while experience shall not have demonstrated "its impracticability, there will always be reason to distrust the patriotism of those who in any "quarter may endeavor to weaken its hands."

CHAPTER NOTES
XXXII

1. Federalist, No. 43.

2. Since this passage was written, the affairs of Greece have assumed somewhat of a different aspect. The Turkish fleet has been accidentally destroyed by the combined powers, and the French have landed a body of men, with an apparent intention to promote the independence of this afflicted country.

3. There is, however, a restriction on this point, which must be noticed. No new state can be formed or erected within the jurisdiction of any other state, nor can any state be formed by the junction of two or more states or parts of states, without the consent of the legislatures of the states concerned as well as of congress.

4. It is with great deference that the author ventures to dissent from this part of the opinion of the learned chief justice of the Supreme Court in the, case of *Cohen v. Virginia*, 6 Wheaton, 390. it was not the point in controversy, and seems to have been introduced in that flow of luminous discussion for which he is so remarkable, by way of an-

swer to part of the arguments of counsel. Every thing that falls from such a quarter excites to reflection, and the opinion having gone forth to the world, it seems a duty on him who professes to take a general view of the Constitution, to notice whatever may in his apprehension amount to the slightest error in principle.

5. Some doubts having been entertained whether this address was not written by another hand, it is due to the memory of this great man to mention, that by the researches of The Pennsylvania Historical Society, it has been fully ascertained that it was the entire work of the president.

APPENDIX, NO. I.

PERHAPS the following view of the elections of president and vice president, since the retirement of President Washington, may not be uninteresting.

In 1796, the votes were given under the first system, as heretofore explained. The highest in votes became the president, and the next highest, the vice president.

1796

John Adams, who had been vice president eight years had	71 votes
Thomas Jefferson	68 votes
Thomas Pinckney	59 votes
Arron Burr	30 votes

1800

Thomas Jefferson	73 votes
Arron Burr	73 votes
John Adams	64 votes
Thomas Pinckney	63 votes

The equality of the votes for Mr. Jefferson and Mr. Burr produced an arduous contest in the house, the history of which is worth preservation.

The declaration of the votes took place in the senate chamber, on Wednesday, the 11th of February. After the declaration that a choice had not been made by the electors, and that it devolved on the house of representatives, the house convened in its own chamber, and furnished seats for the senate, as witnesses. The house had previously adopted rules, that it should continue to ballot, without interruption by other business, and should not adjourn, but have a permanent session until the choice be made; and that the doors of the house shall be closed during the balloting, except against the officers of the house.

The following was directed to be the mode of balloting:

Each state had a ballot box in which the members belonging to it, having previously appointed a teller, put the votes of the state, the teller on the part of the United States having then counted the votes, duplicates of the rest were put by him into two general ballot boxes. Tellers being nominated by each state for the purpose of examining the general ballot boxes, they were divided into two parts, of whom one examined one of the general ballot boxes, and the other examined the other. Upon comparing the result, and finding them to agree, the votes were stated to the speaker, who declared them to the house.

The number of states was at that time 16 — nine were necessary to a choice. On the first ballot Mr. Jefferson had eight states, Mr. Burr six, and two were divided.

The first ballot took place about 4 o'clock, P.M. Seven other ballots, with similar results succeeded, when a respite took place, during which the members retired to the lobbies and took refreshment. At three o'clock in the morning of the 12th, two other ballots took place, and at 4 o'clock in the morning, the twenty-first trial. At 12 at noon, of the 12th, the twenty-eighth ballot took place, when the house adjourned to the next day, having probably, in secret session, dispensed with the rule for the permanent session. On Friday, the 13th, the house proceeded to the thirtieth ballot without a choice, and again adjourned to the next day. On Saturday, the 14th, the ballotings had the same result. On Tuesday, the 17th, at the thirty-sixth ballot, the speaker declared at one o'clock, that Mr. Jefferson was elected, having the votes of New York, New Jersey, Pennsylvania, Virginia, Kentucky, Georgia, Tennessee, North Carolina, Maryland, four votes for Jefferson and four blanks, and Vermont one vote for Jefferson and one blank vote. Thus ended the contest, and it merits the attention of the enemies of republican institutions, who are fond of anticipating the occurrence of tumult and violence on such occasions. The decorum with which the whole was conducted, and the ready and peaceable acquiescence of the minority, evince both the sound texture of the Constitution, and the true character of the American people.

The election in 1804, was under the present system —

1804

Thomas Jefferson	162 votes
Charles C. Pinckney	44 votes
George Clinton for vice president	162 votes
Rufus King	14 votes

1808

James Madison for president	122 votes
Charles C. Pinckney	47 votes
George Clinton for vice president	113 votes
Rufus King	47 votes

1812

James Madison for president	128 votes
DeWitt Clinton	89 votes
Elbridge Gerry for vice president	128 votes
Jared Ingersoll	57 votes

1816

James Monroe for president	183 votes
Rufus King	34 votes
Daniel D. Tompkins for vice president	113 votes

The scattering votes in the above statements are not given.

1824

The votes given were as follows – for

Andrew Jackson as president	99 votes
John Quincy Adams	84 votes
William H. Crawford	41 votes
Henry Clay	37 votes

Of whom the three first were returned to the house, and no one of them having a majority of the whole number of votes, the selection devolved upon the house of representatives, and it terminated in the choice of Mr. Adams.

We annex a statement, to explain the manner in which this constitutional power is exercised, by which it will be seen, that the votes of a majority of the members of each state constitute the vote of the state.

States	Adams	Jackson	Crawford
Maine	7	--	--
New Hampshire	6	--	--
Vermont	5	--	--
Massachusetts	12	--	--
Connecticut	6	--	--
Rhode Island	2	--	--
New York	18	2	14
New Jersey	1	5	--
Pennsylvania	1	25	--
Delaware	--	--	1
Maryland	5	3	1
Virginia	1	1	19
North Carolina	1	2	10
South Carolina	--	9	--

Georgia	--	--	7
Alabama	--	3	--
Missouri	1	--	--
Indiana	--	3	--
Mississippi	--	1	--
Tennessee	--	9	--
Kentucky	8	4	--
Ohio	10	2	2
Illinois	1	--	--
Louisiana	2	1	--

Thus 13 states voted for Adams, 7 for Jackson, and 4 for Crawford. John C. Calhoun was elected vice president by a great majority of the electoral colleges.

In the election of 1828, the great majority of votes, in favor of Andrew Jackson, rendered a recourse to the house of representatives unnecessary.

Of the 261 electors, 178 voted for General Jackson and 83 for Mr. Adams. John C. Calhoun obtained 171 votes for vice president, 83 were given for Richard Rush, and 7 for William Smith of South Carolina.

APPENDIX, NO. II.

IN page 75 [*page 95 this edition*] notice is taken of the difficulties under which congress labored during the confederation, in respect to enforcing the observance of treaties, and the letter from congress to the several states prepared by Mr. Jay is referred to.

As an historical document valuable in every respect, we here insert it: —

"Friday, April 13, 1787.

"The secretary for foreign affairs, having in pursuance of an order of congress, reported the draught of a letter to the states, to accompany the resolutions passed the 21st day of March, 1787: the same was taken into consideration, and unanimously agreed to as follows:

"SIR — Our secretary for foreign affairs has transmitted to you copies of, a letter to him, from our minister at the court of London, of the 4th day of March, 1786, and of the papers mentioned to have been enclosed with it.

"We have deliberately and dispassionately examined and considered the several facts and matters urged by Britain, as infractions of the treaty of peace on the part of America, and we regret that in some of the states, too little attention appears to have been paid to the public faith pledged by that treaty.

"Not only the obvious dictates of religion, morality and national honor, but also the first principles of good policy, demand a candid and punctual compliance with engagements constitutionally and fairly made.

"Our national Constitution having committed to us the management of the national concerns with foreign states and powers, it is our duty to take care that all the rights which they ought to enjoy within our jurisdiction by the laws of nations and the faith of treaties, remain inviolate. And it is also our duty to provide that the essential interests and peace of the whole confederacy, be not impaired or endangered by deviations from the line of public faith, into which any of its members may from whatever cause be unadvisedly drawn.

"Let it be remembered, that the thirteen independent sovereign states have, by express delegation of power, formed and vested in us a general though limited sovereignty, for the general and national purposes specified in the confederation. In this sovereignty they cannot severally participate, (except by their delegates,) nor with it have concurrent jurisdiction; for the ninth article of the confederation most expressly conveys to us the sole and exclusive right and power of determining on war and peace, and of entering into treaties and alliances, &c.

"When therefore a treaty is constitutionally made, ratified and published by us, it immediately becomes binding on the whole nation, and superadded to the laws of the land, without the intervention of state legislatures. Treaties derive their obligation from being compacts between the sovereign of this and the sovereign of another nation; whereas laws or statutes derive their force from being the acts of a legislature competent to the passing of them. Hence it is clear that treaties must be implicitly received and observed by every member of the nation; for as state legislatures are not competent to the making of such compacts or treaties, so neither are they competent in that capacity, authoritatively to decide on, or ascertain the construction and sense of them. When doubts arise respecting the construction of state laws, it is not unusual nor improper for state legislatures, by explanatory or declaratory acts, to remove those doubts: but, the case between laws and compacts or treaties is in this widely different, for when doubts arise respecting the sense and meaning of a treaty, they are so far from being cognizable by a state legislature, that the United States in congress assembled, have no authority to settle and determine them: for as the legislature only, which constitutionally passes a law, has power to revise and amend it, so the sovereigns only, who are parties to the treaty, have power by mutual consent and posterior articles, to correct or explain it.

"In cases between individuals, all doubts respecting the meaning of a treaty, like all doubts respecting the meaning of a law, are in the first instance mere judicial questions, and are to be heard and decided in the courts of justice having cognizance of the causes in which they arise, and whose duty it is to determine them according to the rules and maxims established by the laws of nations for the interpretation of treaties. From these principles it follows of necessary consequence, that no individual state has a right by legislative acts to decide and point out the sense in which their particular citizens and courts shall understand this or that article of a treaty.

"It is evident that a contrary doctrine would not only militate against the common and established maxims and ideas relative to this subject, but would prove no less inconvenient in practice than it is irrational in theory; for in that case the same article of the same treaty might by law be made to mean one thing in New Hampshire, another thing in New York, and neither the one nor the other of them in Georgia.

"How far such legislative acts would be valid and obligatory even within the limits of the state passing them, is a question which we hope never to have occasion to discuss. Certain, however it is, that such acts cannot bind either of the contracting sovereigns, and consequently cannot be obligatory on their respective nations.

"But if treaties, and every article in them be, (as they are, and ought to be,) binding on the whole nation, if individual states have no right to accept some articles and reject others, and if the impropriety of state acts to interpret and decide the sense and construction of them, be apparent, still more manifest must be the impropriety of state acts to control, delay or modify the operation and execution of these national compacts.

"When it is considered that the several states assembled by their delegates in congress, have express power to form treaties, surely the treaties so formed are not afterwards to be subject to such alterations as this or that state legislature may think expedient to make, and that too without the consent of either of the parties to it; that is in the present case without the consent of all the United States, who collectively are parties to this treaty on the one side, and his Britannic majesty on the other. Were the legislatures to possess and to exercise such power, we should soon be involved as a nation, in anarchy and confusion at home, and in disputes which would probably terminate in hostilities and war, with the nations with whom we may have formed treaties. Instances would then be frequent, of treaties fully executed in one state, and only partly executed in another; and of the same article being executed in one manner in one state, and in a different manner, or not at all, in another state. History furnishes no precedent of such liberties taken with treaties under form of law in any nation.

"Contracts between nations, like contracts between individuals, should be faithfully executed, even though the sword in the one case, and the law in the other, did not compel it. Honest nations, like honest men, require no constraint to do justice; and though impunity and the necessity of affairs, may sometimes afford temptations to pare down contracts to the measure of convenience, yet it is never done but at the expense of that esteem, and confidence and credit, which are of infinitely more worth, than all the momentary advantages which such expedients can extort.

"But although contracting nations cannot, like individuals, avail themselves of courts of justice to compel performance of contracts; yet an appeal to heaven and to arms is always in their power, and often in their inclination.

"But it is their duty to take care that they never lead their people to make and support such appeals, unless the sincerity and propriety of their conduct affords them good reason to rely with confidence on the justice and protection of heaven.

"Thus much we think it useful to observe, in order to explain the principles on which we have unanimously come to the following resolution, viz.

"'Resolved, That the legislatures of the several states cannot of right pass any act or acts for interpreting, explaining, or construing a national treaty, or any part or clause of it; nor for restraining, limiting, or in any manner impeding, retarding or counteracting the operation and execution of the same; for that on being constitutionally made, ratified and published, they become in virtue of the confederation, part of the law of the land, and are not only independent of the will and power of such legislatures, but also binding and obligatory on them.'

"As the treaty of peace, so far as it respects the matters and things provided for in it, is a law to the United States which cannot by all or any of them be altered or changed, all state acts establishing provisions relative to the same objects which are incompatible with it, must in every point of view be improper. Such acts do nevertheless exist; but we do not think it necessary either to enumerate them particularly, or to make them severally the subjects of discussion. It appears to us sufficient to observe and insist, that the treaty ought to have free course in its operation and execution, and that all obstacles interposed by state acts be removed. We mean to act with the most scrupulous regard to justice and candor towards Great Britain, and with an equal degree of delicacy, moderation and decision towards the states who have given occasion to these discussions.

"For these reasons we have in general terms,

"'Resolved, That all such acts or parts of acts as may be now existing in any of the states, repugnant to the treaty of peace, ought to be forthwith repealed; as well to prevent their continuing to be regarded as violations of that treaty, as to avoid the disagreeable necessity there might otherwise be of raising and discussing questions touching their validity and obligation.'

"Although this resolution applies strictly only to such of the states as have passed the exceptionable acts alluded to, yet to obviate all future disputes and questions, as well as to remove those which now exist, we think it best that every state without exception should pass a law on the subject. We have therefore,

"'Resolved, That it be recommended to the several states to make such repeal, rather by describing than reciting the said acts; and for that purpose to pass an act declaring in general terms that all such acts, and parts of acts repugnant to the treaty of peace between the United States and his Britannic majesty, or any article thereof, shall be, and thereby are repealed; and that the courts of law and equity in all causes and questions cognizable by them respectively, and arising from or touching the said treaty, shall decide and adjudge according to the true intent and meaning of the same: any thing in the said acts, or parts of acts, to the contrary thereof in any wise notwithstanding.'

"Such laws would answer every purpose, and be easily formed. The more they were of the like tenor throughout the states the better. They might each recite that,

"Whereas certain laws or statutes made and passed in some of the United States, are regarded and complained of as repugnant to the treaty of peace with Great Britain, by reason whereof not only the good faith of the United States pledged by that treaty, has been drawn into question, but their essential interests under that treaty greatly affected. And whereas justice to Great Britain, as well as regard to the honor and interests of the United States, require that the said treaty be faithfully executed, and that all obstacles thereto, and particularly such as do or may be construed to proceed from the laws of this state, be effectually removed. Therefore,

"Be it enacted by and it is hereby enacted by the authority of the same, that such of the acts or parts of acts of the legislature of this state, as are repugnant to the treaty of peace between the United States and his Britannic majesty, or any article thereof, shall be, and hereby are repealed. And further, that the courts of law and equity within this state be, and they hereby are directed and required in, all causes and questions cognizable by them respectively, and arising from or touching the said treaty, to decide and adjudge according to the tenor, true intent and meaning of the same, any thing in the said acts or parts of acts, to the contrary thereof in any wise notwithstanding.

"Such a general law would, we think, be preferable to one that should minutely enumerate the acts and clauses intended to be repeated: because omissions might accidentally be made in the enumeration, or questions might arise, and perhaps not be satisfactorily determined, respecting particular acts or clauses, about which, contrary opinions may be entertained. By repealing in general terms all acts and clauses repugnant to the treaty, the business will be turned over to its proper department, viz. the judicial; and the courts of law will find no difficulty in deciding whether any particular act or clause, is, or is not contrary to the treaty. Besides, when it is considered that the judges in general, are men of character and learning, and feel as well as know the obligations of office, and the value of reputation, there is no reason to doubt that their conduct and judgments relative to these, as well as other judicial matters, will be wise and upright.

"Be pleased, sir, to lay this letter before the legislature of your state, without delay. We flatter ourselves they will concur with us in opinion, that candor and justice are as necessary to true policy as they are to sound morality, and that the most honorable way of delivering ourselves from the embarrassment of mistakes, is fairly to correct them. It certainly is time that all doubts respecting the public faith be removed, and that all questions and differences between us and Great Britain, be amicably and finally settled. The states are informed of the reasons why his Britannic majesty still continues to occupy the frontier posts, which by the treaty he agreed to evacuate; and we have the strongest assurances that an exact compliance with the treaty on our part, shall be followed by a punctual performance of it on the part of Great Britain.

"It is important that the several legislatures should, as soon as possible, take these matters into consideration; and we request the favor of you to transmit to us an authenticated copy of such acts and proceedings of the legislature of your state, as may take place on the subject and in pursuance of this letter.

"By order of congress,

(Signed)

"ARTHUR ST. CLAIR, President."

No one can wish to see the country again reduced to such difficulties and disgrace. Still less that by a total dissolution of the Union, we should be left without even such a defective confederation as this was. But we cannot leave the subject without an additional remark.

As soon as the Constitution was adopted, all legislative measures for the purpose of enforcing existing treaties, either on the part of the United States or the states, became at once unnecessary. The institution of the judicial power was itself adequate to the desired effect. The partial views and local interests which. might have influenced state legislatures, or the high tone which might be jealously imputed to the general legislature, were equally avoided. The people, by the adoption of the Constitution, had themselves legislated on the subject, and the judicial principle, in regular and dignified procedure, carried their legislation into effect.

APPENDIX, NO. III.

For the purpose of convenient reference the entire Constitution is here inserted, including the amendments.

CONSTITUTION
OF THE UNITED STATES OF AMERICA.

We the people of the United States, in order to form a more perfect union, establish justice, ensure domestic tranquility, provide for the common defence, promote the general welfare, and secure the blessings of liberty to ourselves and our posterity, do ordain and establish this Constitution for the United States of America.

Article I.

Section 1.

1. All legislative powers herein granted, shall be vested in a congress of the United States, which shall consist of a senate and house of representatives.

Section 2.

1. The house of representatives shall be composed of members chosen every second year by the people of the several states, and the electors in each state shall have the qualifications requisite for electors of the most numerous branch of the state legislature.

2. No person shall be a representative who shall not have attained to the age of twenty-five years, and been seven years a citizen of the United States, and who shall not, when elected, be an inhabitant of that state in which he shall be chosen.

3. Representatives and direct taxes shall be apportioned among the several states which may be included within this Union, according to their respective numbers, which shall be determined by adding to the whole number of free persons, including those bound to service for a term of years, and excluding Indians not taxed, three-fifths of all other persons. The actual enumeration shall be made within three years after the first meeting of the congress of the United States, and within every subsequent term of ten years, in such manner as they shall by law direct. The number of representatives shall not exceed

one for every thirty thousand, but each state shall have at least one representative; and until such enumeration shall be made, the state of New Hampshire shall be entitled to choose three, Massachusetts eight, Rhode Island and Providence Plantations one, Connecticut five, New York six, New Jersey four, Pennsylvania eight, Delaware one, Maryland six, Virginia ten, North Carolina five, South Carolina five, and Georgia three.

4. When vacancies happen in the representation from any state, the executive authority thereof shall issue writs of election to fill such vacancies.

5. The house of representatives shall choose their speaker and other officers; and shall have the sole power of impeachment.

Section 3.

1. The senate of the United States shall be composed of two senators from each state, chosen by the Legislature thereof, for six years; and each senator shall have one vote.

2. Immediately after they shall be assembled in consequence of the first election, they shall be divided as equally as may be into three classes. The seats of the senators of the first class shall be vacated at the expiration of the second year, of the second class at the expiration of the fourth year, and of the third class at the expiration of the sixth year, so that one-third may be chosen every second year; and if vacancies happen by resignation, or otherwise, during the recess of the legislature of any state, the executive thereof may make temporary appointments until the next meeting of the legislature, which shall then fill such vacancies.

3. No person shall be a senator who shall not have attained to the age of thirty years, and been nine years a citizen of the United States, and who shall not, when elected, be an inhabitant of that state for which he shall be chosen.

4. The vice president of the United States shall be president of the senate, but shall have no vote, unless they be equally divided.

5. The senate shall choose their other officers, and also a president *pro tempore*, in the absence of the vice president, or when he shall exercise the office of president of the United States.

6. The senate shall have the sole power to try all impeachments. When sitting for that purpose, they shall be on oath or affirmation. When the president of the United States is tried, the chief justice shall preside; and no person shall be convicted without the concurrence of

two-thirds of the members present.

7. Judgment in cases of impeachment shall not extend further than to removal from office, and disqualification to hold and enjoy any office of honor, trust or profit under the United States; but the party convicted, shall nevertheless be liable and subject to indictment, trial, judgment and punishment, according to law.

Section 4.

1. The times, places, and manner of holding elections for senators and representatives, shall be prescribed in each state by the legislature thereof: but the congress may at any time by law, make or alter such regulations, except as to the places of choosing senators.

2. The congress shall assemble at least once in every year, and such meeting shall be on the first Monday in December, unless they shall by law appoint a different day.

Section 5

1. Each house shall be the judge of the elections, returns, and qualifications of its own members, and a majority of each shall constitute a quorum to do business; but a smaller number may adjourn from day to day, and may be authorized to compel the attendance of absent members, in such manner, and under such penalties as each house may provide.

2. Each house may determine the rules of its proceedings, punish its members for disorderly behavior, and, with the concurrence of two-thirds, expel a member.

3. Each house shall keep a journal of its proceedings, and from time to time publish the same, excepting such parts as may in their judgment require secrecy; and the yeas and nays of the members of either house on any question, shall, at the desire of one-fifth of those present, be entered on the journal.

4. Neither house, during the session of congress, shall, without the consent of the other, adjourn for more than three days, nor to any other place than that in which the two houses shall be sitting.

Section 6.

1. The senators and representatives shall receive a compensation for their services, to be ascertained by law, and paid out of the treasury of the United States. They shall in all cases, except treason, felony, and breach of the peace, be privileged from arrest during their

attendance at the session of their respective houses, and in going to and returning from the same; and for any speech or debate in either house, they shall not be questioned in any other place.

2. No senator or representative shall, during the time for which he was elected, be appointed to any civil office under the authority of the United States, which shall have been created, or the emoluments whereof shall have been increased during such time; and no person holding any office under the United States, shall be a member of either house during his continuance in office.

Section 7.

1. All bills for raising revenue shall originate in the house of representatives; but the senate may propose or concur with amendments as on other bills.

2. Every bill which shall have passed the house of representatives and the senate, shall, before it become a law, be presented to the president of the United States. If he approve he shall sign it, but if not he shall return it, with his objections to that house in which it shall have originated, who shall enter the objections at large on their journal, and proceed to reconsider it. If after such reconsideration two-thirds of that house shall agree to pass the bill, it shall be sent, together with the objections, to the other house, by which it shall likewise be reconsidered, and if approved by two-thirds of that house, it shall become a law. But in all such cases the votes of both houses shall be determined by yeas and nays, and the names of the persons voting for and against the bill shall be entered on the journal of each house respectively. If any bill shall not be returned by the president within ten days, (Sundays excepted,) after it shall have been presented to him, the same shall be a law, in like manner as if he had signed it, unless the congress by their adjournment prevent its return, in which case it shall not be a law.

3. Every order, resolution, or vote to which the concurrence of the senate and house of representatives may be necessary, (except on a question of adjournment,) shall be presented to the president of the United States; and before the same shall take effect, shall be approved by him, or being disapproved by him, shall be re-passed by two-thirds of the senate and house of representatives, according to the rules and limitations prescribed in the case of a bill.

Section 8.

The congress shall have power

1. To lay and collect taxes, duties, imposts and excises, to pay the debts and provide for the common defense and general welfare of the United States; but all duties, imposts and excises shall be uniform throughout the United States:

2. To borrow money on the credit of the United States:

3. To regulate commerce with foreign nations, and among the several states, and with the Indian tribes:

4. To establish an uniform rule of naturalization, and uniform laws on the subject of bankruptcies throughout the United States:

5. To coin money, regulate the value thereof, and of foreign coin, and fix the standard of weights and measures:

6. To provide for the punishment of counterfeiting the securities and current coin of the United States:

7. To establish post-offices and post-roads:

8. To promote the progress of science and useful arts, by securing for limited times to authors and inventors the exclusive right to their respective writings and discoveries:

9. To constitute tribunals inferior to the supreme court:

10. To define and punish piracies and felonies committed on the high seas, and offences against the law of nations:

11. To declare war, grant letters of marque and reprisal, and make rules concerning captures on land and water:

12. To raise and support armies, but no appropriation of money to that use shall be for a longer term than two years:

13. To provide and maintain a navy:

14. To make rules for the government and regulation of the land and naval forces:

15. To provide for calling forth the militia to execute the laws of the Union, suppress insurrections, and repel invasions:

16. To provide for organizing, arming, and disciplining the militia, and for governing such part of them as may be employed in the service of the United States, reserving to the states respectively, the appointment of the officers, and the authority of training the militia according to the discipline prescribed by congress:

17. To exercise exclusive legislation in all cases whatsoever, over such district, (not exceeding ten miles square,) as may, by cession of particular states, and the acceptance of congress, become the seat of the government of the United States, and to exercise like authority

over all places purchased by the consent of the legislature of the state in which the same shall be, for the erection of forts, magazines, arsenals, dock-yards, and other needful buildings: — And

18. To make all laws which shall be necessary and proper for carrying into execution the foregoing powers, and all other powers vested by this Constitution in the government of the United States, or in any department or officer thereof.

Section 9.

1. The migration or importation of such persons, as any of the states now existing shall think proper to admit, shall not be prohibited by the congress prior to the year one thousand eight hundred and eight, but a tax or duty may be imposed on such importation, not exceeding ten dollars for each person.

2. The privilege of the writ of habeas corpus shall not be suspended, unless when in cases of rebellion or invasion the public safety may require it.

3. No bill of attainder or ex post facto law shall be passed.

4. No capitation, or other direct, tax shall be laid, unless in proportion to the census or enumeration herein before directed to be taken.

5. No tax or duty shall be laid on articles exported from any state. No preference shall be given by any regulation of commerce or revenue to the ports of one state over those of another; nor shall vessels bound to, or from, one state, be obliged to enter, clear, or pay duties in another.

6. No money shall be drawn from the treasury, but in consequence of appropriations made by law; and a regular statement and account of the receipts and expenditures of all public money shall be published from time to time.

7. No title of nobility shall be granted by the United States: And no person holding any office of profit or trust under them, shall, without the consent of the congress, accept of any present, emolument, office, or title of any kind whatever, from any king, prince or foreign state.

Section 10.

1. No state shall enter into any treaty, alliance, or confederation; grant letters of marque and reprisal; coin money; emit bills of credit; make any thing but gold and silver coin a tender in payment of

debts; pass any bill of attainder, ex post facto law, or law impairing the obligation of contracts, or grant any title of nobility.

2. No state shall, without the consent of the congress, lay any imposts or duties on imports or exports, except what may be absolutely necessary for executing it's inspection laws; and the net produce of all duties and imposts, laid by any state on imports or exports, shall be for the use of the treasury of the United States; and all such laws shall be subject to the revision and control of the congress. No state shall, without the consent of congress, lay any duty of tonnage, keep troops, or ships of war in time of peace, enter into any agreement or compact with another state, or with a foreign power, or engage in war, unless actually invaded, or in such imminent danger as will not admit of delay.

Article II.

Section 1.

1. The executive power shall be vested in a president of the United States of America. He shall hold his office during the term of four years, and together with the vice president, chosen for the same term, be elected, as follows:

2. Each state shall appoint, in such manner as the legislature thereof may direct, a number of electors, equal to the whole number of senators and representatives to which the state may be entitled in the congress: but no senator or representative, or person holding an office of trust or profit under the United States, shall be appointed an elector.

3. The electors shall meet in their respective states, and vote by ballot for two persons, of whom one at least shall not be an inhabitant of the same state with themselves. And they shall make a list of all the persons voted for, and of the number of votes for each; which list they shall sign and certify, and transmit, sealed, to the seat of the government of the United States, directed to the president of the senate. The president of the senate shall, in the presence of the senate and house of representatives, open all the certificates, and the votes shall then be counted. The person having the greatest number of votes shall be the president, if such number be a majority of the whole number of electors appointed; and if there be more than one who have such majority, and have an equal number of votes, then the house of representatives shall immediately choose by ballot one of them for president; and if no person have a majority, then from the five highest on the

list the said house shall in like manner choose the president. But in choosing the president the votes shall be taken by states, the representation from each state having one vote; a quorum for this purpose shall consist of a member or members from two-thirds of the states, and a majority of all the states shall be necessary to a choice. In every case, after the choice of the president, the person having the greatest number of votes of the electors shall be the vice president. But if there should remain two or more who have equal votes the senate shall choose from them by ballot the vice president.

4. The congress may determine the time of choosing the electors, and the day on which they shall give their votes; which day shall be the same throughout the United States.

5. No person except a natural born citizen, or a citizen of the United States, at the time of the adoption of this Constitution, shall be eligible to the office of president; neither shall any person be eligible to that office who shall not have attained to the age of thirty-five years, and been fourteen years a resident within the United States.

6. In case of the removal of the president from office, or of his death, resignation, or inability to discharge the powers and duties of the said office, the same shall devolve on the vice president, and the congress may by law provide for the case of removal, death, resignation, or inability, both of the president and vice president, declaring what officer shall then act as president, and such officer shall act accordingly, until the disability be removed, or a president shall be elected.

7. The president shall, at stated times, receive for his services, a compensation, which shall neither be increased nor diminished during the period for which he shall have been elected, and he shall not receive within that period any other emolument from the United States or any of them.

8. Before he enter on the execution of his office, he shall take the following oath or affirmation:

9. "I do solemnly swear, (or affirm,) that I will faithfully execute the office of president of "the United States, and will to the best of my ability, preserve, protect, and defend the Constitution "of the United States."

Section 2.

1. The president shall be commander in chief of the army and navy of the United States, and of the militia of the several states, when

called into the actual service of the United States; he may require the opinion, in writing, of the principal officer in each of the executive departments, upon any subject relating to the duties of their respective offices, and he shall have power to grant reprieves and pardons for offences against the United States, except in cases of impeachment.

2. He shall have power, by and with the advice and consent of the senate, to make treaties, provided two-thirds of the senators present concur; and he shall nominate, and by and with the advice and consent of the senate, shall appoint ambassadors, other public ministers and consuls, judges of the supreme court, and all other officers of the United States, whose appointments are not herein otherwise provided for, and which shall be established by law: but the congress may by law vest the appointment of such inferior officers as they think proper, in the president alone, in the courts of law, or in the heads of departments.

3. The president shall have power to fill up all vacancies that may happen during the recess of the senate, by granting commissions which shall expire at the end of their next session.

Section 3.

1. He shall from time to time give to the congress information of the state of the Union, and recommend to their consideration such measures as he shall judge necessary and expedient; he may on extraordinary occasions, convene both houses, or either of them, and in case of disagreement between them with respect to the time of adjournment, he may adjourn them to such time as he shall think proper; he shall receive ambassadors and other public ministers; he shall take care that the laws be faithfully executed, and shall commission all the officers of the United States.

Section 4.

1. The president, vice president, and all civil officers of the United States, shall be removed from office on impeachment for, and conviction of, treason, bribery, or other high crimes and misdemeanors.

Article III.

Section 1.

1. The judicial power of the United States, shall be vested in one Supreme Court, and in such inferior courts as the congress may from

time to time ordain and establish. The judges, both of the supreme and inferior courts, shall hold their offices during good behavior, and shall, at stated times, receive for their services, a compensation, which shall not be diminished during their continuance in office.

Section 2.

1. The judicial power shall extend to all cases, in law and equity, arising under this Constitution, the laws of the United States, and treaties made, or which shall be made, under their authority; to all cases affecting ambassadors, other public ministers and consuls; to all cases of admiralty and maritime jurisdiction; to controversies to which the United States shall be a party; to controversies between two or more states, between a state and citizens of another state, between citizens of different states, between citizens of the same state claiming lands under grants of different states, and between a state, or the citizens thereof, and foreign states, citizens or subjects.

2. In all cases affecting ambassadors, other public ministers and consuls, and those in which a state shall be party, the supreme court shall have original jurisdiction. In all the other cases before mentioned, the supreme court shall have appellate jurisdiction, both as to law and fact, with such exceptions, and under such regulations as the congress shall make.

3. The trial of all crimes, except in cases of impeachment, shall be by jury; and such trial shall be held in the state where the said crimes shall have been committed; but when not committed within any state, the trial shall be at such place or places as the congress may by law have directed.

Section 3.

1. Treason against the United States, shall consist only in levying war against them, or in adhering to their enemies, giving them aid and comfort. No person shall be convicted of treason unless on the testimony of two witnesses to the same overt act, or on confession in open court.

2. The congress shall have power to declare the punishment of treason, but no attainder of treason shall work corruption of blood, or forfeiture, except during the life of the person attainted.

Article IV.

Section 1.

1. Full faith and credit shall be given in each state to the public acts, records and judicial proceedings of every other state. And the congress may by general laws prescribe the manner in which such acts, records and proceedings shall be proved, and the effect thereof.

Section 2.

1. The citizens of each state shall be entitled to all privileges and immunities of citizens in the several states.

2. A person charged in any state with treason, felony, or other crime, who shall flee from justice, and be found in another state, shall, on demand of the executive authority of the state from which he fled, be delivered up, to be removed to the state having jurisdiction of the crime.

3. No person held to service or labor in one state, under the laws thereof, escaping into another, shall, in consequence of any law or regulation therein, be discharged from such service or labor, but shall be delivered up on claim of the party to whom such service or labor may be due.

Section 3.

1. New states may be admitted by the congress into this Union; but no new state shall be formed or erected within the jurisdiction of any other state; nor any state be formed by the junction of two or more states, or parts of states, without the consent of the legislatures of the states concerned as well as of the congress.

2. The congress shall have power to dispose of and make all needful rules and regulations respecting the territory or other property belonging to the United States; and nothing in this Constitution shall be so construed as to prejudice any claims of the United States, or of any particular state.

Section 4.

1. The United States shall guarantee to every state in this Union a republican form of government, and shall protect each of them against invasion; and on application of the legislature, or of the executive, (when the legislature cannot be convened,) against domestic violence.

Article V.

1. The congress, whenever two-thirds of both houses shall deem it necessary, shall propose amendments to this Constitution, or, on the application of the legislatures of two-thirds of the several states, shall call a convention for proposing amendments, which, in either case, shall be valid to all intents and purposes, as part of this Constitution, when ratified by the legislatures of three-fourths of the several states, or by conventions in three-fourths thereof, as the one or the other mode of ratification may be proposed by the congress; Provided, that no amendment which may be made prior to the year one thousand eight hundred and eight, shall in any manner affect the first and fourth clauses in the ninth section of the first article; and that no state, without its consent, shall be deprived of its equal suffrage in the senate.

Article VI.

1. All debts contracted and engagements entered into, before the adoption of this Constitution, shall be as valid against the United States under this Constitution, as under the confederation.

2. This Constitution, and the laws of the United States which shall be made in pursuance thereof; and all treaties made, or which shall be made, under the authority of the United States, shall be the supreme law of the land; and the judges in every state shall be bound thereby, any thing in the constitution or laws of any state to the contrary notwithstanding.

3. The senators and representatives before mentioned, and the members of the several state legislatures, and all executive and judicial officers, both of the United States and of the several states, shall be bound by oath or affirmation, to support this Constitution; but no religious test shall ever be required as a qualification to any office or public trust under the United States.

Article VII.

1. The ratification of the conventions of nine states, shall be sufficient for the establishment of this Constitution between the states so ratifying the same.

AMENDMENTS TO THE CONSTITUTION.

Article I.

Congress shall make no law respecting an establishment of religion, or prohibiting the free exercise thereof; or abridging the freedom of speech, or of the press; or the right of the people peaceably to assemble, and to petition the government for a redress of grievances.

Article II.

A well regulated militia being necessary to the security of a free state, the right of the people to keep and bear arms shall not be infringed.

Article III.

No soldier shall, in time of peace, be quartered in any house, without the consent of the owner; nor in time of war, but in a manner to be prescribed by law.

Article IV.

The right of the people to be secure in their persons, houses, papers, and effects, against unreasonable searches and seizures, shall not be violated, and no warrants shall issue, but upon probable cause, supported by oath or affirmation, and particularly describing the place to be searched, and the persons or things to be seized.

Article V.

No person shall be held to answer for a capital, or otherwise infamous crime, unless on a presentment or indictment of a grand jury, except in cases arising in the land or naval forces, or in the militia, when in actual service, in time of war or public danger; nor shall any person be subject for the same offence to be twice put in jeopardy of life or limb; nor shall be compelled, in any criminal case, to be a witness against himself, nor be deprived of life, liberty, or property, without due process of law; nor shall private property be taken for public use without just compensation.

Article VI.

In all criminal prosecutions, the accused shall enjoy the right to a speedy and public trial, by an impartial jury of the state and district wherein the crime shall have been committed, which district shall have been previously ascertained by law, and to be informed of the nature and cause of the accusation; to be confronted with the witnesses against him; to have compulsory process for obtaining witnesses in his favor, and to have the assistance of counsel for his defense.

Article VII.

In suits at common law, where the value in controversy shall exceed twenty dollars, the right of trial by jury shall be preserved; and no fact tried by a jury shall be otherwise re-examined in any court of the United States, than according to the rules of the common law.

Article VIII.

Excessive bail shall not be required, nor excessive fines imposed, nor cruel and unusual punishments inflicted.

Article IX.

The enumeration in the Constitution of certain rights, shall not be construed to deny or disparage others retained by the people.

Article X.

The powers not delegated to the United States by the Constitution, nor prohibited by it to the states, are reserved to the states respectively, or to the people.

Article XI.

The judicial power of the United States shall not be construed to extend to any suit in law or equity, commenced or prosecuted against one of the United States by citizens of another state, or by citizens or subjects of any foreign state.

Article XII.

1. The electors shall meet in their respective states, and vote by ballot for president and vice president, one of whom, at least, shall not be an inhabitant of the same state with themselves; they shall name in their ballots the person voted for as president, and in distinct ballots the person voted for as vice president; and they shall make distinct lists of all persons voted for as president, and of all persons voted for as vice president, and of the number of votes for each, which lists, they shall sign and certify, and transmit sealed to the seat of the government of the United States, directed to the president of the senate;

the president of the senate shall, in the presence of the senate and house of representatives, open all the certificates, and the votes shall then be counted: The person having the greatest number of votes for president, shall be the president, if such number be a majority of the whole number of electors appointed; and if no person have such majority, then from the persons having the highest numbers not exceeding three, on the list of those voted for as president, the house of representatives shall choose immediately, by ballot, the president. But in choosing the president, the votes shall be taken by states, the representation from each state having one vote; a quorum for this purpose shall consist of a member or members from two-thirds of the states, and a majority of all the states shall be necessary to a choice. And if the house of representatives shall not choose a president whenever the right of choice shall devolve upon them, before the fourth day of March next following, then the vice president shall act as president, as in case of the death or other constitutional disability of the president.

2. The person having the greatest number of votes as vice president, shall be the vice president, if such number be a majority of the whole number of electors appointed, and if no person have a majority, then from the two highest numbers on the list, the senate shall choose the vice president: a quorum for the purpose shall consist of two-thirds of the whole number of senators, a majority of the whole number shall be necessary to a choice.

3. But no person constitutionally ineligible to the office of president, shall be eligible to that of vice president of the United States.

The last amendment listed here is the Twelfth Amendment, which was ratified in 1804. Since that time, the following amendments have been added:

AMENDMENT	*YEAR RATIFIED*	
Thirteenth	*1865*	
Fourteenth	*1868*	*Enacted**
Fifteenth	*1870*	
Sixteenth	*1913*	
Seventeenth	*1913*	
Eighteenth	*1919*	
Nineteenth	*1920*	
Twentieth	*1933*	
Twenty-first	*1933*	

Twenty-second	*1951*
Twenty-third	*1961*
Twenty-fourth	*1964*
Twenty-fifth	*1967*
Twenty-sixth	*1971*

**The term "enacted" is used in relation to the forced enactment of the Fourteenth Amendment. During reconstruction, the radicals in Congress forced the enactment of this amendment. The free will of the people of the South and several Northern States was ignored as the radicals forced this amendment onto the Constitution. It is the belief of many that this amendment was never legally ratified and is pinned to the Constitution with bloody bayonets. This was done in direct violation of the American principle of government by the consent of the governed. The reader is directed to the following sources for more information on this subject:*

1. Forrest McDonald, "Was the Fourteenth Amendment Constitutionally Adopted?" The Georgia Journal of Southern Legal History, *Vol. 1, No. 1 Spring/Summer 1991.*
2. Joint Resolution, No. 1 State of New Jersey, cited in The South Was Right!, *Addendum VIII, Kennedy & Kennedy, second edition, Pelican Publication, Gretna, Louisiana.*
3. David Lawrence, "The Worst Scandal In Our History," U.S. News and World Report, *9-2-57 & 1-26-70.*

Editors' Commentary on the Constitution From Republic of Sovereign States to Globalist Empire— The Pre-War Constitution: 1787-1861

St. George Tucker On the U.S. Constitution: Pre-War[88]

In 1803, a mere fifteen years after the adoption of the United States Constitution, St. George Tucker published the first authoritative analysis of the Constitution of the new republic, the United States

88 The following abstract is taken from *View of the Constitution of the United States, With Selected Writings*, Clyde Wilson, Ed., (Liberty Fund, Inc., Indianapolis, IN: 1999). Note: Any text or phrases within brackets [*] are inserted by author of this abstract and not St George Tucker.

of America. Tucker's view of the Constitution has been described as, "a key document of Jeffersonian republicanism."[89] Tucker is little known in modern America and his view of the Constitution was overturned by the adjudication of the bayonet. Yet his view of the Constitution, like the view of his Northern counter-part, William Rawle, was the guiding view of American Constitutional law and jurisprudence until the election of Abraham Lincoln. Both William Rawle of Pennsylvania and St. George Tucker of Virginia viewed the Constitution as a compact among the people of sovereign states. As such both men understood that a government by consent could not exist at the point of a bayonet. They embraced the view that a union of free men could only be "perpetual" if men were content with their government — very similar to a "perpetual" marriage union. As long as free men were content with their government, the union would be perpetual. But free men cease to be free men if they are compelled to remain in a government not of their choice. Modern Americans often fail to understand that free men do not live in a prison — if you can't leave, you are not free. As the Declaration of Independence affirms, free men possess the right to freely give or withdraw their consent to government. As both Rawle and Tucker, one a Northerner and one a Southerner, point out, in these United States this consent is given not by Americans in a general context but Americans as citizens of their sovereign state.

Both Rawle and Tucker held a strong States' Rights view of the Constitution which included the right of secession. In modern America the States' Rights view is usually described as the view held by those who promoted slavery and racial discrimination. The modern negative view of States' Rights is not based on fact but on emotion. Both Rawle and Tucker were abolitionists and Tucker was also a critic of laws that discriminated against free people of color. Tucker's views on equality before the law places him over one hundred and fifty years ahead of the modern Civil Rights movement, yet he was a strong States' Rights man.

St. George Tucker was born in Bermuda in 1752 and relocated to Virginia in 1771. Tucker studied law at William and Mary under George Wythe, a signer of the Declaration of Independence and Chief Justice of Virginia. Tucker served in the Virginia militia during the War for American Independence from the beginning to the end

89 Clyde Wilson, bid, VII.

of the war. He was cited for his distinguished service under General Nathanial Green at the Battle of Guilford Courthouse in North Carolina and was wounded during the Battle of Yorktown, Virginia. During the latter days of the government under the Articles of Confederation, Tucker served as a delegate to the Annapolis Convention which called for the Philadelphia Constitutional Convention. In 1790 he succeeded his old law professor, George Wythe, as professor of law at William and Mary College. It was during this time as a law professor that Tucker edited and published Blackstone's *Commentaries on the Laws of England*. Blackstone's *Commentaries* was at that time "the leading legal text of the English-speaking world."[90] Since Blackstone's work was full of monarchist views, Tucker edited Blackstone's *Commentaries* so as to make it appropriate for American students who were republicans, not monarchists. In 1813 President James Madison appointed Tucker to be the United States District Judge for Virginia. As Dr. Clyde Wilson noted, "As a jurist Tucker never wavered from the principles he had set forth as a professor of law."[91] In other words until his death (1827), Tucker never abandon his strict States' Rights view of the Constitution something almost unheard of in modern Federal Judges.

The following text is a summary of Tucker's view of (1) the Constitution — who created it and empowered it; (2) the nature of sovereignty — what is sovereignty, where does it reside in these United States, can it be overthrown; and, (3) the union — where did it originate and is it perpetual.

The Constitution

In the new government [union under the Constitution], *as under the old* [under the Articles of Confederation], *the general powers are limited, and that the states, in all unenumerated cases, are left in the enjoyment of their sovereign and independent jurisdictions.*[92]

Tucker, who is writing just a few years after the formation of the union under the Constitution, will often refer to the union as a "confederacy" or a "confederate government." This terminology was in common usage prior to the War for Southern Independence. The government of the seceded states of the South having been denoted "The Confederate States of America," most modern readers usually

90 Ibid, IX.

91 Ibid, X.

92 Tucker, 93.

associate the term "confederate" to the seceded Southern states. Yet, this was not true at the founding of these United States. For example, Alexander Hamilton in Federalist No. 9 pronounces the form of government under the Constitution to be a confederacy.[93] Hamilton points out that under a confederate type of government many small republics can unite for their common good to form a larger republic. Having united for their common good in a confederation, the member states of a confederacy retain all areas of government not entrusted (by their free and unfettered consent) to the general government. The vast residue of self-government is therefore reserved to the individual member states. While each member state of the new union would submit to the general authority of the union, the union "would still be, in fact and in theory, an association of States, or a confederacy."[94] Hamilton then quotes Montesquieu's *The Spirit of the Laws* where he notes that in a confederacy, such as the one Hamilton is proposing the States adopt, states were not unconditionally bound to the new government. Montesquieu noted that, "the confederacy may be dissolved, and the confederates preserve their sovereignty."[95]

Tucker makes it clear who the author is, i.e., the empowering agent, of the Federal Constitution: "The Constitution of the United States of America, then, is...freely voluntarily, and solemnly entered by the several states of North-America, and ratified by the people thereof."[96] This is a clear reflection of the words of Article VII of the Constitution. Tucker also notes that the Constitution is a compact among the states:

> It is a compact; by which it is distinguished from a charter, or grant; which is either the act of a superior to an inferior; or is founded upon some consideration moving from one of the parties, to the other, and operates as an exchange, or sale; but here the contracting parties, whether considered as states, in their politic capacity and character; or as individuals, are all equal; nor is there anything granted from one to another; but each stipulates to part with, and to receive the same thing, precisely, without any

93 Alexander Hamilton as cited in, George W. Carey and James McClellan, Edt., The Federalist (Kendall/Hunt Publishing Co., Dubuque, IA: 1990), 38-41.
94 Ibid.
95 Charles de Secondat, Baron de Montesquieu, as cited in Federalist No. 9, Carey and McClellan, 40.
96 Tucker, as cited in, Wilson, 91.

> distinction or difference in favor of any of the parties. … Therefore, when the convention at Philadelphia had made their report, the ordinary legislatures, with great propriety, recommended the appointment of state-conventions, for the sole and especial purpose of considering the propriety of adopting the constitution, thus proposed by the conventions of the states.[97]

Thus, Tucker explains that the Constitution was, from beginning to end, the child of "we the people" of the sovereign states. Each state acting totally independent from any other regulating, coaching, or instructing power. As shall be explained subsequently, this essential element of state sovereignty is one of many fine points of Constitutional history that Abraham Lincoln and his adoring minions refused to recognize. Tucker proceeds to further stress the compact nature of the Constitution and also notes that the government, i.e., Union, under the Constitution did not exist until given life by the people of the sovereign states:

It is a compact by which the federal government is bound to the several states, and to every citizen of the United States. Although the federal government can, in no possible view, be considered as a party to a compact made anterior to its existence, and by which it was, in fact, created; yet as the creature of that compact, it must be bound by it, to its creators, the several states in the union, and the citizens thereof. Having no existence but under the constitution, nor any rights, but such as that instrument confers; and those very rights being in fact duties; it can possess no legitimate power, but such as is absolutely necessary for the performance of a duty, prescribed and enjoined by the constitution. Its duties, then, becomes the exact measure of its powers; and whenever it exerts a power for any other purpose, than the performance of a duty prescribed by the constitution, it transgresses its proper limits, and violates the public trust.[98]

Continuing his discussion of who created the new government under the Constitution, Tucker then proceeds to confer upon the new nation the title of a "confederal republic," and explains why this is a correct title:

> The constitution of the United States, then being that instrument by which the federal government hath been creat-

97 Ibid, 91, 118-19.

98 Ibid, 120-21.

> ed;...the government, thus, established, may be pronounced to be a confederal republic, composed of several independent, and sovereign democratic states, united for their common defense, and security against foreign nations, and for the purposes of harmony, and mutual intercourse, between each other; each state retaining an entire liberty of exercising, as it thinks proper, all those parts of its sovereignty, which are not mentioned in the constitution, or act of union, as parts that ought to be exercised in common.[99]

As Tucker demonstrates, the people of the sovereign states, acting freely and for their own specific benefit created the government (aka, the Union or federal government) under the Constitution. Beyond just the process of creation, Tucker proves that the Constitution is given, i.e., granted, its power from the states. Therefore, it can be surmised that the states, acting in their sovereign capacity, granted unto the federal government any and all the authority the federal government can legally exercise.

Sovereignty

From the moment of the revolution they became severally independent and sovereign states, possessing all rights, jurisdiction, and authority, that other sovereign states...possess and bound by no ties but of their own creation.[100]

"The sovereign state" and the word "sovereignty" is often seen in any discussion of the creation of these United States and the adoption of the Constitution. As a noted legal expert has stated, "Sovereignty is the ability to execute any thought or idea without limitation."[101] It is more than obvious that only God can act in such a manner. The closest that man can come to such a situation is the action of government. In an autocratic monarchy, sovereignty is said to reside in the monarch; in an empire, sovereignty resides in the emperor; in a dictatorship, sovereignty resides in the hands of a tyrant, but in a "democratic" republic, sovereignty resides in the people. Complete sovereignty is not the possession of each individual of society but rather in the collective body politic of the people as expressed in their constitution.

---

99 Ibid, 121.

100 Ibid, 100.

101 Francis Lieber, *On Civil Liberty and Self Government* (J. B. Lippincott and Co., Philadelphia, PA: 1853), 270.

As Tucker points out, the American people's "body politic" consists of their state government to which they have given their consent by the act of adopting their state constitution. This consent to be governed is essential if their government is to be denoted a "free government."

> But no people can ever be free, whose government is founded upon the usurpation of their sovereign rights; for by the act of usurpation, the sovereignty is transferred from the people, in whom alone it can legitimately reside, to those who by that act have manifested a determination to oppress them.[102]

Generally speaking, in 1803, the central government of these United States of America under both the Articles of Confederation and the Constitution demonstrate a distinct and unique concept of sovereignty as opposed to the governments of Europe.[103] Tucker explains America's unique from of government. In the United States the people of each state are sovereign and the government is their servant and agent, not their lord and master:

> The American revolution seems to have given birth to this new political phenomenon: in every state a written constitution was framed, and adopted by the people, both in their individual and sovereign capacity, and character. By this means the just distinction between the sovereignty, and the government, was rendered familiar to every intelligent mind; the former [sovereignty] was found to reside in the people, and to be unalienable from them; and the latter [government] in their servants and agents; by this means, also, government was reduced to its elements; its object was defined, its principles ascertained; its powers limited, and fixed; its structure organized; and the functions of every part of the machine so clearly designated, as to prevent any interference, so long as the limits of each were observed. The same reasons operated in behalf of similar restrictions in the federal constitution. ... But to guard

102 Tucker, 28.

103 In the 1560s the local governments now making up modern day Netherlands became an early example of European efforts to withdraw their consent from a monarch (King Phillip of Spain) and form a free Republic, see Berendse & Lucas, *The Act of Abjuration-The Dutch Declaration of Independence* (1581) (Elsevier Boeken, Amsterdam, the Netherlands: 2014), 14-5. Also see, Lucas, *The Act of Abjuration as Model for the Declaration of Independence—Thomas Jefferson and the Art of Imitation, in The Act of Abjuration-Inspired and Inspirational* (Wolf Legal Publishers, Nijmegen, the Netherlands: 2011), 173-89.

> against encroachments on the powers of the several states, in their politic character, and of the people, both in their individual and sovereign capacity, an amendatory article was added, immediately after the government was organized, declaring; that the powers not delegated to the United States, by the constitution, nor prohibited by it to the states, are reserved to the states, respectively, or to the people [Tenth Amendment]. And, still further, to guard the people against constructive usurpations and encroachments on their rights, another article declares; that the enumeration of certain rights in the constitution, shall not be construed to deny, or disparage, others retained by the people [Ninth Amendment declaring the existence of unenumerated rights not specifically listed in the Constitution. The right of nullification or secession are such rights].[104]

If, sovereignty resides with the people in their political community,[105] that is, their state, as Tucker asserts, can sovereign states be alienated from the exercise of their sovereign rights? In other words, can a sovereign state be deprived of its sovereignty? Tucker positively answers that question:

> It is likewise a maxim of political law that sovereign states cannot be deprived of any of their rights by implication; nor in any manner whatever by their own voluntary consent, or by submission to a conqueror.[106]

Tucker clearly points out that the conquest of a state or people cannot form the basis of a legitimate government regardless of the passage of time:

> The acquiescence of the people of a state under any *usurped* authority for *any length of time*, can never deprive them of the right of resuming the sovereign power onto their own hands, whenever they think fit, or are able to do so, since that right is perfectly unalienable. ... The sovereign power therefore always resides ultimately, and in contemplation, whatever be the form of government [emphasis added].[107]

---

104 Tucker, 104-5.

105 John C. Calhoun used the term "sovereign community."

106 Tucker, 94.

107 Ibid, 33.

As noted in the Declaration of Independence, rights are given to man from the "Creator" and are therefore, "unalienable." A free people's right to live under a government by their consent cannot be destroyed by the action of their government nor by the action of an invader who conquers a free people. Yes, their rights can be abridged, trampled upon, and suppressed, but those rights are never destroyed because God-given rights are permanent. Any government that exercises its authority without the consent of the governed is merely a government that exists by the "fruits of internal violence and struggles,"[108] and has, therefore, destroyed legitimate government — it has morphed into an illegitimate government. As Tucker notes, "Legitimate government, then, can be established only by the voluntary consent of the society."[109]

Tucker then stipulates that these states, i.e., body politic, can at their volition recall or reclaim any and all rights delegated to their agent. This principle is based upon sound American political principle:

> When any government shall be found inadequate, or contrary, to the purposes of its institution, a majority of the community hath an indubitable, unalienable and indefeasible right to reform, alter or abolish it, in such manner as shall be judged most conducive to the public weal.[110]

The usage of the term "alter or abolish" by Tucker is noteworthy in itself. This phrase is taken from the Declaration of Independence which announced to the world that in America government was to serve the people but the people do not serve the government. Tucker notes that the federal government of these United States exists by the "free consent and suffrages of the people of the several states, separately, and independently taken, and expressed."[111] The people of each sovereign state have the unalienable right to judge for themselves how they are governed. As to the actual act of secession, that is, withdrawing their consent by the recalling of delegated rights, Tucker informs the reader thusly:

> The dissolution of these systems happens, when all the confederates by mutual consent, or some of them, voluntarily

108 Ibid, 29.
109 Ibid, 32.
110 Ibid, 34.
111 Ibid.

> abandon the confederacy, and govern their own states apart; or a part of them form a different league and confederacy among each other.[112]

Tucker explains that to form a new government under the Constitution, the states that were united under the Articles of Confederations had to accede to the new union under the Constitution. This act of acceding to the new union was in fact an act of secession from the old union under the Articles of Confederation.

> Yet the seceding states, as they may be not improperly termed, did not hesitate, as soon as nine states had ratified the new constitution, to supersede the former federal government and establish a new form…of federal union.[113]

Even though under the *first* constitution of the United States (Articles of Confederation) the government or Union was explicitly declared to be perpetual and that Union could only be changed by the *unanimous* consent of all states, that did not prevent sovereign states from seceding from the old government to form the new union under the Constitution. The act of establishing a new government under the Constitution was justified not by the law under the Articles of Confederation but rather by the fact that as citizens of a sovereign state the people had the ultimate right to "alter or abolish" any government. What was true in 1788 was equally true in 1861 and true to this day. As Tucker notes:

> We may infer that right has not been diminished by any new compact which they may since have entered into, since none could be more solemn or explicit than the first, nor more binding upon the contracting parties. Their obligation, therefore, to preserve the present constitution, is not greater than their former obligations were, to adhere to the articles of confederation; each state possessing the same right of withdrawing itself from the confederacy without the consent of the rest, as any number of them do, or ever did possess. Prudence … will dictate, that governments established by compact should not be changed for light or transient causes; but should a long train of abuses and usurpations, pursuing invariably the same object, evince a design in any one of the confederates to usurp a do-

---

112 Ibid, 84.

113 Ibid.

minion over the rest; or, if those who are entrusted to administer the government...should manifest a design to invade their sovereignty, and extend their own power beyond the terms of compact...and to reduce them to a state of obedience, and finally to establish themselves in a state of permanent superiority, it then becomes not only the right, but the duty of the states respectively, to throw off such government, and to provide new guards for their future security. To deny this, would be to deny to sovereign and independent states, the power which, as colonies, and dependent territories, they have mutually agreed they had a right to exercise, and did actually exercise, when they shook off the government of England, first, and adopted the present constitution of the United States.[114]

In the preceding review of St George Tucker's analysis of the Constitution, he clearly views sovereignty in these United States as residing with the people of each state and not in the American people in the aggregate. Equally true, Tucker holds firm to the view that the rights of sovereignty are inalienable. This attribute, just as any right, can be abused and denied but never destroyed. The right of a sovereign community to recall any and all of its delegated rights remain even if the state has suffered invasion, conquest, and occupation.

Union

If the bond of union be the voluntary consent of the people, the government may be pronounced to be free; where constraint and fear constitute that bond, the government is no longer the government of the people, and consequently they are enslaved.[115]

As to the nature of the new union under the Constitution, Tucker notes that "the union is in fact, as well as in theory, an association of states, or a confederacy. The state governments not only retain every power, jurisdiction, and right not delegated to the United States, by the constitution, nor prohibited by it to the states, but they are constituent and necessary parts of the federal government."[116] As already noted, Tucker affirms the fact that the new union exists because the Constitution was adopted, thus replacing the older first union under the Articles of Confederation. Since the union, like the federal

114 Ibid, 86.
115 Ibid, 27.
116 Ibid, 92.

government itself, is a product of the Constitution, neither the government nor the union can exist before the Constitution.[117]The states forming the new union did so for their mutual benefit, they were not creating a controlling entity.

> Their [states] submission to its [union] operation is voluntary; its councils, its sovereignty is an emanation from theirs, not a flame by which they have been consumed, nor a vortex in which they are swallowed up. Each is still a perfect state, still sovereign, still independent, and still capable, should the occasion require, to resume the exercise of its functions, as such, in the most unlimited extent.[118]

In the preceding text Tucker makes it clear that the actions of the states *vis-à-vis* the creation of the new union is a voluntary act and one from which they retain the right and power to "resume the exercise of its function," i.e., secede. This act of resuming delegated powers is the act of a sovereign state. Tucker demonstrates that the article of ratification of several states proclaimed that they maintained the right to recall any delegated power if said power was used to their determent. For example, Virginia's ratification document declares the ratification was being done "in the name and in behalf of the people of Virginia,"[119] and further states:

> We the delegates of the people of Virginia … do in the name and behalf of the people of Virginia, declare and make known, that the powers granted under the constitution, being derived from the people of the United States, may be resumed by them, whenever the same shall be perverted to their injury or oppression. [120]

The sovereign nature of the member states of the new union is displayed in several state constitutions including the very Yankee state of Massachusetts. The Constitution of Massachusetts declared that, "the people of the commonwealth have the sole and exclusive right to governing themselves as a free, sovereign, and independent state."[121] New Hampshire adopted a new state constitution three years after the adoption of the Federal Constitution and proclaimed: "The people of

117 Ibid, 33.
118 Ibid, 136.
119 Ibid, 111.
120 Ibid.
121 Ibid, 341.

this Commonwealth have the sole and exclusive right of governing themselves as a free, sovereign, and independent State."[122] In 1803 Louisiana was admitted to the union. The Constitution of Louisiana declared Louisiana to be "a free and independent state."[123] A union of such free, independent, and sovereign states creates a union of free men that is made "perpetual" by the good will and mutual benefit of the states of the union. As Tucker points out, "where constraint and fear constitute that bond" of the union, freedom ends and political slavery begins.

Lincoln vs Tucker

Advocates of big government always clothe their grab for power in high and praiseworthy rhetoric: socialists are struggling to uplift the workers; communists are bringing economic freedom to the masses; Nazis are trying to free the workers from the parasitic influence of an alien culture; and Lincoln was saving the Union and freeing the slaves.[124]

It should be obvious to any student of the Constitution that the views expressed in 1803 by St. George Tucker, a founding father, and the views expressed and acted upon by Abraham Lincoln cannot be compared but must be contrasted. Having a different view on Constitutional interpretation is not a crime. Using that different view as an excuse to compel, by unconstitutional military invasion with its attendant death and destruction, a people to accept those radically different views is more than simply criminal, it is tyrannical! The exercise of such tyrannical force sounds the death-knell for free republican institutions.

There are three main areas of American governmental philosophy where Tucker and Lincoln disagree: (1) where does sovereignty reside; (2) who established the Union; (3) and, the perpetual nature of Union.

First: Determining the location of sovereignty is more than just an academic exercise. The War for Southern Independence centered upon the question of whether the states individually or the federal government was sovereign. If, as Lincoln proposed, the federal government or as some would say, the whole of the American people as

122 *The American's Guide to the Constitutions of the United States of America* (Trenton, NJ: Moore and Lake, 1813), 341.

123 Ibid.

124 Benson and Kennedy, *Lincoln's Marxists* (Pelican Publishing Co., Gretna, LA: 2011), 96.

represented by the federal government, was sovereign then secession was illegal. In that case, the attempt at secession would be nothing less than an act of rebellion. Lincoln boldly stated that the states were not sovereign and ridiculed the idea of state sovereignty: "Much is said about the 'sovereignty' of the States; but the word, even, is not in the national Constitution; nor, as is believed, in any of the State constitution."[125] Here Lincoln completely rejects the very words of the Ninth Amendment which clearly states that just because a right is not "enumerated," i.e., mentioned separately such as in counting or naming each right separately, that does not mean the people do not hold said right. The word "marriage" does not exist in the Constitution, does that mean that marriage is not allowed under the Constitution? Lincoln also was incorrect when he stated that the word sovereignty did not exist "in any of the State constitutions." As already noted in New Hampshire the word does exist, as it does in other state constitutions, and in Louisiana's Constitution, she proclaims herself to be "a free and independent state." A free and independent state is a sovereign state and a sovereign state is a free and independent state. Tucker, who was a major participant of both the War for American Independence and the formation of the government under the Constitution, puts the question to rest with the statement, "From the moment of the revolution they [the thirteen original states] became severally independent and sovereign states ... bound by no ties but of their own creation."[126] It is obvious that Lincoln was wrong on these points.

Second: Lincoln's view of who established the Union (today referred to as the federal government), is completely at odds with St. George Tucker's view. Lincoln stated that "The Union is older than the States and, in fact, created them as States." According to Lincoln, the Union begat the States, whereas, Tucker insists that the States begat the Union: "The union is in fact, as well as in theory, an association of states, or, a confederacy."[127] How was the Union created? As Tucker points out, it was done by the free act of so many sovereign states. The Union, under the Constitution, sprang into life when nine sovereign states adopted it as their form of central government. As Article 7 of the Constitution expresses, the new federal government

125 Abraham Lincoln, "July 4th Message to Congress," 4 July 1861. For a more complete review of subject see, *Lincoln Marxist*, Chapter 9.

126 Tucker, 100.

127 Ibid, 92.

would exist among only those states so ratifying the Constitution. Neither the Union nor the government under the Constitution existed before the adoption of the Constitution: "A constitution is a thing antecedent to a government, and a government, is only the creature of a constitution." With these words Tucker destroys Lincoln's vaunted announcement that the Union created the States. Also, these words of Tucker demonstrate that the states created the Union. It is somewhat ironic that one major 20th century historical figure did agree with Lincoln's view of the Union creating the states: "These states did not and could not possess sovereign rights of their own. Because it was the Union that created most of these so-called states."[128] The author of this statement was Adolph Hitler.

Third: If, as Lincoln declared, no state or group of states can remove themselves from the Union, then said Union is perpetual. Here again we must contrast the views of Lincoln, who was not a founding father, with Tucker, who was a founding father. Lincoln stated, "But if the destruction of the Union, by one, or by part only, of the States, be lawfully possible, the Union is less perfect than before the Constitution, having lost the vital element of perpetuity. It follows from these views that no State, upon its mere motion, can lawfully get out of the Union."[129]Lincoln asserts that perpetuity of the Union is a vital element in the government of the United States. The fact is that nowhere in the Constitution is the word "perpetual" or "perpetuity" even mentioned. The Declaration of Independence clearly and unequivocally states that governments can and MUST be "altered or abolished" by the people when it falls out of favor with the people. The only place where "perpetual" is mentioned is in the Articles of Confederation. But despite the claim of being perpetual, the simple historical fact is that the government/union under the Articles of Confederation was not perpetual. It was not perpetual because the sovereign states withdrew from that government/union as they acceded to the new government/union under the Constitution. As for Lincoln's assertion that perpetuity is a vital element of government/union, one only has to refer to the words of Patrick Henry, "The first thing I have at heart is American *liberty*, the second thing is American *union*."[130] Henry, as

128 Adolf Hitler, *Mein Kampf* (Hurst and Blackett, LTD., New York: 1942), 312. Also see, Benson and Kennedy, *Lincoln's Marxist*, chapter 3.

129 Abraham Lincoln, "First Inaugural Address," 6 March 1861.

130 Patrick Henry, as cited in, William W. Henry, *Patrick Henry: Life, Correspondence and Speeches* (1891: Sprinkle Publication, Harrisonburg, VA: 1993), III, 449.

well as Madison in the Federalist Paper No. 43, plainly state that liberty (Henry) and/or the safety and happiness of a society (Madison) are the points in which "all political institutions aim, and to which all such institutions must be sacrificed."[131] A union is a "political institution." Madison did not proclaim that all institutions *except* the union must be sacrificed but rather "*all such institutions must be sacrificed.*" In other words, in the republic of republics of our founding fathers, liberty always trumps union. Tucker notes that after the adoption of the Constitution, each state "is still a perfect state, still sovereign, still independent, and still capable, should the occasion require, *to resume the exercise of its functions, as such, in the most unlimited extent* [emphasis added]."[132] The act of resuming "the exercise of its functions... in the most unlimited extent," is what patriots of 1861 called secession.

This review demonstrates just how radically different St. George Tucker and Abraham Lincoln viewed the power of the federal government. Alexander Hamilton and Thomas Jefferson also held very different views of the nature of the Constitution and American government. But the sad fact is that Hamilton and Jefferson did not usher in a war of aggression, conquest, and impoverishment of a whole class of people as did Lincoln! Modern-day sycophants of Lincoln will excuse his war on the ground that it was "necessary to save the Union." One is left perplexed and wondering, "What kind of Union did Lincoln saved?" Tucker proclaims that any union or government that does not exist on the basis of the *consent* of the governed is nothing less than "*political slavery.*" When Americans refuse to embrace a government by consent, they by that very act are embracing a "union" akin to the union of a lamb's throat and the jaws of a wolf. This is not the type of union that America's Founding Fathers, such as St. George Tucker, fought to create.

John C. Calhoun On Government and the U.S. Constitution: Pre-War

Calhoun was one of the greatest political philosophers and Constitutional scholars produced in the United States. Yet, just like Rawle and Tucker, he is ignored today because his conservative views of government and the Constitution stand in sharp contrast to America's

131 James Madison, 'Federalist Paper No. 43,' as cited in, Carey and McClellan, 228.
132 Tucker, 136.

dominant, politically correct views held by America's ruling elites. The following is taken from two of Calhoun's books. It demonstrates the close political agreement between Judge Rawle from Pennsylvania and Senator Calhoun from South Carolina. Calhoun's book *A Disquisition on Government* explains the basic philosophy that shaped early American ideas on government, why man needs government, the Devine origins of rights protected by government, and the danger posed by all forms of government. He takes up the discussion of the U.S. Constitution in *A Discourse on the United States Constitution* which follows this section. [*The following are direct quotes from Calhoun's book except for comments by editors in brackets*].

A Disquisition on Government

Man is so constituted as to be a social being. His inclinations and wants, physical and moral, irresistibly impel him to associate with his kind; ... In no age or country has any society or community ever been found whether enlightened or savage, without government of some description.[133]

[Calhoun notes that there is something within man that makes government necessary] "... it impels man to associate with his kind, renders it impossible for society to exist without government."[134]

[But while man is created for the social state, he is so constituted as to], "feel more intensely what affects him directly, than what affects him indirectly though others; or, to express it differently, he is so constituted, that his direct or individual affections are stronger than his sympathetic or social feelings."[135]

...our nature which makes us feel more intensely what affects us directly than what affects us indirectly through others, necessarily leads to conflict between individuals...hence, the tendency to a universal state of conflict...if not prevented by some controlling power... This controlling power, wherever vested, or by whomsoever exercised, is *government.*[136]

To the Infinite Being, the Creator of all. ... To man, he has assigned the social and political state, as best adapted to develop the great capacities and faculties, intellectual and moral, with which he

---

133 Calhoun, John C., *A Disquisition on Government in The Works of John C. Calhoun*, Vol I. (Appleton & Co., New York, 1851), 1-2.

134 Calhoun, *A Disquisition on Government*, 2.

135 Calhoun, *A Disquisition on Government*, 3.

136 Calhoun, *A Disquisition on Government*, 4.

has endowed him [man]; and has, accordingly, constituted him so as not only to impel him into the social state, but to make government necessary for his preservation and well-being.[137]

But government ... has itself a strong tendency to disorder and abuse of its powers ... [Government] must be administered by men in whom, like others, the individual are stronger than the social feelings. And hence, the powers vested in them to prevent injustice and oppression on the part of others, will, if left unguarded, be by them converted into instruments to oppress the rest of the community. That, by which this is prevented ... is what is meant by *constitution* ... when applied to *government*.[138]

Constitution is the contrivance of man, while government is of Divine ordination. Man is left to perfect what the wisdom of the Infinite ordained, as necessary to preserve the [human] race.[139]

How can those who are invested with the powers of government be prevented from employing them, as the means of aggrandizing themselves, instead of using them to protect and preserve society?[140]

Power can only be resisted by power — and tendency by tendency.[141] [This is one of the most important statements ever uttered for the benefit of those who wish to establish or maintain liberty within a free Republic. Calhoun then addresses the false hope that voting (suffrage) alone will provide adequate protection from an abusive government].

Suffrage ... it would be a great and dangerous mistake to suppose, as many do, that it is, of itself, sufficient to form constitutional governments. To this erroneous opinion may be traced one of the causes, why so few attempts to form constitutional governments have succeeded.[142]

[Suffrage] would, unaided by other provisions, leave the government an absolute as it would be in the hands of irresponsible rulers.[143]

The right of suffrage, of itself, can do no more than give complete control to those who elect, over the conduct of those they have elect-

137 Calhoun, *A Disquisition on Government*, 6-7.

138 Calhoun, *A Disquisition on Government*, 7.

139 Calhoun, *A Disquisition on Government*, 8.

140 Calhoun, *A Disquisition on Government*, 8.

141 Calhoun, *A Disquisition on Government*, 12.

142 Calhoun, *A Disquisition on Government*, 13.

143 Calhoun, *A Disquisition on Government*, 13.

ed.[144]

If the whole community had the same interests … then the right of suffrage, of itself, would be all-sufficient to counteract the tendency of the government to oppression and abuse of its powers …[if] The interest of all being the same … all would have like interests as to what laws should be made, and how they should be executed.

But such is not the case. On the contrary, nothing is more difficult than to equalize the action of the government, in reference to the various and diversified interests of the community; and nothing more easy to aggrandize and enrich one or more interests by oppressing and improvising the others; and this too, under the operation of laws… Nor is this the case in some particular communities only. It is so in all.[145] [Note that Calhoun explains how government can oppress its people "under the operation of laws"]

…the right of suffrage, by placing the control of the government in the community must, from the same constitution of our nature which makes government necessary to preserve society, lead to conflict among its different interests — each striving to obtain possession of its [government] powers, as the means of protecting itself against the others; or of advancing its respective interests, regardless of the interests of others … a struggle will take place between the various interests to obtain a majority, in order to control the government.[146] [Modern Americans have seen this as the great Red States-Blue States divide in national presidential elections. When Obama won, he spent his time promoting policies that were deemed oppressive by Red State conservatives, but when Trump won, his policies were deemed oppressive by Blue State "progressives." By 2020 there were dire predictions of a coming second civil war between the Red States and Blue States].

The advantages of possessing the control of the powers of the government and, thereby, [gaining control] of its honors and emoluments, are, of themselves … ample to divide … a community into two great hostile parties.[147]

[The ability of the numerical majority to tax the numerical minority and thereby transfer wealth from the minority to the majority became an issue for the South in the early 1800s. Bounties for one

144 Calhoun, *A Disquisition on Government*, 13.
145 Calhoun, *A Disquisition on Government*, 15.
146 Calhoun, *A Disquisition on Government*, 16.
147 Calhoun, *A Disquisition on Government*, 17.

becomes burdens for the other].

" … the unequal fiscal action of the government is, to divide the community into two great classes…"

The effect, then of every increase [in taxation] is, to enrich and strengthen the one and impoverish and weaken the other.[148]

The dominant majority, for the time, would, in reality, through the right of suffrage, be the rulers — the controlling, governing, and irresponsible power.[149]

… the right of suffrage, without some other provision, cannot counteract this tendency of government [to abuse its powers].[150]

[The majority party in a democracy would be the dominant party]. Being the [dominant] party in possession of the government, they will, from the same constitution of man which makes government necessary to protect society, be in favor of the powers granted by the constitution, and opposed to the restrictions intended to limit them. As the major and dominant party, they will have no need of these restrictions for their protection. The ballot-box, of itself, would be ample protection to them [the dominant or majority party].[151] [The dominant party does not need and indeed, does not want, a constitution that limits its power to use government to enrich those who belong to the dominant party. In today's economy they would be known as crony capitalist — or as President Eisenhower stated "the military-industrial-complex"].

The minor, or weaker party, on the contrary, would take the opposite direction — and regard them [constitutional restrictions or limits on government powers] as essential to their protection against the dominant party.[152]

The party in favor of the restrictions [on government powers] would be overpowered. At first, they might command some respect, and do something to stay the march of encroachment; but they would, in the progress of the contest, be regarded as mere abstractionists; and, indeed, deservedly, if they should indulge the folly of supposing that the party in possession of the ballot-box and the physical force of the country, could be successfully resisted by an appeal to reason, truth, justice, or the obligations imposed by the constitution.

148 Calhoun, *A Disquisition on Government*, 21.
149 Calhoun, *A Disquisition on Government*, 22.
150 Calhoun, *A Disquisition on Government*, 24.
151 Calhoun, *A Disquisition on Government*, 32.
152 Calhoun, *A Disquisition on Government*, 32.

For when these, of themselves, shall exert sufficient influence to stay the hand of power, then government will be no longer necessary to protect society, nor constitutions needed to prevent government from abusing its powers. The end of the contest would be the subversion of the constitution, either by the undermining process of construction — where its meaning would admit of possible doubt — or by substitution in practice what is called party-usage, in place of its [the constitution's] provisions — or, finally, when no other contrivance would subserve the purpose, by openly and boldly setting them [constitutional restrictions on government powers] aside.[153] [The ultimate end of a political struggle between the numerical dominant party and the smaller party is (1) the separation of the smaller party from the government dominated by the larger party and the establishing of a new government for the smaller party (secession as in 1776 and 1861) or (2) the domination and destruction of the smaller party in a violent war waged by the larger party].

[Recognizing that no part of a constitution is self-enforcing Calhoun describes the means by which the minority party could enforce the constitutional restrictions and thereby protect its rights against an aggressive majority. He terms it a "concurrent majority" by which each party is allowed a negative on the acts of the other]. The concurrent majority is ... to give to each interest or portion of the community a negative on the others. It is this mutual negative among its various conflicting interests, which invests each with the power of protecting itself — and places the rights and safety of each, where only they can be securely placed, under its own guardianship.[154] [The American left uses this "negative" today by establishing "sanctuary cities" in violation of Federal law. Unfortunately, the American right is not allowed to use the same to protect its values].

The numerical majority is as truly a single power, ... as completely as the absolute government of one or of the few.[155]

And hence, the great and broad distinction between governments is — not that of the one, the few, or the many — but of the constitutional and the absolute.[156] [Today American government is one of absolute power. The federal government is supreme].

But absolute governments, of all forms, exclude all other means

153 Calhoun, *A Disquisition on Government*, 33-4.

154 Calhoun, *A Disquisition on Government*, 35.

155 Calhoun, *A Disquisition on Government*, 36.

156 Calhoun, *A Disquisition on Government*, 37.

of resistance to their authority, than that of force; and, of course, leave no other alternative to the governed, but to acquiesce in oppression, however great it may be, or to resort to force to put down the government.[157]

[Calhoun explains how governments are preserved or maintained over time]. This principle, in constitutional governments, is *compromise* — and in absolute governments, is force.[158] [In 1776 the King of England elected force and in 1861 Northern President Lincoln who controlled the numerical majority also elected force despite numerous attempts to avoid war].

[Calhoun describes the insidious decay of a constitutional republic under the control of the numerical majority, predicting that it will ultimately become a criminal enterprise]. At this stage, principles and policy would lose all influence in the elections; and cunning, falsehood, deception, slander, fraud, and gross appeals to the appetites of the lowest and most worthless portions of the community, would take the place of sound reason and wise debate.[159]

The numerical majority, perhaps, should usually be one of the elements of a constitutional democracy; but to make it the sole element, in order to perfect the constitution and make the government more popular, is one of the greatest and most fatal of political errors.[160]

By giving to each interest, or portion, the power of self-protection, all strife and struggle between them for ascendency, is prevented; and, thereby, not only every feeling calculated to weaken the attachment to the whole is suppressed, but the individual and the social feelings are made to unite in one common devotion to country.[161]

Neither religion nor education can counteract the strong tendency of the numerical majority to corrupt and debase the people.[162]

The progress of a people rising from a lower to a higher point in the scale of liberty, is necessarily slow — and by attempting to precipitate [accelerate] we either retard, or permanently defeat it.[163]

It is only through an organism [the concurrent majority] which vests each with a negative, in some one form or another, that those

157 Calhoun, *A Disquisition on Government*, 37.
158 Calhoun, *A Disquisition on Government*, 37.
159 Calhoun, *A Disquisition on Government*, 41-2.
160 Calhoun, *A Disquisition on Government*, 45.
161 Calhoun, *A Disquisition on Government*, 48.
162 Calhoun, *A Disquisition on Government*, 51.
163 Calhoun, *A Disquisition on Government*, 56.

who have like interests in preventing the government from passing beyond its proper sphere, and encroaching on the rights and liberty of individuals, can co-operate peaceably and effectually in resisting the encroachments of power and thereby preserve their right and liberty.[164]

And hence, in no governments, except those that rest on the principle of the concurrent or constitutional majority, can the people guard their liberty against power; and hence, also, when lost, the great difficulty and uncertainty of regaining it by force.[165]

A Discourse on the Constitution and Government of the United States

[The government of the United States means] a federal, in contradistinction to a national government.[166]

[A national government would possess the ultimate power to judge the limitations, if any, imposed by the Constitution on the federal government. In a national government, power is maintained in Washington, DC, and privileges, under the control of the federal government, flow down to the people; but in a true federal system, power, especially the power to judge the constitutionality of federal acts, is maintained at the local (state) level. It is the difference between a centralized, all powerful, supreme federal government vs. a Constitutionally limited Republic of Sovereign States].

That the States, when they formed and ratified the constitution, were distinct, independent, and sovereign communities.[167]

During their colonial condition, they formed distinct communities — each with its separate charter and government—and in no way connected with each other, except as dependent members of a common empire. ... voting and acting as separate and distinct communities — and not in the aggregate, as composing one community or nation.[168]

"We the people of the United States," means, We, the people of the

164 Calhoun, *A Disquisition on Government*, 60-1.

165 Calhoun, *A Disquisition on Government*, 61.

166 Calhoun, *A Discourse on the Constitution and Government of the United States, in The Works of John C. Calhoun*, Vol I. 114. Herein after cited as *On the Constitution.*

167 Calhoun, *On the Constitution*, 119.

168 Calhoun, *On the Constitution*, 123.

several States of the Union. The inference is irresistible. And when it is considered that the States of the Union were then members of the confederacy [union under the Articles of Confederation] and that, by the express provision of one of its articles, "each State retains its sovereignty, freedom, and independence," the proof is demonstrative, that —"We, the people of the United States of America," mean that people of the several States of the Union acting as free, independent, and sovereign States.[169] [The first draft of the Constitution contained a list of all thirteen States but the list was removed by the Committee on Style, because it was not certain that all of the States would choose to join the new union under the proposed constitution].[170]

"*United States*" was used in a geographical and not a political sense.[171] [Emphasis in the original, italics in quotes belong to Calhoun].

[The] constitution was ordained and established *by* the several States, as *distinct, sovereign communities*; and that it was ordained and established by them for *themselves* — for their common welfare and safety, as distinct and *sovereign communities.*[172]

That it [the Constitution] was not over *the several States*, is settled by the seventh article beyond controversy. It declares, that the ratification by nine States be sufficient to establish the constitution between the States so ratifying. "Between" necessarily excludes "*over*" as that which is *between* States cannot be over them.[173]

But the question still remains, *over whom* was it [the Constitution] ordained and established? … It was over *the government* which it created.[174]

It is an acknowledged principle, that sovereigns may, by compact, modify or qualify the exercise of their power, without impairing their sovereignty.[175]

The theory of the nationality of the government, is, in fact, founded on fiction.[176]

The term, "federal" implies a league — and this, a compact be-

169 Calhoun, *On the Constitution*, 128.
170 Calhoun, *On the Constitution*, 133.
171 Calhoun, *On the Constitution*, 134.
172 Calhoun, *On the Constitution*, 130.
173 Calhoun, *On the Constitution*, 130.
174 Calhoun, *On the Constitution*, 131.
175 Calhoun, *On the Constitution*, 139.
176 Calhoun, *On the Constitution*, 140.

tween sovereign communities.[177]

Among them [the powers retained by the people of sovereign states in the federal union under the Constitution] is included the high sovereign power, by which they ordained and established [government] and by which they can modify, change or abolish them at pleasure. This, with others not delegated, are those which are reserved to the people of the several States respectively.[178] [We the people of the Sovereign States retained unenumerated powers, as per the Ninth Amendment, such as the States' Rights of nullification and secession. An aggressive and genocidal war waged by the numerical majority may suppress these rights but these rights are among the "unalienable rights" belonging to Americans and can never be destroyed — they live on regardless of the suppression enacted by battalions of bloody bayonets or the passage of time].

[The] act establishing the constitution is, itself, a federal and not a national act.[179]

If it [the Union under the Constitution] had been formed by the people as one nation … the will of the majority of the whole people of the Union would have bound the minority that the idea of a national government involves in it, not only authority over individual citizens, but an indefinite supremacy over all persons and things, so far as they are objects of lawful government — that among the people consolidated into one nation, this supremacy is completely vested in the government; that State government and all local authorities, are subordinate to it and may be controlled, directed or abolished by it at pleasure.[180] [Calhoun is here describing a supreme federal government—a form of government both Federalist and anti-Federalists expressly declared they did not intend to create under the Constitution].

[The constitution making powers] … emanating from the people, as forming a *sovereign community* — creates the government — the other, as a representative appointed to execute its powers, enacts laws to regulate and control the conduct of the people, regarded as *individuals.*[181]

[*E pluribus unum*] Abroad — to the rest of the world — they

177 Calhoun, *On the Constitution*, 141.

178 Calhoun, *On the Constitution*, 144.

179 Calhoun, *On the Constitution*, 150.

180 Calhoun, *On the Constitution*, 151.

181 Calhoun, *On the Constitution*, 192.

are but one. It is only at home, in their interior relations, that they are many; and it is to this twofold aspect that their motto *E pluribus unum* appropriately and emphatically applies.[182]

[Describing the first 12 Amendments to the Constitution] … they are intended to guard against improper constructions of the constitution, or the abuse of the delegated powers by the government.[183]

[Calhoun explains the division of powers which is unique to the American system of government as designed by the Founding Fathers]. The great, original, and primary division, as has been stated, is that of distinct, independent, and sovereign States. It is the basis of the whole system. The next in order is the division into the constitutional-making [we the people within our specific sovereign states] and the law-making powers [Congress and State legislatures]. The next separates the delegated and the reserved powers, by vesting the one [delegated powers] in the government of the United States and the other in the separate governments of the respective States, as co-ordinate governments; and the last, distributes the powers of government between the several departments of each [the so-called co-equal branches of government — executive, legislative, and judicial].[184]

Two great parties, which arose with the formation of the constitution and which, finally, assumed the names of "*Federal*" and "*Republican*."[185] [Federalists being consolidationists who wanted a strong central government, followed the thinking of Hamilton. Jeffersonian Republicans being strict constructionists who wanted a constitutionally limited federal government, followed the thinking of Jefferson and Madison].

[No part of the Constitution is self-enforcing] … the constitution of the United States is a written instrument; for this, of itself, cannot possibly enforce the limitations and restrictions which it imposes.[186] [As Calhoun notes, it is not the federal government that has the ultimate authority to determine the limitations imposed upon itself by the Constitution, but the Sovereign States who are the principles who created the Constitution — the federal government being merely the agent of the Sovereign States].

182 Calhoun, On the Constitution, 201.
183 Calhoun, On the Constitution, 211.
184 Calhoun, On the Constitution, 216.
185 Calhoun, On the Constitution, 227.
186 Calhoun, On the Constitution, 234.

If, then, neither the constitution, nor any thing appertaining to it, furnishes means adequate to prevent the encroachment of the delegated on the reserved powers, they must be found in some other part of the system, if they are to be found in it at all. And, further — if they are to be found there, it must be in the powers not delegated. … But, if they are to be found in the reserved powers, it must be in those vested in the separate governments of the several States, or in those retained by the people of the several States, in their sovereign character.[187]

[Discussing the means available to those holding the reserved powers — the Sovereign States — to resist encroachment on its reserved powers by the government of delegated powers — the federal government — Calhoun noted the ultimate ineffectiveness of relying exclusively upon representation in the Federal Congress or the Federal Judiciary]. To rely upon them to counteract a tendency so strong and steady, would be as idle as to rely on reason and justice, as a means to prevent oppression and abuse of power on the part of government, without the aid of constitutional provisions. Nothing short of a negative, absolute or in effect, on the part of the government of a State, can possibly protect it against the encroachments of the government of the United States, whenever their powers come in conflict.[188] [Nullification by the Sovereign State is the ultimate means of enforcing the limitations on federal acts — nullification is a way to maintain the Union and thereby avoid the necessity of secession].

[Rejecting the principle that under our Constitution a Sovereign State has the right to nullify oppressive acts of its agent, the federal government, would have the following results] …The effect would be to raise one from an equal to a superior — and to reduce the other from an equal to a subordinate; … to sink it into a dependent corporation.[189]

[If the federal government can judge the extent of its power, then so can the Sovereign State. The two are equal — co-ordinate governments — and when a conflict arises, there arises a constitutional standoff in which neither has the Constitutional authority to compel the other].[190]

187 Calhoun, *On the Constitution*, 236.

188 Calhoun, *On the Constitution*, 241.

189 Calhoun, *On the Constitution*, 242.

190 See Hamilton's discussion in *Federalist* Number 31 and 32 regarding the Federal/State equilibrium.

The party, in the convention, which favored a supreme national government, [Hamilton, *et al.*] clearly saw that the separate governments of the several States would have the right of judging of the extent of their powers, as between the two governments, unless some provision should be adopted to prevent it. This is manifested from the many and strenuous efforts which they [Hamilton, *et al.*] made to deprive them [the Sovereign States] of the right, by vesting the government of the United States with the power to veto or overrule their [States] acts, when they might be thought to come in conflict with its [Federal] powers. These efforts were made in every stage of the proceedings of the convention, and in every conceivable form — as the journals will show.[191] … they were all made but not one adopted.[192] [The Founding Fathers *did not* create a supreme federal government to sit in judgment over the States. Lincoln and his cronies did what the Founding Fathers deliberately and openly avoided — the creation of a supreme federal government. The Founding Fathers' work was accomplished via the consent of the governed, whereas Lincoln's work was accomplished via coercion, i.e., aggressive war].

The fact that they were proposed [proposals in the Constitutional Convention to give the federal government veto powers over State legislation] and so urged, proves, conclusively, that it was believed, even by the most distinguished members of the national party [Federalist], that the former had no right to enforce its measures against the latter, where they disagreed as to the extent of their respective powers — without some express provision to that effect; while the refusal of the convention to adopt any such provision, under such circumstances, proves, equally conclusively, that it was opposed to the delegation of such powers to the [federal] government.[193]

It was well known, that there was a powerful opposition to the adoption of the constitution of the United States. It originated in the apprehension, that it would lead to the consolidation of all power in the government of the United States. ... The alarm became so great as to threaten the defeat of the ratification by nine States … it was particularly great in Virginia.[194] [That opposition being led by Patrick Henry].

[To obtain Virginia's ratification it was necessary to include a pro-

191 Calhoun, *On the Constitution*, 244.

192 Calhoun, *On the Constitution*, 246.

193 Calhoun, *On the Constitution*, 246.

194 Calhoun, *On the Constitution*, 247.

vision in her ratification document specifically reserving the right to withdraw from the compact of the Union based solely upon the will of the people of Virginia. New York and Rhode Island included similar language in their ratification — reserving the right of secession]. [195]

[Ratifying States, North and South, recommend an amendment with wording similar to the Tenth Amendment proving that States' Rights was not just a "Southern thing" conjured to defend first slavery and then white supremacy]. [196]

[The Supremacy Clause — Article VI, Sec. 2 — Calhoun's reply to those who would claim that the supremacy clause grants the federal government unlimited authority over the Sovereign States composing the Union]. It is sufficient, in reply, to state, that the clause is declaratory; that it vests no new power whatever in the government, or in any of its departments. … And, hence, the supremacy of laws and treaties is expressly restricted to such as are made in pursuance of the constitution, or under the authority of the United States; which can, in no case, extend beyond the delegated powers.[197]

[This is in perfect agreement with the writings of a High Federalist Alexander Hamilton as expressed in the Federalist Papers.

But it will not follow from this doctrine that acts of the larger society [Federal] which are not pursuant to its constitutional powers, but which are invasions of the residuary authorities of the smaller societies [States], will become the supreme law of the land. These will be merely acts of usurpation and will deserve to be treated as such.[198]

It will not, I presume, have escaped observation, that it *expressly* confines this supremacy to laws made *pursuant to the Constitution.*[199]

There is no position which depends on clearer principles than that every act of a delegated authority, contrary to the tenor of the commission under which it is exercised, is void. No legislative act, therefore, contrary to the Constitution can be valid.[200]

The operative words in the Supremacy Clause are "pursuant to the Constitution" not "supreme law of the land" the latter being merely the effect of the former. The question remains as to who decides if the

---

195 Calhoun, *On the Constitution*, 248-9.
196 Calhoun, *On the Constitution*, 251.
197 Calhoun, *On the Constitution*, 252-3.
198 Hamilton in Federalist Papers No. 33, page 108; in *The Federalist, Great Books of the Western World*, Robert M. Hutchins, Ed., (The University of Chicago: 1952).
199 Hamilton in Federalist Papers No.33, page 109.
200 Hamilton in Federalist Papers No.78, page 231.

federal government is acting in a manner that is not "pursuant to the Constitution?" Should the actor (the federal government) be allowed to judge whether its acts are constitutional or should the final judge be the principles who created the federal government — we the people within our respective Sovereign State? Which method would be most likely to prevent the encroachment upon reserved rights?]

In this respect, as well as their supremacy in regard to each other [Federal and State], in their respective spheres, they stand on the same level. Neither has any advantage, in either particular, over the other.[201]

[Calhoun answers those who advocate the principle of federal supremacy.] It is manifest, that they who contend for this right to its full extent, overlook the distinction, in this respect, between single governments [national or a supreme federal government], vested with all the powers appertaining to government, and co-ordinate governments, in a system where the powers of government are divided between two or more, as is the case with us.[202]

[On nullification] But the several States, as weaker parties, can protect the portion not delegated … a negative on its [the federal government's] acts, when they disagree as to the extent of their respective powers.[203]

[On the relationship between the federal and state governments in our co-ordinate system of government.] The effect of this is, to make each, as against the other, the guardian and protector of the powers allotted to it, and of which it is the organ and representative.[204]

[Evidence of the equality between federal and state governments is seen in the way in which the Founding Fathers treated suggestions of federal supremacy at the Constitutional Convention and during the ratifying conventions in each Sovereign State.] By refusing to vest the government of the United States with a veto on the acts of the separate governments of the several States, in any form or manner whatever.[205]

[The Constitution was created] … as a constitution for the United States not over them; and established, not over, but between the States ratifying it; and hence, a State acting in its sovereign capacity, and in

---

201 Calhoun, *On the Constitution*, 258.
202 Calhoun, *On the Constitution*, 265.
203 Calhoun, *On the Constitution*, 266.
204 Calhoun, *On the Constitution*, 266.
205 Calhoun, *On the Constitution*, 267.

the same manner in which it ratified and adopted the constitution, may be guilty of violating it as a compact, but cannot be guilty of violating it as a law.[206]

[Those who deny that the Constitution is a compact do so in an effort to protect their unconstitutional theory of federal supremacy.] And hence, those who are unwilling to admit the consequences, have been found to deny that the constitution is a compact; in the face of facts as well established as any in our political history, and in utter disregard of that provision of the constitution, which expressly declares, that the ratification of nine States shall be sufficient to establish it "*between the States so ratifying the same*."[207] [Article VII, Sec. 1 demonstrates that the Constitution is a compact between mutually equal sovereign states.]

[On why the amending process was intentionally set to require such a large number of States to constitute a constitutional majority — three fourths of the States.] I say, as large a proportion as three fourths — for the larger the proportion required to do an act [amending the Constitution], the less is the danger of the power being used for the purpose of oppression and aggrandizement.[208]

The federal government never will make an appeal to the amending power, in a case of conflict [with States regarding reserved powers], unless compelled — nor, indeed, willingly in any case, except with a view to enlarge the powers it has usurped by construction.[209]

It [Federal supremacy] would be a revolution in the character of the system. It would virtually destroy the relation of co-ordinates between the federal government and those of the several States, by rendering the negative of the latter [State nullification], in case of conflict with it [federal government], of no effect … thereby, elevate the federal government to the absolute and supreme authority of the system, with liberty to assume, by construction, whatever power the cupidity or ambition of a dominant party or section might crave.

It would, in a word, practically transform the federal, into a consolidated national government, against the avowed intention of its framers — the plain meaning of the constitution itself — and the understanding of the people of the States, when they ratified and

206 Calhoun, *On the Constitution*, 277.

207 Calhoun, *On the Constitution*, 278.

208 Calhoun, *On the Constitution*, 293.

209 Calhoun, *On the Constitution*, 298.

adopted it.[210]

[On the impact of state nullification] … where a State acting in her sovereign character, and as a party to the constitutional compact, has interposed, and declared an act of the federal government to be unauthorized by the constitution—and, therefore, null and void.… In such case, the State is not bound to acquiesce. It may choose whether it will, or whether it will not secede from the Union.[211]

[The mutual negative between the two co-ordinate governments is the only means available to prevent encroachments by the federal government upon the reserved rights of Sovereign States.] [212]

[Absent a means to enforce the reserved rights of the States, the Constitution becomes a mere parchment barricade.[213]] The written restrictions and limitations of the constitution, would oppose no effectual resistance. They would all be gradually undermined by the slow and certain process of construction; which would be continued until the instrument itself, would be of no more force or validity than an ordinary act of Congress — nor would it be more respected. The opposing construction of the minority would become the subject of ridicule and scorn — as mere abstractions — until all encroachments would cease to be opposed.[214] ["The slow and certain process of construction." As Thomas Jefferson warned, the Constitution, "… is a mere thing of wax in the hands of the judiciary, which they may twist and shape into any form they please."[215] Here we see the genesis of the living constitution — a plaything for America's ruling elite!]

[Mutual respect is key to maintaining a Constitutional Union.] They [States] freely and voluntarily created it, for the common good of each and of all — and will cherish and defend it so long as it fulfils these objects. If it's safe-keeping cannot be entrusted to its creators [Sovereign States], it can be safely placed in the custody of no other hands.[216]

[Those favoring a supreme federal government.] They assume that the courts of the States are always *right* when they decide in favor of

---

210 Calhoun, *On the Constitution*, 299.

211 Calhoun, *On the Constitution*, 300.

212 Calhoun, *On the Constitution*, 302-3.

213 Madison's words in Federalist No, 48, 157.

214 Calhoun, *On the Constitution*, 305.

215 Jefferson cited in, Quirk & Bridwell, *Judicial Dictatorship* (Transaction Publishers, New Brunswick, NJ: 1995), 3.

216 Calhoun, *On the Constitution*, 312.

the government of the United States, and always *wrong* when they decide in favor of the power of their respective States.[217]

But if the State courts should have a strong leaning in favor of the powers of their respective States, what reason can be assigned, why the Supreme Court of the United States should not have a leaning, equally strong, in favor of the federal government? If one…cannot be trusted in making decisions…on what principle can the other be trusted in making a decision adverse to the reserved powers?[218]

The Federalist, maintained that the government was partly federal and partly national, notwithstanding it calls itself "the government of the United States" and notwithstanding the convention repudiated the word *national* and designated it by the name of "*federal*" in their letter laying the plan before the old Congress[219] [the Congress under the Articles of Confederation].

[Calhoun points out the origin of the Deep State, a bureaucratic ruling elite and its crony capitalist allies] Another of its effects [federal supremacy] has been to engender the most corrupting, loathsome and dangerous disease, that can infect a popular government — I mean that known by the name of "*the Spoils*." It is a disease easily contracted under all forms of government — hard to prevent, and most difficult to cure, when contracted; but of all the forms of governments, it is, by far, the most fatal in those of a popular character.[220] [A government infected by "*the Spoils*" in Calhoun's day is the same as today's federal government of crony capitalism, the military industrial complex, and Wall Street's financial elites.]

… the Alien and Sedition acts, and other measures of the government having a tendency to change its character from a federal to a national government.[221] [The Alien and Sedition Acts were nullified by Kentucky and Virginia in 1798 under the leadership of Thomas Jefferson and James Madison.]

The more the powers of the system are centralized in the federal government, the greater will be its power and patronage; proportionate with these, and increasing with their increase, will be the desire to possess the control over them, for the purpose of aggrandizement; and the stronger this desire, the less will be the regard for principles,

217 Calhoun, *On the Constitution*, 326.
218 Calhoun, *On the Constitution*, 327.
219 Calhoun, *On the Constitution*, 342.
220 Calhoun, *On the Constitution*, 347.
221 Calhoun, *On the Constitution*, 353.

and the greater the tendency to unite for sectional objects — the stronger section with a view to power and aggrandizement — the weaker, for defense and safety.[222] [Thus, Calhoun predicts the actions of Republicans, and Northern commercial interests as they slowly moved toward war against the numerical minority of the South. What those who wanted a supreme federal government could not accomplish via constitutional methods, they accomplished via aggressive war. This ends our study of the pre-War Constitution. We now move to the Republican attack against the Constitution during Reconstruction.][223]

The U.S. Constitution Post-War: Reconstruction 1867-1877

Laws comprising any legal system have two distinct aspects. Laws have a strict written denotation known in common usage as the letter of the law. But laws also have a connotation set by the spirit of the age in which the law was written. This is known as the spirit of the law. It may be possible to fulfill the letter of the law while actually destroying the spirit of the law. The spirit of our original Constitution was to limit the power of the central government while protecting the liberties of the people within their sovereign states. Prior to the War for Southern Independence, the Northern element used the method of loose construction to attack the spirit of the Constitution. The attempt to destroy the spirit of the Constitution reached its most destructive form when the North chose to use military force against the sovereign community in each of the Southern states to prevent them from recalling their delegated rights, powers or authority and establishing a government of their own.

It should be noted that it is far more reasonable to assume a constitutional right of the Southern states to secede from a union from which they had formally and voluntarily acceded than it is to find justification, on constitutional grounds, for the act of armed aggression on the part of the dominant Northern element against the Southern people. This is especially true when we realized that the term "perpetual union" was not included in the Constitution even though it was a part of the Articles of Confederation that preceded the Constitution!

---

222 Calhoun, *On the Constitution*, 371.

223 See, Kennedy & Kennedy, *Yankee Empire: Aggressive Abroad and Despotic at Home* (Shotwell Publishing, Columbia, SC: 2018).

The act of armed aggression by the North to force a new form of government upon the people of the South was in reality an attack upon the original spirit of the Constitution. The attack was an overwhelming success. By the end of the war the South lay prostrate, her armies were physically exhausted, a large portion of her male population was either dead or maimed, her political leader was imprisoned, her white population was disenfranchised, and her economy was totally destroyed. But worst of all, the spirit of the original Constitution was dead!

The end of the war did not mark the end of hostilities. The death of the spirit of the original Constitution was not enough to satisfy the dominant Northern element (Republicans). The letter of the law had to be destroyed as well — lest these Southerners regain their nerve and attempt to use political power to enforce Constitutional limitations on the North's federal government. The Northern element knew that to complete its conquest the letter, as well as the spirit, of the law had to be destroyed. In a political sense, the second attack, on the letter of the law, was as disastrous for the Southern people as the armed invasion had been.

How was this radical change in the American government accomplished? There are only two choices available to the stronger element seeking a change in the form of a constitutional republic: (1) it can use the slow method of loose construction to gradually erode the limitations imposed on federal power by the constitution, or (2) it can use its stronger position — its control of the federal government — to wage aggressive, even genocidal, war against the smaller element. After defeating the smaller element, the victor can put in place puppet governments to rule its conquered people and then dictate the new form of government that the smaller element must accept. As with all empires, consent is replaced with coercion. While both methods were used and, in a manner, are still being used, against the Southern people, it is the latter, armed aggression that forced the greatest change — a change from a constitutionally limited Republic of Sovereign States to a supreme federal government which has evolved into a Globalist Empire.[224] This radical change in American government has been acknowledged and celebrated by liberal/progressive, constitutional scholars:

---

224 See, Kennedy & Kennedy, *Yankee Empire: Aggressive Abroad and Despotic at Home* (Shotwell Publishing, Columbia, SC: 2018), 75-131; 297-310.

"After the Civil War, the power of the nation was firmly established and the arguments for "states' rights" disappeared from the halls of Congress and most of the nation."[225]

Enter Reconstruction

The South's failure in the War for Southern Independence is the primary factor determining the development of America's new form of government — a new, mailable, constitution that recognized no limitations on the federal governments' rulership (domination) over the once sovereign states. Federal acts that were considered unconstitutional prior to the War for Southern Independence became normal post war. States' Rights as exercised prior to the War died and became no more than States' Privileges — privileges exercised only with the permission of the supreme federal government. Post-war the federal government became the sole judge of its own powers.

The War and Reconstruction marked the end of the American Constitutional Republic of Sovereign States. The officially accepted history (history written and enforced by the victor) conveniently ignores the distinction between the American government that evolved after the War as compared to the American government before the War. Just as Imperialists of ancient Rome attempted to keep the trappings (flags, banners, symbols, names, etc.) of the old Roman Republic, the Northern victor convinced Americans that the current federal government is a legitimate descendant and a natural continuation of the Original American Republic of 1776. The truth is that the victor's history is mere propaganda designed to hide its hideous crimes against a people who no longer wanted to be exploited by the Northern majority — a people who wanted to live under a government of their own! A people who wanted a government that would allow them to solve their social problems in a manner that would be best for all of their citizens, but such was not to be. The North used aggressive war to prevent Southern self-determination and then used aggressive, unconstitutional legislation to punish its defeated foe:

"Much of the legislation which Congress passed in the years immediately following the Civil War was designed to punish the Southern states for their attempt to secede from the Union."[226]

---

225 Nowak & Rotunda, *Constitutional Law*, 4th ed. (West Publishing Co., St. Paul Minn., 1991), 19.

226 Nowak & Rotunda, *Constitutional Law*, 4th ed. (West Publishing Co., St. Paul Minn., 1991), 356.

On March 2, 1867 Congress passed the Reconstruction Act. This act abolished civil government in the Southern states. While the United States military occupied its newly conquered territory, Congress used the Reconstruction Act to divided the South into five military districts with a commander of the rank of brigadier general or higher in each district. The United States Army abolished all semblance of civil government, and established military rule — no different than the way all empires treat their newly acquired territories.[227] The Reconstruction Act disenfranchised all voters and directed the army to set up voter registration of its own. The effect was to disenfranchise a large portion of white Southerners and to extend the franchise to illiterates, scalawags, and carpetbaggers.

The Reconstruction Act of 1867 declared the Southern states were not part of the Union. Remember, this was the same Union from which the North had previously said these states could not withdraw! From 1866 to March 2, 1867, the defeated Southern states were accorded the rights of statehood. They participated in the ratification of the Thirteenth Amendment (outlawing chattel slavery) and in the rejection of the Fourteenth Amendment — both Northern and Southern states joined in the rejection of the Fourteenth Amendment. The rejection of the Fourteenth Amendment posed a serious roadblock to the revolutionary schemes of the Republicans in Congress. The Republicans who controlled Congress knew that, even after their successful military conquest of the Southern people, they (Republicans) could not complete their evil designs as long as the South retained even this slight amount of political power. The primary aim of the Republican-initiated invasion and war against the South was to exterminate the South's conservative political power in Congress. To further their evil schemes the Republican majority in Congress decided to eject their conquered foe from Congress and then complete their revolution. In the process the Republican majority in Congress treated the conquered Southern states alternatively as states in the Union and as conquered territories. The treatment afforded the Southern people at the hands of the Republican controlled Congress during Reconstruction stands as historical proof of the extent to which the Federal Empire is willing to go to destroy those who dare to oppose America's new political, commercial, financial, and military empire.

---

227 For a full explanation see, Kennedy & Kennedy, *Yankee Empire: Aggressive Abroad and Despotic at Home* (Shotwell Publishing, Columbia, SC: 2018), 147-77, 219-49.

During Reconstruction the right to vote was denied to a large portion of white citizens, and new elections were ordered with illiterates enfranchised regardless of their lack of education, or qualifications. New legislatures composed of illiterates and others who had little or no governmental experience were elected to carry out the demands of the Republican controlled Congress. Yankee military officers presided over or monitored legislative deliberations in these puppet Southern legislatures. In defiance of the letter and spirit of the original Constitution, new puppet state governments were installed in the South — they were, in fact, bayonet governments. These puppet governments — even though they were not recognized as states in the Union at that time — immediately ratified the Fourteenth Amendment as demanded by the Republican controlled Congress. This was done even though the Secretary of State in Washington had in hand, from the legitimate Southern legislatures, previously enacted resolutions rejecting the proposed amendment. These were the same states that had ratified the Thirteenth Amendment and were then expelled from the Union when they rejected the Fourteenth Amendment. Republicans in Congress realized the Fourteenth Amendment was necessary to give the federal government continuing power to interfere in the internal policies of the once sovereign states. Subsequent to Reconstruction, the Federal Supreme Court used this illegitimate amendment to "incorporate" the Bill of Rights into the exclusive control of the federal government. Pre-war the Bill of Rights applied only to the federal government.[228] Post-war the federal judiciary claimed the right, via the Due Process clause of the Fourteenth Amendment, to be the final judge as to the constitutionality of state law that conflicted with the "progressive" ideological views of the ruling elite in Washington, DC.

The Fraudulent Fourteenth Amendment

The Fourteenth Amendment was pinned to the Constitution via bayonets dripping with Southern blood. After the initial rejection of the Amendment, the Republican controlled Congress reacted by ejecting the South from Congress and established the requirement that before a Southern state would be re-admitted to the Union, they would have to ratify the Fourteenth Amendment. Said ratification has

228 Chief Justice John Marshall speaking for the U.S. Supreme Court acknowledged this in *Barron v. Baltimore*, 32 U.S. 243 (1833). The founders declared "Congress shall not" they did not say "states shall not."

the same legal standing as a confession obtained under the threat of death!

Republicans needed 28 states to ratify the Fourteenth Amendment — at the time (1867) there were 37 states in the Union. Twelve states officially rejected the Amendment (Mississippi's rejection did not reach Washington). To overcome the rejection, Republicans removed the South from Congress and refused to "re-admit" Southern states until they ratified the Fourteenth Amendment. In 1970 the editor of the *U.S. News and World Report*, David Lawrence, published an editorial in which he declared the passage of the Fourteenth Amendment to be "The worst scandal in our history."[229] In 1991 Southern Constitutional scholar Forrest McDonald published an article in *The Georgia Journal of Southern Legal History* explaining the unconstitutional enactment of the Fourteenth Amendment.[230] In 1994 an extensive review of the fraud involved in the passage of the Fourteenth was published in *The South Was Right!* [231] Modern day Yankee "scholars" admit that it was necessary to enact the Fourteenth and Fifteenth Amendments because these amendments were, "the constitutional amendments that consolidated the North's victory."[232] Another liberal "scholar" admitted that the ratification of the Fourteenth Amendment in 1868, "... changed the constitutional landscape. ..."[233]

One of the primary reasons Republicans were determined to pass the Fourteenth Amendment was that with the ratification of the Thirteenth Amendment, abolishing chattel slavery, the South would now have a substantial increase in the number of Southern representatives in the House, because blacks would now be counted the same as whites in the census. Prior to the Thirteenth Amendment slaves were counted as only 3/5s of a person for the purpose of representation in the House of Representatives.[234] The census determines the number

229 Lawrence, David, *U.S. News and World Report*, January 26, 1970, pages 95-6.
230 Republished at: www.abbevilleinstitute.org/review/was-the-fourteenth-amendment-constitutionally-adopted/
231 Kennedy & Kennedy, *The South Was Right!* (Pelican Publishing Co., Gretna, LA: 1994), 167-81; 365-7, 369-74, 375-6, 377-9.
232 *The Oxford Companion to the Supreme Court of the United States*, Kermit L. Hall, Editor In Chief, (Oxford University Press, New York: 1992), 361.
233 O'Brien, David M., *Constitutional Law and Politics, Civil Rights and Civil Liberties*, 2nd edition, Vol. Two (W.W. Norton & Co., New York: 1995), 302.
234 The counting of slaves as only 3/5s of a person was put into the Constitution at the insistence of the North because they feared the South would have too many representatives in Congress and thus outvote the North in Congress.

of representatives for each state. With the additional representatives from the South plus Northern democrats, Republicans stood to lose control of the House. As one Yankee Constitutional scholar noted, the North, "... having won the war, might lose the peace."[235] Republicans answered this challenge by unconstitutionally enacting the Fourteenth and Fifteenth Amendments. The spirit of America's original Constitution was destroyed via war and now Republicans murdered the very letter of America's Constitutional law. After war and Reconstruction, the United States was no longer a Republic of Sovereign States. Thanks to the unconstitutional acts of Republicans, the United States' ruling elite turned the original Republic into a centralized, supreme, federal government that continued to morph into a national and, eventually, a global military, financial, and political empire.[236]

The Constitution Post War & Reconstruction: The Ruling Elite's Constitution

The enactment of the Fourteenth Amendment opened the door for federal judicial activism. This fraudulent amendment allowed the Federal Supreme Court to "incorporate" the "Bill of Rights" into federal jurisdiction and then apply the Constitution against the once sovereign states. Even "progressive" Constitutional scholars have noted the Court's radical departure from Constitutional precedent:

"Judicial supremacy over interpreting the Constitution remains controversial. In Marbury, however, Chief Justice Marshal did not lay claim to judicial supremacy. ..."[237]

The "Due Process" clause of the Fourteenth Amendment now operates as an ongoing Constitutional Convention, allowing the Court's unelected elites to inform citizens of which "rights" they may exercise. Now the Court would invent whole new rights to satiate trendy, leftist, social activism. The "right of privacy" is nowhere in the Constitution but the activist Supreme Court, after discovering it in a prior case, applied it in *Roe v. Wade*. The tendency of judicial activism began in the post-war progressive era. At first, in the *Slaugh-*

235 *The Oxford Companion to the Supreme Court of the United States*, Kermit L. Hall, Editor-in-Chief, 309.

236 See, Kennedy & Kennedy, *Yankee Empire: Aggressive Abroad and Despotic at Home*.

237 *Constitutional Law and Politics, Volume Two, Civil Rights and Civil Liberties*, 2nd edition, David M. O'Brien editor, (W. W. Norton & Co., New York: 1995), 35, 302.

ter Case (1873), the Court refused to use the Amendment to apply federal judicial control over the States, but, during the progressive era, the Court gradually expanded its reach into the rights reserved by the states. In the 1887 *Chicago, Burlington and Quincy Railroad Co. v. Chicago* case, and the 1937 *Gitlow v. New York* case judicial activism and domination over the states began to emerge.[238] By 1965, in *Griswold v. Connecticut*, the Court used the Fourteenth Amendment to justify the discovery of the right of privacy by applying the Bill of Rights to the states. Justice Black warned the Court about using their own interpretation of the Constitution while abandoning the strict language of the Constitution because it would create, "a day-to-day constitutional convention."[239]

The political nature of the Federal Supreme Court's "day-to-day constitutional convention" is demonstrated by reviewing the number of times a subsequent court has reversed "settled-law" or precedent set by a prior Federal Supreme Court. As one scholar noted these reversals document, "… the politics of the changing composition of the high bench."[240] During the 19th century (1800-1899) the Federal Supreme Court reversed itself only 32 times but from 1900 to 1995 the Federal Court reversed itself 174 times. Most demonstrative of the Court's political biases is the fact that of the 174 reversals only 17 occurred from 1900 to 1936. Beginning with the Roosevelt New Deal (liberal-progressive) political era (1937) and counting all reversal up to 1995, the activists Federal Supreme Court reversed "settled-law" 157 times.[241] During the debates on ratification of the Constitution (circa 1787) Robert Yates of New York warned about the Supreme Court's potential danger to liberty when he declared, "This power in the judicial will enable them to mold the government, into almost any shape they please."[242] Chief Justice Charles Evans Hughes, serving from 1930 to 1941, commenting on his and his fellow Justices unlimited powers boldly declared, "We [the Supreme Court Justices] are under a Constitution but the Constitution is what the judges say

---

238 *The Oxford Companion to the Supreme Court of the United States*, Kermit L. Hall, Editor In Chief, 426.

239 Justice Black in dissent, Griswold v. Connecticut, as cited in, *Constitutional Law and Politics, Volume Two, Civil Rights and Civil Liberties*, 2nd edition, 308.

240 O'Brien, David M., *Constitutional Law and Politics*, Vol. 2, 118.

241 O'Brien, David M., *Constitutional Law and Politics*, Vol. 2, 119. Note; O'Brien's work was published in 1995.

242 Anti-Federalist Robert Yates cited in, O'Brien, David M., *Constitutional Law and Politics*, Vol. 2, 26.

it is."[243] In modern America "our" Constitution is the reflection of the trendy political opinions of five or more unelected, elitist, justices. Chief Justice Roberts' decision on Obamacare (the Affordable Care Act of 2010) is a prime example of how political pressure and personal ego can influence the Supreme Court, as opposed to the original intentions of the Founding Fathers who wrote the Constitution and the Sovereign States that ratified it.

Higher Law and a Living Constitution

William H. Seward, Lincoln's Secretary of State, declared that the fight against slavery was part of a "higher law" even higher than the Constitution.[244] The state of Wisconsin enforced this higher law when it nullified the Constitution's fugitive slave clause in 1859 by passing "personal liberty laws." Such state acts are permissible in a Republic of Sovereign States, but Seward, and other Republicans, applied it from a national level against the Southern States — which violates the very terms of the constitutional compact ratified by the Sovereign States. George P. Fletcher, law professor at Columbia University, noted that activist federal judges are re-writing the Constitution to comply with what progressive judges see as "higher law."[245] Judicial review when combined with higher law (living constitution) theories eventually lead to judicial tyranny.

Judicial review, in the hands of a "strict constructionist" judge is like a loaded gun; dangerous, but not necessarily fatal. The modern Supreme Court justices, however, speak of a "living" constitution. By this, they mean they are free to apply current standards — theirs — to fill in gaps in the Constitution, or even to overrule parts of it.[246] Other Constitutional scholars have noted the dangers created by a Supreme Court that is ideologically wedded to the idea of "higher law" or a "living" constitution.

The U.S. Supreme Court's reliance on higher law doctrines, as a rationalization for voiding state policies, is problematical because it

---

243 Chief Justice Hughes as cited in, O'Brien, David M., *Constitutional Law and Politics,* Vol. 2, 32.

244 https://en.wikipedia.org/wiki/Rule_according_to_higher_law

245 George P. Fletcher as cited by, DiLorenzo, *Thomas J., Hamilton's Curse: How Jefferson's Archenemy Betrayed the American Revolution and What It Means for Americans Today* (Crown Publishing Group, New York: 2008), 184.

246 Quirk, William J & Bridwell, R. Randall, *Judicial Dictatorship* (Transaction Publishers, New Brunswick, NJ: 1995), 6.

runs counter to Article VI, which stipulates that "this Constitution, and the Laws made in Pursuance thereof" are supreme.[247]

The progressive's rejection of "original intentions" and embracing of "higher law" or "living" constitutional law has resulted in the Supreme Court looking to not only extra-constitutional but to international law to justify its "progressive" interpretation of the Constitution. One scholar noted, "… from time to time, the U.S. Supreme Court has taken it upon itself to use international law as persuasive authority to interpret various portions of the U.S. Constitution."[248] It is a simple matter to move from "persuasive" to "mandatory" authority — especially if original intentions are no longer mandatory!

Dean Alfange, a liberal legal scholar used the idea of a "living Constitution" to support his advocacy of judicial activism. In 1937 he declared, "… the denial of the right of secession by the *unanswerable argument of superior force* put an end to the claim that the American States were full-fledged and independent sovereignties,"[249] [emphasis added]. In 1941 Professor Edward Corwin wrote in his book *Court Over the Constitution*, "… the National Government is entitled to employ any and all of its powers to forward any and all of the objectives of good government."[250] Five or more justices on an activist Supreme Court can now use the "living Constitution" to determine the definition of "good government."

The Constitutional Republic of Sovereign States as designed by the Founding Fathers, ratified by the Sovereign States, and clearly explained by early Constitutional scholars such as William Rawle, St George Tucker, and John C. Calhoun no longer exist. In its place now stands an empire created by a ruling elite who control a supreme federal government — a government that has the sole right to judge what, if any, Constitutional limitations it must recognize. A ruler who assumes the sole responsibility for determining the limits of his actions is known as a tyrant!

---

247 DeRosa, Marshall L., *The Ninth Amendment and the Politics of Creative Jurisprudence* (Transaction Publishers, New Brunswick, NJ: 1996), 7.

248 Glensy, Rex D., The Use of International Law in U.S. Constitutional Adjudication, http://law.emory.edu/eilr/content/volume-25/issue-1/articles/international-law-constitutional-adjudication.html accessed 2/13/2020.

249 Alfange, Dean, *The Supreme Court and the National Will* (Garden City, NY: 1937), 88; Dean Alfange was born December 2, 1897, in Istanbul, Turkey, migrated to the United States and received his law degree from Columbia Law School.

250 Quirk & Bridwell, *Judicial Dictatorship* (Transaction Publishers, New Brunswick, NJ: 1995), 40.

EPILOGUE

The Sad Results of Rejecting Rawle's View of the Constitution

Professor Jay S. Hoar, while doing a book signing in Dubach, Louisiana in 1986, for his book *The South's Last Boys in Gray*, made the following observation to the Kennedy Twins: "The American people have lived long enough to see the Confederate soldier's worst nightmare come true — a Federal government that cannot be controlled."[251] These words were not spoken by a partisan Southerner but by an author and historian from Maine. Although spoken in a distinctive New England accent, these words would have been embraced and lauded by all defenders of Dixie and the original Constitution of these United States. Professor Hoar's words reflect the feelings of those who have witnessed the 20th century's malignant growth of the Federal government. During this time, a corresponding fear for the well-being and civil liberties of America's future generations dramatically increased among America's traditional Constitutionalists.

The topic of secession reappeared among leftists in America after the 2000 Presidential election. After a very contentious "hanging chad"[252] election victory by the Republican Party in the 2000 presidential election, a cry was raised from leftists for the secession of "progressive" states from the Union. Subsequently to that incident, there was an increased demand for secession from both the left and right. The growing number of Americans who no longer trust the Federal government is a major reason for the renewed interest in secession. The number of Americans who had faith and trust in the Federal government in 1964 was 77 per cent. As of 2019 the "trust" factor of citizens for the Federal government was down to only 17 per cent.[253] Size has a lot to do with why so many Americans feel isolated

---

251 Jay S. Hoar, as cited in James R. Kennedy and Walter D. Kennedy, *The South Was Right!* (Pelican Publishing Co., Gretna, La.: 1994) 219.

252 During the vote counting process for the 2000 presidential election in Florida, many ballots were disputed because two or more "chads" were not removed properly on a disputed ballot. CHAD is an acronym for Card Hole Accumulated Debris which was at the center of the controversy in Florida's 2000 presidential vote.

253 www.pewresearch.org/chart/public-trust-in-government-near-historic-lows/ accessed 2/15/2020.

and removed from their government. The most effective way the average citizen can influence the actions of the Federal government is via his representative in Congress. Yet, because of the large U. S. population a citizen in a Congressional District is only one in approximately 710,767 citizens.[254] In 1790 the U. S. population stood at 3, 929,214.[255] In 2020 U. S. population was 329,064,917.[256] When the Constitution was drafted, the ratio of citizens to their representative was 30,000 citizens to 1 representative. Even that number was considered too large by many but 1 to 710,767 is too large to induce "trust" in the Federal government, thus, the contemporary consideration of secession as a political solution to the radical ideological divide in the United States.

The last decade of the 20th century and the first decade of the 21st century witnessed the resurrection of secession movements around the world. The 19th century and the first half of the 20th century witnessed the rise of empires as large powerful nations conquered, occupied, and exploited smaller nations. This conquest was followed by the suppression of anything that would prove dangerous to the empire's control of its newly acquired territory — this action is known as cultural genocide.[257] But as noted, this worldwide trend of the past 150 years seems to have come to an end as more oppressed people are pursuing cultural and political independence. In the Western Hemisphere the people of Quebec began a push to become independent from Canada. Although not a sovereign nation yet, Quebec's move has led to an almost total cultural independence and a near positive recognition of its right of be free, if the people of Quebec so desire. This has inspired other Canadian Provinces to look into the idea of secession.

With the establishment of the Polish Trade Union *Solidarity* in 1980 and the fall of the Berlin Wall in 1991, secession began to break out all over the former Soviet Bloc world. Leading the way, the Soviet Union's occupied nations of Estonia, Latvia, and Lithuania seceded

---

254 Wyoming has one representative for 568,300 population; Montana has one representative for 994,416 population; whereas, nationally the average is 710,767 citizens per representative in Congress; www.thegreenpapers.com/Census10/FedRep.phtml accessed 2/17/2020.

255 United States Census Bureau www.census.gov/history/www/through_the_decades/overview/1790.html accessed 2/14/20.

256 World Population Report, 2020 http://worldpopulationreview.com/countries/ accessed 2/14/20.

257 Kennedy & Kennedy, *Yankee Empire: Aggressive Abroad and Despotic at Home* (Shotwell Publishing Co., Columbia, SC: 2018), 125-7, 283-96.

from the Soviet Bloc. Many nations such as Yugoslavia and Czechoslovak ceased to exist due to secession, as new nations representing more natural population groupings appeared. People who had been forced to live under a government which did not respect their cultural values and history, simply separated, that is, seceded, from each other and formed governments more to their liking. In 2020, Great Britain seceded from the European Union via an election referred to as Brexit. This secession, Brexit, reflected the Thirteen American Colonies' secession from the British Empire in 1776 and the Confederate States of America's secession from the Yankee Empire in 1861. Thankfully, the European Union did not have a Lincoln as its leader or Great Britain would have faced invasion, impoverishment, the installation of European Union puppet government to rule Great Britain, and then, made subservient to the will of the European Union.

Scotland, which is currently a part of Great Britain, did not endorse Brexit but voted to remain in the European Union. Some in Scotland are now considering secession from Great Britain in order to remain in the European Union. The various secession movements of the late 20th century and early 21st century prove secession can be peaceful, advantageous to all parties, but most importantly, secession maintains the right of people to live under a government based upon the free and unfettered consent of the governed. As pointed out by President Jefferson Davis, CSA, "The alternative to secession is coercion."[258] Coercion is to tyranny, what consent is to freedom.

This resurgence of local sovereignty and self-determination has an American counterpart. With the polarization of the United States into essentially two warring political camps, the subject of secession is raised by members from both political spectrums, left and right. Not only are there several secession groups in the South but similar groups are found from Vermont to California. Secession is no longer a mere "Civil War" subject. Early in the 1990s a book hit the market with the shocking title, *The South Was Right!*. Without reservation the authors, the Kennedy Twins, advocated the right of self-determination, that is, secession, as an unalienable American right and the only antidote to the malignant growth of big government. *The South Was Right!* sold more than 140,000 copies. According to the publisher, a very large number of these books were sold outside of the South.

---

258 Davis, Jefferson, *Rise and Fall of the Confederate Government*, Vol. 1, (1881, William Mayes Coats, Nashville, TN: circa 1980), 177.

Obviously, the concept of secession and learning the Southern view of the War for Southern Independence is alive and well.

With the publication of *The South Was Right!*, for the first time in 150 years Southerners were announcing their moral and legal right to, as proclaimed in the Declaration of Independence, "alter or abolish it [government], and to institute new Government … as to them seem most likely to effect their Safety and Happiness." It is obvious many Southerners and non-Southerners are questioning the legitimacy of an intrusive Federal government. What is being questioned is not the love for America, but the continued loyalty to a government based upon principles which were unacceptable to the Founding Fathers in 1787-88. [259] The Constitution of 1787 established a government which was acceptable to Southerners, but when that government became abusive of its power, a whole generation of Southerners willingly offered their very lives to prevent the Federal government from continuing its encroachment upon the rights and liberties of their People.

Post-war the conquering Federal government punished the South with poverty as it exploited its newly conquered Southern territory. As a result of the War and Reconstruction, Southerners were reduced from the richest to the poorest people in the United States and remain so today — more than 150 years after the War![260] With the extinction of the South's constitutionally conservative political influence in the Federal Congress, Lincoln's newly created supreme Federal government morphed into, first, a North American and then, a global Yankee Empire. Post-War the supreme Federal government became, as predicted by General Robert E. Lee in 1870, a centralized tyranny that is, "aggressive abroad and despotic at home." [261]

In 1992, a book was published which also questioned how Americans can continue living with a government that claimed the right to unquestioned control of every aspect of American life. Post-war "progressive" elements successfully created a huge and uncontrollable "Deep State" Federal government. The "progressive" ruling elite have

---

259 Founding Fathers include the men who debated the ratification or rejection of the proposed Constitution in the legislature of their specific Sovereign State. It was, in fact, the Sovereign States, not a group of Founding Fathers, who gave life to the new Union under the Constitution.

260 See, Kennedy & Kennedy, *Punished With Poverty-the Suffering South* (Shotwell Publishing Co., Columbia, SC: 2016).

261 See, Kennedy & Kennedy, *Yankee Empire: Aggressive Abroad and Despotic at Home* (Shotwell Publishing Co., Columbia, SC: 2018).

waged war upon Americans who hold traditional American values—the once prosperous American middle-class, who are now referred to as "deplorables," "irredeemables," and "bitter clingers." It was noted: "Since 1965, the Hamiltonian vision of human nature and government has supplanted the Jeffersonian one. The 25-year Court-led Revolution to establish equality of results has given us an ugly landscape and a bitterly divided and bankrupt country."[262]

The Federal government's ever-increasing power has been noted by non-Southerners as well as the traditional States' Right Southerners. A *Wall Street Journal* article titled 'Federal Mandates Crush States,' noted the governor of Ohio took issue with the aggressive power play of the Federal government.[263] Such Federal Mandates are often styled "unfunded Federal mandates." An unfunded Federal mandate is a Federal law that commands the states to perform an act without any Federal compensation. As the article noted, even Northern governors were now sounding the alarm about the loss of States' Rights. According to the, then, Governor of Ohio, these unfunded Federal mandates would cost the people of Ohio $356 million in 1994 and a total of $1.74 Billion by 1995.

Federal mandates pre-empt state programs such as schools, police protection, and highways. The reality of contemporary civil liberties in the USA is that the people at the state and local level exercise only those rights that are permitted by the ultimate dispenser of rights and privileges, the supreme Federal government. Contrast contemporary American "rights" with those contemplated by William Rawle, St. George Tucker, and John C. Calhoun.

In 1993 when the Kennedy Twins republished the first edition of Rawle's textbook, the national debt was just over $3.5 trillion. In 2020, the national debt was just over $23 trillion and climbing![264] As the governor of Ohio noted in 1994, the Federal government now issues orders to its inferiors, the once sovereign states. This same supreme and over-grown Federal government is unable to control its malignant spending habit. The United States is suffering from a chronic case of "Bigness."[265] As F. H. Buckley notes in his book on American

---

262 William J. Quirk and Randall Bridwell, *Abandoned: The Betrayal of the American Middle Class Since World War II* (Madison Books, Lanham, MY: 1992), 218.
263 *The Wall Street Journal*, January 31, 1994, editorial page.
264 The Concord Coalition, www.concordcoalition.org/ accessed 2/14/20.
265 F.H. Buckley, *American Secession: The Looming Threat Of A National Breakup* (Encounter Books, NY & London: 2020), ix.

secession, Rome fell not as a small republic but only after the disease of "bigness" had turned it into an empire. It became a victim of success, "The great mistake was bigness."[266] As with all empires, bigness promotes spending. To support its spending, empires often turn to taxation and inflation of currency to finance its spending habit. As natural as flies to honey, corruption, fraud, and bribery will flow to a government with large amounts of money to dispense. Today there are almost twice as many military-industrial lobbyists as there are Congressmen. Now multiply these lobbyists by a multitude of other agencies and businesses and it becomes clear just how corrupt the Deep State has become. Big government needs big taxes. Big taxes lead to huge amounts of money being spent. Deep State corruption is assured because, there is no one, other than the elite who control the supreme Federal government, to determine how Federal dollars are spent or how big the government can become.

Rawle's *A View of the Constitution* describes a federal government limited by the specific language of a constitution. In Rawle's view, the federal government possesses no constitutional right to infringe upon the liberties of the states and the people thereof. As a document explaining the right of secession, Rawle's textbook offers the people of America the solution to a federal government that has grown completely out of control! It was Rawle's hope such a solution as secession would never become necessary but it was and remains an unalienable right of a free people. As always, secession serves as a warning to any government that wishes to deny to its citizens their unalienable rights and liberties. In *The South Was Right!*, and *Dixie Rising-Rules for Rebels*[267] Southerners are called upon to initiate the struggle to return the Federal government to its proper role in the governing of these United States. The challenge has been issued to take up once again the Cause for which our ancestors struggled in 1776 and 1861.

This challenge announces to the world that we demand a radical reformation of the current unconstitutional, supreme, Federal government. If our Northern neighbors cannot be rallied to the cause of limited constitutional government, then the South should join the people of the former Soviet Union who in the early 1990s seceded from their union. And also, join the people of Great Britain who in 2020 seceded from the European Union. The right of self-government

---

266 Ibid, 51.

267 Kennedy, James Ronald, *Dixie Rising-Rules for Rebels* (Shotwell Publishing Co., Columbia, SC: 2017).

and the right to consent to or withdraw consent from one's government is enshrined in America's most revered document, the Declaration of Independence. No American should shy away from embracing the principles announced in the Declaration of Independence.

For Americans who, like Patrick Henry, understand that in a free society liberty always trumps government, [268] Rawle's textbook inspires our dreams of living with a Federal government whose Constitutional limits are ultimately enforced by "we the people" within our respective Sovereign State. In such a system all non-delegated rights and sovereignty will be reserved to the states and the people thereof. As Rawle demonstrates, this is the only legitimate form of government for these United States but as Rawle also demonstrates, if this free government is denied the people, then there is a constitutional alternative — secession. Hopefully our Northern neighbors will join in the struggle to radically reform the current unconstitutional, supreme, Federal government and thereby prevent the necessity of another secession movement.

Deo Vindice

268 "The first thing I have at heart is American liberty, the second in American union." Patrick Henry, as cited in William Wirt Henry, *Patrick Henry: Life, Correspondence and Speeches* (1891, Sprinkle Publication, Harrisonburg, VA: 1993) III, 449.

INDEX

A

B

C

D

L

M

N

O

P

Q

R

S

T

U

V

Index
Annotation Notes and Addendums[269]

269 This index includes *only* words and phrases used in annotation notes and addendums. See Rawle's index for his work.

About The Authors

THE KENNEDY TWINS were born in Mississippi; both now reside in Louisiana. Ron and this twin brother Donnie have authored 17 books including the bestselling book *The South Was Right!* which sold more than 135,000. The following Kennedy books are in current publication: *Yankee Empire: Aggressive Abroad and Despotic at Home* (RK & DK); *Rawle's View of the Constitution-Secession as Taught at West Point* (RK & DK); *Confederate Myth Buster* (DK); *Dixie Rising-Rules for Rebels* (RK); *When Rebel Was Cool-Growing-Up in Dixie* (RK, release date summer 2020); *The Redneck Dictionary-How to Speak Southern* (RK, release date fall 2020) and *Be Ye Separate* (RK, release date fall 2020).

Ron is past Division Commander, Louisiana Sons of Confederate Veterans (SCV), in 2018 he was appointed Deputy of Heritage Promotions National SCV. He is a frequent speaker at SCV, Southern Heritage and other pro-Liberty groups. Ron received a Master in Health Administration (MHA) from Tulane University in New Orleans, a Master of Jurisprudence in Healthcare Law (MJ) from Loyola University Chicago, and a Bachelor's degree from University of Louisiana Monroe. He retired in April 2015 after serving more than 20 years as Vice-President of Risk Management for a Louisiana based insurance company.

Donnie is past Division Commander of Louisiana SCV, he was appointed Chief of Heritage Operations for the National SCV in 2018. He is a frequent speaker at SCV, Southern Heritage and other pro-Liberty groups. Donnie received a Bachelor's degree from the University of Louisiana Monroe and is a graduate of Charlotte Memorial Medical Center School of Anesthesia. He is a registered respiratory therapist (RRT), registered nurse (RN), and certified registered nurse anesthetist (CRNA).

Authors' website: www.kennedytwins.com

www.ingramcontent.com/pod-product-compliance
Lightning Source LLC
Chambersburg PA
CBHW060640310726
48982CB00003B/830

* 9 7 8 1 9 4 2 8 0 6 2 8 8 *